CW00972704

To I........
with best
wishes.

More of the
same, except
women!

By the same authors:
Toon Tales – a Euro-Geordie pilgrimage
ISBN 0-9548437-0-0
© 2004 Toon Publishing Ltd

Toon Odyssey
- *the pilgrimage goes on*

'*The Fatwa didn't work*' – sunderland Sentinel

'*Not them again*' – Boro Bugle

'*Topical yet timeless, now endless*' - anon

'*Mixed metaphors, who needs 'em? The Toon, that's who*' – another anon

Photographs

Front cover photo: UEFA Cup Final, Lisbon, by Brian Robertson & Barry Robertson

Centre photos: people and places of the odyssey (courtesy of Sarah & Chris Wilkie, Don Faulds, Alec McHale, & the authors)

toon odyssey

- the pilgrimage goes on

by

Peter Cain

and

Barry Robertson

First published in Great Britain in 2005 by
Toon Publishing Limited
129/131 New Bridge Street
Newcastle upon Tyne NE1 2SW

e-mail: toonpublishing@yahoo.co.uk
website: http://www.freewebs.com/toonpublishing/

1 3 5 7 9 10 8 6 4 2

A CIP catalogue record for this book is available from the British Library

ISBN 0-9548357-1-9

Printed and bound in Great Britain
by Biddles Ltd, King's Lynn, Norfolk

Contents

Acknowledgments

Our many thanks go to all of the following: Malcolm Colling for advice, inspiration, and proof-reading; Brian Robertson for cover and website development; Sarah and Chris Wilkie, Don Faulds, and Alec McHale for additional photos; Didier de Almeida for computer wizardry; Niall and Biffa at nufc.com and Mark Jensen at The Mag and Mike Jolliffe for their wise words; John Gibson, Paul Robertson and Paul McMillan at the Evening Chronicle for the articles and words of encouragement; Jon Harle at BBC Radio Newcastle for the lively interview; Biddles for their helpfulness and printing expertise; Ian Robertson for the company set-up; Steve and Oliver for ticket help; Thanos Stubos for telling us about the *Gavri*; Jiri Muller for knowing the way to Teplice; and of course to wives, families, and friends; not forgetting the big happy family that is the Toon Army.

'Toon Odyssey – *the pilgrimage goes on*' is the second and final instalment of a seven-part trilogy charting the path of Newcastle United's glittering success in Europe and beyond. Unfortunately, it doesn't get very far. Less than that even, because, like Ulysses' Odyssey, it goes round in a circle and brings you exactly back to where you started. In the Toon, and trophyless. You might have had some really good times, met a few challenges, fought a few battles, lost a few men (Bellamy for one), and seen some new places, but when all's said and done, that's your lot. And that really is our lot in life, to win more than we lose, yet to come third or fifth. Because ultimate success and Newcastle United are not on the most intimate of terms. In fact, they split up a few decades ago.

Never mind, the Euro-Geordie pilgrimage continues, and the Toon Army carries on regardless. Once again, it was an odd sort of odyssey in which we meandered blissfully around Europe soaking up the atmosphere, good will and sometimes awful smells of continental football (and continental drains that left much to be desired). From Athens via Fatima to Cardiff, we followed the pilgrims' and druids' trails in our search and hope for a miracle. Once again, it just didn't happen, but we still had a great time sipping the *vino* in the tavernas and cafés as we basked in the Aegean sun and the reflected glory of antiquity. Oh, and also supping French ale in the shadow of a Peugeot car plant.

The good humour and eternal optimism of the Toon faithful stood in marked contrast to the sheer unbelievable gannins-on at the club itself. For it was a season that saw NUFC stagger from the ridiculous to the even more ridiculous and ultimately self-destruct on the field as Bowyer and Dyer engaged in fisticuffs when all we wanted to do was celebrate the colossus Alan Shearer's decision to stay on for another year. But the writing had been on the wall back in

August when Sir Bobby was sent packing in the tattiest of circumstances. Why such a public washing of dirty linen just after the season had got under way? Could things not have been sorted out in a dignified manner in the close season? And once it had been decided to give Sir Bobby the chance he definitely deserved to stay at the helm for one last season, could the club not have seen that through? Even after sacking him, they still had to pay him and it sounds like they can't even do that properly. Only after he had gone did they start looking for a replacement. Now there's forward planning for you. And did we get the people's choice? Then of course there was the Bellamy episode. Plus various off-the-field incidents in which obscenely overpaid employees made Newcastle United a laughing stock once again. In many ways, you could even feel sorry for Graeme Souness. Has he ever had such a tough job? Would he too have turned us down if he'd known what he was going to be letting himself in for? On the other hand, who in their right mind would turn down a job like that, and a seat right on the half-way line to go with it?

We'd written in the dedication page of our first book, *Toon Tales,* that if we actually won something this season, then the powers that be at the club would be able to look us in the eye and tell us that the actions they'd taken at the end of August 2004 had been justified. And come April, we were still in two cup competitions for the first time ever at that late stage in a season, and it looked like Springtime for Freddy and Geordieland. But of course it was not to be. How could we have deluded ourselves so? Because that's the way we Geordies are. A week so full of promise ended in utter humiliation after not really turning up either in Lisbon (two-nil aggregate lead turns into a two-four drubbing) or in Cardiff (we hate Man U and we hate Man U, but we wish we were a bit like them on the park). And yes, there were the old excuses – long season, so many games, don't have the strength in depth. No, we certainly don't have the strength in depth. So isn't it about time that something was seriously done about it? We had to wait until just a handful of games away from season's end and the goalless draw at home to the smoggies before we were safe from relegation. The top teams were safe before Christmas. No, we weren't going to qualify for Europe through our league position.

So we were told that we would be applying for the Intertoto. The question is: don't the Intertoto people have standards to maintain? But if they're not proud, then neither should we be. It just means re-arranging our holidays and heading for the beaches (do they have any?) of Slovakia or Hungary or Turkey, then Armenia or France or Switzerland or who knows where? The pilgrimage will be starting earlier next season. And remember, the first Intertoto competition was great fun: Lokeren, 1860 Munich, and Troyes. Hope springs eternal, as it has to if you follow the Toon.

And all success is relative, as we found out on Einstein's patch during our earlier pilgrimage. Believe it or not, our efforts in the 2004/05 season have taken us up the UEFA Rankings to the point where we are now the fifteenth top-seeded team in Europe! Ahead of Chelsea (really), Roma, Sporting Lisbon (yes), Celtic, Monaco, Ajax, and many other good teams. And based on this season's European results alone, rather than the five-year cumulative total which decides seedings, we are actually fifth. Which means that compared to all but four other teams, we've had a great ride along the way, even if we failed the penultimate challenges in Lisbon and Cardiff. So some reasons to be cheerful too!

To set the scene and to answer a few questions that you might have, we thought we should repeat a few explanations from last year's introduction. Please bear in mind that we don't claim to be football experts. We're just fans - Toon Army wallahs. So we're not trying to analyse the why's and wherefores of every game; nor are we attempting detailed match reports, because the media in their various forms do that better than we can - though we have gone into more detail on the games this time. What we're trying to do is give a taste of what it was like being there (before, during and after) amidst all the distractions of being in the middle of a boisterous crowd.

Sometimes we say things just for effect - there's such a thing as irony so we don't always mean exactly what we say; if you're non-anglo, we know some of you have a particular problem in spotting irony, so don't get too upset: it's your fault not ours (did you spot it?); stereotypes are useful and fun, so we use them, but don't read too much into them - there's always some element of truth in them, but by no means everyone conforms to the same trait.

There are two of us writing this, Barry and Pete, and sometimes we ramble on in different directions over the same ground. We are Geordies born and bred, but we don't live in the Toon. We live in Belgium and Germany, and have done for well-nigh a quarter of a century now. So our angle on getting to the games and finding match tickets is different to most and we hope this adds to the interest. Getting tickets certainly can be an adventure in itself sometimes! We also hope that our insiders' experiences of everyday living in Europe make some of the stories more interesting for you, and maybe can even help you with some advice on surviving your own trips to *le continent*!

Collaborating on the writing has been a great experience and big fun: you learn a lot; including that sometimes identities need to blur to keep the narrative flowing, so the 'I' in this book is often a composite person, neither one of us nor the other, but both of us (and sometimes maybe it's you!); we all create our own personal realities and meanings from our different experiences of the same events – no two histories are the same – just read a match report of a game you went to yourself to see what we mean.

With our usual pig-headed refusal to look reality in the face (and Newcastle United must be the ultimate alternative to reality), the Toon Army turned the 2004/05 UEFA Cup campaign into a further celebration of us all being Geordies with the continent of Europe at our feet. Here we now are, all in the market together, where most people even use the same money, flitting backwards and forwards across borders as if it were nothing at all. It's great. Watching football and having a bit crack and a few pints together is much more fun than bombing the shit out of each other. And so much cheaper. Our grandparents and great-grandparents could only dream of doing this. And if they got to some of the same destinations in their day, it was probably for the worst of all possible reasons. They'd be proud of the way it is now. Spreading Geordie good will, that's what it's aal aboot. Geordieland gave the world proper railways, plenty of ships, loads of coal, stottie cakes and broon. And now our European cousins can come and hear the Blaydon Races sung in their very own bars.

Well, here goes! UEFA Cup take-off time again. How've you been keeping since we left off at last year's Cup Final in Gothenburg? There've certainly been some changes, though but! It's Pete and Barry here again, jotting down our impressions as we set off on a new Euro-Geordie pilgrimage, with a strong hint of odyssey this year, following the Toon around our Cup campaigns. We join Barry somewhere in the stratosphere and heading in a south-easterly direction across the full extent of Europe.

Looking around me on this chocka plane, I'm flanked on one side by a large, heavily perfumed lady from, as far as I can understand, Sakhnin's near neighbour, the Lebanon, and on the other, by her more svelte friend with one-year-old daughter on her lap. Fore and aft, we're surrounded by a big contingent wearing long black coats and top hats, shiny white shirts, sideburns and wispy beards. They're in a jolly mood and they put me in mind of a male version of those Monty Python Grannies. Having been drawn out of UEFA's own top hat against Hapoel Bnei Sakhnin of Israel, this has to be par for the course. When I'd first got on the plane, I'd half-wondered for a moment whether Toon fans were getting dressed up for the occasion, much as you'd seen Viking helmets in Vålerenga, sombreros in Mallorca, berets and strings of onions in Marseille, and breathing apparatus at Boro. The colours were right!

The draw for the first round was made at lunchtime on the twenty-seventh of August. As usual, you could follow it on the Internet at www.uefa.com, though quite often the BBC website updates the details quicker. We were placed in Group Three, which meant that we would play either CSKA Sofia, Rapid Vienna, Djurgårdens from Sweden, (Mott the) Hapoel Bnei Sakhnin of Israel, or Temuri Ketsbaia's old team, Dinamo Tbilisi from Georgia. Quite a mixed bunch, with the pick for me from the tourism point of view probably being the Swedish team. I assumed that if we drew the Israeli side, then the away leg would be moved to somewhere like Cyprus, as I seemed to recall that had been the usual practice over recent years.

This is the first round proper of the 2004/05 UEFA Cup, where we make our entry into the competition. There has already been the customary Intertoto summertime qualifying competition. Like last year, Schalke 04, from Newcastle's twin town Gelsenkirchen, and our fellow 2003/04 semi-finalists Villarreal passed through successfully, this time along with Lille. Any of those three would be most worthy opponents and really good places to visit in future rounds. In the subsequent UEFA Cup qualifying round, Hapoel Benny Sakhnin overcame the challenge of Partizan Tirana, home of the largest Norman Wisdom fan club in the world. And we all know that Norman is a big Toon fan. There really are Geordie connections everywhere you look. A trip to Albania some time wouldn't go amiss.

I could feel it in my bones that we were going to play the Israeli or the Georgian team. I took a look on the Internet to see what Tbilisi might be like. When I saw the map, I realised that I'd actually already been to Georgia twenty-six years ago when I was a student and I'd travelled through Europe in a VW Caravette, ending up by the Black Sea on the Turkish-Georgian border. At the time, I'd thought of it as being Russia, and even now I was a bit surprised to know I'd been there. I checked for hotels and found that there was a Marriott Hotel, and very reasonable it looked too, with Internet access, health club, and a pool – hopefully indoors in view of the weather - at about ninety euros a night. Nowhere is so different any more, I thought, but read on! I got a lot more worried when I chanced upon the British Embassy site and read such things as 'we advise against travel to the breakaway regions' and 'you should avoid travelling alone in Georgia and take precautions against the high levels of crime, including kidnapping' and 'you should be aware of the risk of indiscriminate terrorist attacks'. Under the heading of air safety, it gave the interesting news that 'aircraft maintenance procedures on some flights are not always properly observed.' With respect to kidnapping, it went on to give the unnerving advice to 'consider with your employers and family a 'what if' action plan.' That did it for me. I was sure we were headed for Tbilisi, but I didn't think I'd be looking for a ticket.

It was a relief to hear that we were drawn against Hartlepool Bnei Sakhnin, though that was going to be a bit of a challenge too. They hail from the remote town of Sakhnin in the North of Israel, not far from Nazareth and the Sea of Galilee, or from the border with the Lebanon, where my neighbour on the plane was from. It's an Arab club that plays in the Israeli League (well Berwick play in the Scottish League). In the run-up to the match, some wag suggested that Sakhnin should play their home tie in Gateshead as they would feel at home there, and then some slightly better-informed joker reckoned that, in the circumstances, South Shields would be a more appropriate venue.

Amidst the intractable problems of the Middle East, a little football club offers a glimmer of hope for mutual respect. They have our very best wishes, and we're sure yours too. It was a very nice touch from the club to donate a tidy sum to the town of Sakhnin after the tie was all over to help build a school for the local children. How strangely appropriate that of all the eighty clubs in the first round draw, we should be paired together - the Holy Lands were to meet at last!

Of course, we weren't the only British team in the draw. We weren't even the only North-East team, as our southern neighbours Middlesbrough found themselves playing Pavel Srnicek's first club, Banik (don't panic) Ostrava in the Czech Mate Republic. That would have been a good draw for us, giving us the chance to renew contacts with Pav in some way. Hearts got drawn against Braga of Portugal, which would also have been a very nice place to go. Last and very much least, Millwall found themselves up against Ferencvaros of David Ginola wonder-goal fame. So that was Millwall finished pretty sharpish, wasn't it? There was one other English-speaking (of sorts!) team in the competition and they would certainly have been my favourite destination if only we'd been put in the same Group, and that was Shelbourne of Ireland. Why can't we ever get drawn to go over to Ireland? Retracing Big Jack and Wor Jackie's footsteps.

While I was still looking at the draw, the news came on Radio Five that UEFA considered Tel Aviv to be a safe venue and so we would be asked to play there! So it wasn't going to be Cyprus, then. A check of the UEFA website showed that they had indeed played the qualifying round in Tel Aviv, so it looked pretty conclusive. UEFA have this year decided that all matches against Israeli teams are to be played at the Ramat Gan (let's gan) national stadium in Tel Aviv, where, according to their judgment, the safety of players and spectators can be guaranteed. A lifetime guarantee, no quibbles.

The home leg was played first and a disappointing crowd of just 30,221 turned up at SJP to see the first Arab-Israeli side ever to play in England, or Geordieland for that matter, in a serious competition. They were pretty hard up apparently, and to our great credit NUFC coughed up for a team coach to bring them up from Heathrow. The coach didn't think he could manage all those piggy-back shuttle runs, however, so they sent a trip bus instead. What were your thoughts, Pete?

Well Barry, I'm a bit of a traditionalist at heart, and the first thought that flashed through my mind when I heard the draw was: the Eurovision Song Contest. What a wonderful concept! Don't you just love it? Well I used to, and so did wor lass. Every year, we'd religiously get the beers, crisps and peanuts in for the televisual extravaganza, which often took place on the same day as the Grand National – so you could have a flutter on both. Equally religiously, we'd make sure we had our copy of the local telly magazine, which always ran a helpful two-page spread with the title of each country's song, the name of the singer or group, a bit gossip about them and a little box at the side in which to award your points. Sometimes, we would award the points (zero) even before we heard the song! But in most cases, we would follow the traditional pattern and allocate marks after each song and then, at the end of the evening (and in my case, several bottles of Veltins Pils later), we would compare our winners with the real one – and generally, ours were better!

We no longer watch the Eurovision Song Contest. It's not because it has suddenly become crap. No. Lets face it, it was always crap – right from the outset. But it was also great fun. We stopped watching when they changed the rule that forced each country to sing in its own language – or at least in one of its languages. It was so pants-pissingly funny to listen to crappy pop songs in Icelandic, Danish or Phlegmish. Now that the own-language rule has gone, every country uses whichever language it likes, which nine times out of ten is a Mickey Mouse variety of English. The winning song, which is straight onto the radio ten minutes after the contest has ended, is invariably, er, crap. *Plus ça change*.

When we were watching back in the good old days, some strange thoughts would drift through my increasingly sozzled brain as the evening wore on and the contestants took us on a kind of tour of Europe and, well, beyond... Suppose, just suppose for one awful moment, that for some strange inexplicable reason, the United Kingdom got kicked out of the song contest because nobody wanted to play with us any more. Let's say, for argument's sake, because it had been a case of *Royaume Uni nul points* just once too often. Or maybe because Britain couldn't get on with any of its neighbours. No, hang on, that actually is the case anyway, and we're still in Eurovision! Okay, supposing those neighbours really didn't want to be on the same planet as us. Would there be an alternative? Or would we languish eternally in a chronic state of abject and restless songcontestlessness? This really puzzled me, taxed my brain, drove me almost to despair for a long time. Then, as if from on high, there came the inspirational answer! Of course, that's it! The answer was so simple: we would just start singing in the Middle-East-O-Vision song contest instead. We would be made every bit as welcome as Gateshead were made to feel when they applied to join the Scottish League. Piece of cake! That was that conundrum sorted. But wait a minute. What if a similar fate befell Newcastle United and for some inexplicable reason we were no longer welcome in the UEFA Cup? Again, the answer is simple. We would simply play in the Sandy-Top-Bit-Of-Africa Cup! And wouldn't they just love us!

But this was the UEFA-vision football contest, and it didn't take more than a couple of minutes to see from my sat-in-comfy-chair-in-front-of-the-telly-with-cool-beer-in-hand position that Hetton-le-Hole Saccharin were certainly tough tacklers, driven on by a determined and aggressive manager, as witness two fouls in the very first minute of the match. And they were doing their best to show us their true European footballing credentials. They had obviously prepared well by watching videos of Italian club sides of the seventies, as they evinced all the best Italo-skills of that era: ankle-tapping, time-wasting, play-acting and being generally disagreeable. This was a Eurovision night to forget in a hurry. Kluivert's brace of first-half goals at the Gallowgate End (the second a powerful forty-first minute header that toured the frame of the goal pinball-style before crossing the line) gave us a semblance of hope that we might possibly just manage to overcome the cream of the Israeli league on aggregate. Phew, lucky we weren't playing the cream of the Scottish Second Division – we'd have been done for. But Mr Souness helpfully explained afterwards that they had knocked us 'out of our rhythm'. How? '...with a three-card trick.' Could have been Sir Bobby talking. Anyway, Barry, hoo's it gannin' up-a-height in that plane?

Sitting uncomfortably, Pete! I had looked into how to travel to Tel Aviv and found that there was a direct plane from Brussels, although the schedule is quite unusual. You arrive at twenty past midnight on the Wednesday night, have the whole of Thursday to explore Tel Aviv, go to the match in the evening and then head straight to the airport to catch the plane at a quarter past one on Thursday night and arrive back in Brussels at six o'clock in the morning. All for the extortionate price of one thousand two hundred euros, which is not far off a thousand pounds. When you're shelling out the shekels at that rate, you'd expect first-class treatment. Or at any rate better treatment and more space than I was getting on board this plane.

Turning back

Have you ever seen or heard of the film 'Fargo'? Me neither, until Pete and Harvey told me about it while we were sitting in Mallorca in the storm before the UEFA Cup match last year. I got it out of the local library when I was back home and it's not bad at all, in fact it's well worth watching. One of the best bits is right at the start when a solemn caption appears announcing that all of the events you are about to see are based on real events – only the names have been changed to protect the characters' anonymity. If you plan to ever watch 'Fargo', then go and rent it now before you read the next bit or, alternatively, skip the next paragraph.

You watch the whole film, growing more and more incredulous that such things could really have happened. Then, just after the villain has been apprehended while failing to force the last limb down through the garden wood chipper, you're told that no, they had made it all up after all and it never really happened. A very temporal experience – the film makers were playing with you and your capacities to suspend your belief all along.

Welcome back, film fans! Well, the same kind of thing's just happened to you here, because after all that we decided that our Eurovision-trip across the airwaves to teleview the home leg against Sakhnin had been enough and that we'd give Tel Aviv a miss, thank you very much. The plane I was sitting in was actually headed for Athens for the next round, not for Tel Aviv. Don't ask me why I was surrounded by Middle-Easterners. It's a mystery to me. What's that, Pete?

Well Barry, I would say our decision was purely geographical. There is just no getting away from geography, is there? You're kind of stuck with it and in it. History you can ignore – well at least for a while, but it has a nasty habit of catching up with you, grabbing you by the scruff of the neck and rubbing your nose in the mess you've just done on the carpet. You don't believe me? Well, ask France! But geography? No way. It's just too real, man. Try leaving the Toon for smoggieland but heading north instead of south – it just doesn't work, or at least it would take a long, long time. By the same token, try applying to play in the African Nations Cup if your name is Iceland! Your map will tell you 'Ya norron, bonny lad.'

Oh yes, and then there was another teeny-weeny reason why we didn't go to Tel Aviv: *c'est la vie.* Notwithstanding the UEFA lifetime guarantee, it happens to be one of the most dangerous places on every God's earth. Buses bursting into a million pieces, some of them potentially pieces of you. Rocket-firing jets screaming across the sky. Suicide bombers. No, that was a trip we just weren't going to make.

So instead of a description of a trip we didn't actually go on, let's turn our thoughts instead to the Vikings and all the spam they ate. While on the subject, here's some helpful advice on how to deal with those scammy spammy e-mails you sometimes receive from less than scrupulous people. If you have a bit of time to spare, you can turn them into a spot of fun, as long as you reply using someone else's computer and e-mail address. My favourites are those Nigerian ones. You know the sort of thing:

'Dear Friend,

Please allow me to introduce myself. I am the third nephew of the late Robert Mutogo, the former Minister of Corruption, who so tragically blew up while combing his hair. In accordance with his final will and testament I have been instructed to contact you with a view to arranging a financial settlement that will be very much to your esteemed advantage. My dear friend, please know that the sum involved is considerable, and therefore that discretion is of the essence. We need to be on our guard. The four million US dollars will be made over, for your security and peace of mind, to a Swiss bank account, which my uncle's executor shall open on your behalf at the Zurich main branch of Union Bank of Switzerland. Unfortunately, time is running against us and we must act with haste before enemies of the state and of my late uncle attempt to stop these monies from reaching you, the rightful heir. Please, have confidence in me, as I know you will, my brother in the Lord. We need urgently to have your bank account details. In turn, you can transfer the associated transfer and account-opening fee of seven thousand dollars to the following account...

Please, waste no time. May God's blessing be upon you.

Randy Belchers Mutogo III'

Here's a good answer:

'My Dearest Friend and Brother in the Lord. Or may I call you 'marra'?

I am truly grateful for the confidence you have placed in me. Of course it comes as no surprise that your uncle Robert has remembered me in his will, after all we went through together. How fondly I remember those times we would sit together in the Gallowgate End watching Jackie Milburn play! 'Howay man, Jackie', uncle Robert would shout, 'stick the baal in the net, man.' And sometimes, when we were standing next to each other having a piss at half time he would say: 'Ye knaa, bonny lad, if a iver get to be Minister of Corruption a'm ganna see yee aal reet when a'm deed! Mind, enjoy it while ye can, 'coz ye cannit tek noot wi' ye, that's for shooa! A want ye te promiss ye'll get yasell a season ticket.'

And you can be sure, Dearest Friend, Dearest Marra, that I solemnly made that promise.

And of course you are right. We must be cautious, we must be prudent. We can take no chances. For evil-doers lurk everywhere. Why only the other day, a strange and haggard person clad in red and white stripes - I couldn't be sure whether he was a follower of the mackems or the Athenian *Gavri* - whispered to me as I walked along the way:

'Beware the Ides of April.'

'Woddya mean, like?' quoth I.

'Coz' that's when yiz'll play the Boro - or Manchester and Lisbon, man!' came the eerie response.

And just then a black cat was crushed by the wheels of a No 34 bus. I realised in an instant that the soothsayer must have been a mackem, transmoggified. And behold, from its entrails I could see the future. And the future was not orange. Nay, it was black and white.

Therefore, Dear Marra, we must meet this very weekend at Amsterdam *Centraal Station*, at ten thirty in the morning outside the main platform-level buffet. Please bring my money in two black and white holdalls. For ease of recognition, I shall be wearing a black and white tartan kilt with matching tammy shanta and a ginger shoulder-length wig.

Till then, I shall remember you in my prayers, O beloved cousin and marra.

Pete'

Then the reply:

'Dear Marra, for indeed you may call me thus. Can you fly down to Africa to discuss details?'

To which the response is:

'Cortainly bonny lad. Hoo's aboot Windhoek? In order to blend in with the locals, I shall be wearing black and white striped *lederhosen*.'

Our five-one rout of Hapless Benny Hill Sakhnin in Tel Aviv gave us a seven-one aggregate victory, which swept us into the draw for the next round. Tell us about it, Barry.

Well, the next round was the Group Stage where we would play in a league of five teams, playing four games each. This replaced the old format of two rounds of home and away legs, and ensured that every team, rather than just half of them, played four games and none risked being knocked out after only two games. This helps to spread the money more evenly amongst the weaker teams, which seems a fairly laudable aim to me. Since we were seeded fourth out of forty, we were in the pot with the other favourites, so we were protected from being drawn against the best teams.

The draw took place, as usual at lunchtime, on the fifth of October at the UEFA headquarters in Nyon. The teams were split into five pots, with Pot One containing the Toon and the other seven teams with the highest UEFA rankings. The next pot held the ninth to sixteenth-ranked teams, and so on down to the fortieth-ranked team in the last pot, who turned out to be Dinamo Tbilisi. Boro, who'd overcome Banik Ostrava with ease and a four-one scoreline, though amid regrettable scenes of crowd trouble at the Czech ground, were in Pot Three. The principle of the draw was that there would be eight Groups, each containing one team from each pot, giving eight balanced Groups. Looking at the teams in the different pots, my dream draw to avoid too many good teams while going to some nice places would have been something like Real Zaragoza for nostalgic reasons, Utrecht, Alemannia Aachen or Hearts, and Standard Liège or Beveren. I didn't get a single wish! Instead, we ended up in Group D with Sporting Lisbon, Sochaux, Panionios and Dinamo Tbilisi. It could have been much worse and showed the advantage of being amongst the top seeds. Meanwhile Boro had been a lot less lucky and were drawn with big names Lazio, Villarreal and Partizan Belgrade and minnows Egaleo.

It was funny that we'd avoided Dinamo Tbilisi in the first round only to be drawn with them for real in the group stage. There was a nervous little wait while UEFA worked out which games each team would play at home and which away. Tbilisi on a wintry December night wasn't a very attractive prospect, so I was pleased to see that it would be Tbilisi and Sporting Lisbon coming to St. James's, while we would travel to Sochaux in France and Panionios in Athens. From the competition point of view, the most famous football names in our group were Sporting Lisbon and Dinamo Tbilisi, but neither club is what it used to be. On the other hand, some unkind souls might say that we have never been what they used to be either. For instance, in Dinamo Tbilisi's state-sponsored glory days in 1979, one hundred and ten thousand fans had packed their stadium to see them beat a Liverpool team including Graeme Souness three-nil in the European Cup. Times have changed. Sochaux sounded familiar because I remembered that they had caused a shock by knocking Borussia Dortmund out of last year's UEFA Cup. Whereas I'd never heard of Panionios and had to look on Google to find out that they played in a suburb of Athens. This was to be our first destination in the group stage, and a very nice one too.

What did you make of it, Pete?

What a brilliant draw for the group stage! Panionios, Dinamo Tbilisi, Sporting Lisbon and Sochaux. Thank goodness that Tbilisi was a home game – don't think we would have gone to Georgia. Mind, it really is ridiculous: fancy including a club from the peanut capital of America in the UEFA Cup! But seriously, that particular bit of the former Soviet Union is decidedly dodgy at the best of times, and in that respect has much in common with Israel. So all in all, no regrets about missing out on a (possibly rainy) Geordie night in Georgia. But what a pity we wouldn't be getting a chance to visit Lisbon, as Sporting were coming to Tyneside in a fixture that would bring back fond memories of a glorious night back in late November 1968. I was there, standing in the Popular... But Athens was a mouth-watering prospect alright!

No sooner had the draw been made than the well-oiled ticket-procurement machinery slipped into gear. Barry's brother Ian got in the application at NUFC, as did Chris and Sarah, plus Don tried for a couple of extras just in case. The game was to take place on a Thursday evening, of course, so taking the Friday off and staying on till the Sunday was the obvious move. Barry had been to Athens a couple of times before to attend meetings and had stayed at a peach of a hotel called the Saint George. Perched half-way up Mount Lycabettus and only a few minutes' stroll away from the centre of town, it affords a spectacular view of the entire city - but more especially of the Acropolis. It even gave us a discount, so Chris, Sarah, Barry and I booked five-star rooms for three-star prices. You should check out its www.sglycabettus.gr website and look for a good deal when next you're in that neck of the woods.

The night before the match arrives and we re-join Barry where he left off earlier somewhere in the skies over Europe.

The lass in front of me on this Olympic Airways flight is reading a Greek paper. What a way to write! You can't understand one *iota* of it. Except the one *iota* bit. There's a photo of Bill Clinton jogging, and in Greek it looks as if he's called *Mpil Klivtov*. I must find out how they write Newcastle in Greek. Hold on, maybe it's on the match ticket... no, it's written in good old-fashioned Geordie. Pity Prince Philip's nowhere to be seen when you really need him, he'd be able to tell us in a shot, and translate it into German as well. I dare say there must have been a good deal of whooping and hollering and Zorba's dancing and much downing of *retsina* and *ouzo* and *schnapps* in the Royal household back in the summertime after the European Championships Final, though but!

The night-time temperature as we land out of a starlit sky at the Olympics-funded *Eleftherios Venizelos* – 'above us only gods' - Airport in Athens at just before midnight is nineteen degrees. Centigrade. At the end of October. How the other half do live! Mind, the bus drivers' union here must be really strong as, despite it being a brand new airport, they make you alight from the plane onto the runway and pile onto a bus, instead of letting you walk across a gangway straight into the airport. A tad old-fashioned.

As we pass through customs, a horrifying thought suddenly strikes me. I hope they don't check my bag, otherwise they're going to see I've brought my bins with me. Maybe I shouldn't have brought them, but I clean forgot. Because they're illegal in Greece, aren't they? And here I am, British and a potential plane-spotter spy in a Greek airport of all places. But it's too late, and I just have to hope they let me through without seeing my binoculars – they're just mini ones after all. Luckily, they must be half asleep with it being late and I slip through the net. I'm taking no chances, mind, so I resolve not to take them out of my bag until I'm safely out of Greece again. I don't want to be thrown into some Greek slammer and miss this match and, who knows, the Sochaux one too.

But the airport's smart and sparkling and, as we wander around looking for the train, the man at the train ticket office attracts our attention with a strange whistly 'pissst' sound. It turns out that the Greeks have this funny habit of pisssting to attract each other's attention. It's not in any way a gesture of insolence as it would be in most other countries. It seems perfectly normal and friendly in Greece. So having got 'pisssted', I catch the spotless Aegean turquoise train to take me the forty-five minutes into town.

The trains are made by Bombardier, the people from Canada who brought you the Channel Tunnel trains and those boxy aeroplanes with propellers facing the wrong way that put out forest fires in the Adirondacks. The new trains certainly make a change from the dusty old round-the-houses charabanc ride that you used to have to endure from the old Athens East and West airports. The Olympic Games seem to have had a similar effect on Athens to what they had on Barcelona. Not only do they have a new airport and rail system, but also they've pedestrianised lots of the city centre and generally smartened the place up. So when are they bringing the Olympics to the Toon, then? Mind, the money didn't stretch to finishing off those half-built temples up on that there Acropolis rock. They still had the scaffolding up when we were there!

Well, the train's just brought one member of the Toon to the scene of the Olympics, so that's a start, I suppose. Now I need to find a taxi to get up to our St. George Hotel, 'Wor Geordie', on Mount Lycabettus, one of the other rocks rising above the city sprawl. The taxi drivers outside the Larissa Central Station only speak Greek. Much as there aren't many cabbies ootside wor own Central Station who taak oot but Geordie, like. It takes a while before I pronounce the hotel's name near enough to be intelligible to them. Ten minutes and five euros later, I am in the hotel and it's well past midnight. I drop my stuff off and take a couple of photos from my balcony over to the floodlit Parthenon, which is just about on the same level a kilometre away. (I've just noticed that you can read that in two ways! Some of you may be having visions of me carrying two photos across town and up to the Parthenon. Well, I didn't mean that!) I then head down to the bar to see if I can get a bite to eat and a nightcap. There are three lasses in red and white scarves waiting for the lift too.

'Are you here for the Boro match?'

'What Boro? We're Gunners girls, us lot.'

'How did you do, then?'

'Oh, we scraped a draw. Two-two. We need a new keeper.'

'Well, you can't have ours.'

'Who's that then?'

'Shay Given and Steve Harper, of course.'

'Geordies! What you doin' 'ere? We didn't see any of you lot around today.'

'Don't you know we're playing here tomorrow? And Middlesbrough too. Not against each other, mind. Against two little teams, Panionios and another one.'

'My old man's a Geordie.'

'Better than a dustman! Well, where is he? Isn't he here? It would be a great double-header, your match tonight and his tomorrow.'

'No fear mate, we don't want him here spoiling our fun. We left them all at home! We're off out on the town now. See ya.'

It's now after one, and the only place left open in the hotel is the armchair-filled basement yuppie bar where little bottles of beer cost more than four quid. It's sparsely populated by what you might imagine Greek TV stars could look like, plus a Middlesbrough couple who retire soon after, leaving me to down my solitary bottle of Mythos beer before heading off too. These posh hotels can offer you a below-half-price off-season deal on a nice room with an incredible view, but they can't offer you the late-night atmosphere that you'd get over in the Plaka or Psiri districts. The next day, I find I could have gone just across the street into a little park with a late-night open-air taverna, but I wasn't to know at the time.

In the morning, I go up to the rooftop breakfast terrace to sit in the warm Aegean sunshine and take in the view of the city below and the Acropolis ahead of me. I order just a pot of tea – breakfast is twenty-six euros, and I'm not twenty-six euros hungry. I'm looking forward to a good day. We'll meet up by noon with the rest of the Toon Army and there'll be plenty of time to take in the sights and scenes.

The mobile phone rings and I see Don's name on the display. He's much earlier than I expected.

'Barry? Greetings from Gatwick! The plane's not taken off yet. They're telling us it's a lightning strike by Greek air traffic controllers. They think we might be taking off in an hour or so if we're lucky.'

'Typical! So how late will that make you?'

'Oh, it'll be mid-afternoon at the earliest.'

'Well, you've got plenty of time to get here. The match doesn't start till half past nine. I'm here with the phone on, so you can give me a ring any time and we'll work out a new plan to meet. I suppose it's going to delay everyone. I'll go and check in the hotel and see what they know. Anyway, good luck, and see you later.'

'I most certainly hope so! Bye for now.'

The girl in the hotel reception lets me have a go on her virus-ridden computer and we find out from the Athens airport website that it's not as bad as it could be. Planes are arriving in dribs and drabs, albeit way behind schedule. She then kindly phones them up (the airport people, that is, not the planes), and they confirm that all the flights will eventually get here some time by the late afternoon, so there should be no problems of anyone in our little band actually missing the game, but there won't be much time for anything before the game starts.

How are things with you, Pete?

Canny, man! Athens, eh? What a draw! And hey, the logistics were a doddle. Well it's a holiday sort of place, isn't it? So there are lots of direct flights from just aboot aal ower the shop, including Luxembourg. It was a ten-thirty kick-off from the Grand Duchy, which gave me plenty of time to get Tina to school on the Kirchberg for a quarter to nine, and from there it's only a twenty-minute drive to the Grand Ducal airport at Findel. When you first arrive in this patch, you tend to think of Luxembourg airport – 'above us only a tax haven' - in less than the most complimentary of terms. As in: it is only a third of the size of Newcastle International Airport and resembles what you reckon a provincial airstrip in Communist Poland must have looked like. But in the end, it kind of grows on you, like, and you think that, actually, it's dead canny. It's certainly stress-free. Just one big check-in counter, just small shops. But there's not the hassle of the crowded big places, and there aren't the massive distances to cover on autowalks either. That said, they have recently opened a spanking new terminal B and are currently busy building a third, presumably C – though this being Luxembourg, I wouldn't be surprised if they called it D.

It was only when I'd checked in at the single check-in counter, showing my single, claret-coloured European Union (GB) passport, introduced I think under the Single European Act and was about to enter the spanking new terminal B that I checked the departures board and realised that my single-hop flight to the Greek capital was in fact a two-hops affair calling into Bergamo in Italy (that's Ryanair-speak for Milan). Great, I'd be able to practise my eye-tiddly-eye-tie after only four evening classes which me and wor lass had embarked upon with a view to a mobile-home holiday in *bella Italia*, culminating hopefully in a trip to Pompei and Herculaneum: '*Vorrei una birra grande, per favore*' - which is probably what some poor sod was saying in some sleazy Pompei bar just as the first few salvos of rock and lava came spewing out of Vesuvius on that sultry twenty-fourth of August back in AD 79. 'Wheyabuggama,' he probably said to himself, 'a'd berra get this doon me neck sharpish – giz a double whisky an' aal.'

It just goes to show, mind, you never know what's around the corner, so you have to seize the day – *carpe diem* – and what better way to seize the day than by latching onto the best alternative to reality known to man, following Newcastle United?

Unsurprisingly, the day of the Panionios game was certainly full of surprises. My flight was due to get into Athens at a quarter past one. Chris and Sarah were flying direct from Heathrow and arriving at three o'clock, while Don was coming in from Gatwick, due in at half past twelve, after a six thirty take-off. Greece is one hour ahead of

Germany, Luxembourg and Belgium, and two hours ahead of the UK, don't forget.

When my flight was about to land in Italy after affording only furtive glimpses of the mighty Alps through the cloud, the captain gave us the less than welcome news that Greek public servants, including air traffic controllers, had picked today of all days to stage a lightning strike. Still, it usually doesn't strike twice in the same place. The onward flight was therefore delayed for at least a couple of hours and passengers for Athens were kindly requested to alight and proceed by bus to the transit lounge facilities. So I would be ordering a *birra grande* after all. Once in the bus, it was panic stations all round. No sooner was my mobile switched on than it was buzzing with a text message from Chris saying they were stuck in Heathrow with no departure in sight.

Bergamo airport buffet is pleasant enough and they keep a steady pint of Heineken. Bumped into a few lads from Glasgow who had been at the Inter v Barcelona Champignons League game the night before, won by Inter with the only goal of the game. They had just wanted to savour the atmosphere of the San Siro. Compared notes about travelling around the various grounds of Europe and what great fun it is. Reminded me of the time we bumped into a ground-hopping Toon wallah when we played at Ipswich, I think it was, back in the early eighties. Turned out we had come over on the same ferry from Zeebrugge to Felixstowe that night. Many memories of dossing overnight under the stairs in a sleeping bag on that ship. He had been to see Standard Liège play at home against somebody or other, for no better reason than that he'd always wanted to go and see Standard Liège play at home against somebody or other to see what it was like. Fair enough, if you ask me.

I'll just text Barry to update him on the delay. How are things in Athens while I'm kicking my heels in Bergamo?

I can't complain, Pete! I've just re-emerged into the heat from the cool of the roof-top pool. A couple of large Swedish families were hogging all available sun-loungers, so I jumped straight into the empty pool for a long swim. I'll keep your ticket on me, in case you have to go straight to the ground from the airport. We don't want another mix-up over collecting tickets at the reception like that time in the smoke. We had left tickets for the Wimbledon game in an envelope bearing the words 'For Mr Kelly', and a well-meaning lassie popped the envelope under Mr Kelly's hotel room door – only trouble was, it was the wrong Mr Kelly. Even if you get here really late and we're already in the ground, you can phone and I'll come down to the turnstile and get you through. I'm off for a spot of sightseeing in the metropolis. See you sooner rather than later, I hope.

First stop is at the foot of the Mount Lycabettus funicular railway. Second stop is at the top, the highest point in Athens, where I admire the little old white church with the little old lady giving out little old white candles. Should I light one for the good of the team, I wonder? The view across the metropolis and over to Piraeus and the Aegean Sea is unbeatable, as is the team now the candle's safely glowing away. From this mountain peak, even the Acropolis is below us. I ask a couple of lads if they can point out where the Panionios and Egaleo grounds lie and they are very well-informed, especially considering that they turn out to be Bulgarians working on a short-term IT contract. They love the place, they say.

Back down at ground level in Kolonaki Square, I buy a copy of 'Derby', which is one of the Greek football papers. It's just down the hill from our hotel (Kolonaki Square, that is, not Derby), and judging by the look of the people in the packed pavement cafés, this must be one of the places to see and be seen for afternoon drinks. The Greeks seem to love to get out onto one of these terraces and while away the time over a *frappé* or two. That's a long, cool, milky coffee on the rocks, by the way, and it appears to be the national drink, judging by the quantities dotted around the tables. I wasn't sure what it was, so I just said 'I'll have one of those that everyone else is drinking, please, pet.' Not bad at all. Why the Greeks use a French name, meaning iced milk shake, and not a Greek one is beyond me. The other question is: when do they ever find time to work? That's what the Olympic Committee was asking back in the spring, too. The solution was right under their noses all the time: the Greek government declared a frappé-free period of Greek Orthodox Lent and, hey presto, they got themselves a stadium. Maybe.

You drink your *frappé* very slowly in sips, and you have a glass of iced water to accompany it, to string out the ritual even longer. Which gives me plenty of time to learn Greek so that I can read the 'Derby'. No mention of Brian Clough, Colin Todd or Archie Gemmill anywhere. No, it's full of Panathinaikos and their previous night's two-two draw with Arsenal. That's what the pictures told me. It also had a page or so about Panionios in the middle. You really can't make head nor tail out of anything in Greek: Craig Bellamy looks like *Tkperk Mnelami*, Graeme Souness is *Tkpeiam EoyneE*, Alan Shearer is *Eipep*, and Newcastle is *Nioukaotl*. With a bit of imagination, you can just about get your head around *Nioukaotl*. Especially after a night out in the Bigg Market and a couple of doners from the Turkish kebab shop.

I do believe that the Bigg Market one was the first kebab shop opened in Newcastle, probably in the North-East. As a matter of interest, I also do believe that kebabs reached us before MacDonald's, though it was a close-run thing either way. I was at the university at the time – about 1977 – and my Turkish friends were overjoyed to find Turkish cuisine coming to the North-East, so they used to go down regularly at lunchtimes and pick up an order for all of us. But Turkey's not Greece, though the food's the same, so let's stop talking Turkey. You might on the other hand erroneously believe that MacDonald's is synonymous with Greece, if you're not a good speller.

As I wander aimlessly around, I come upon a home-made reminder of the Olympics: a mock four-lane red running track painted on one of the narrow streets which traverse the old Athens district of Plaka. Nobody can explain how this district came to be named after the Geordie word for plastic. Its slopes lead gently up towards the rock of the Acropolis and are full of tavernas and souvenir shops. The town is nearly empty of Toon fans – I've seen no more than a couple of dozen in dribs of two and drabs of three all day, and not many more Boro fans either.

Another check with the airport and none of our little band is likely to be down town until perhaps eight o'clock. What a waste - being stuck in airport lounges instead of taking in the sights of this great and historic city.

Are you still stuck in Italy, Pete?

Si, but not for long now. A couple of pints of the cool Heineken later and the announcement came through on the tannoy that passengers for Athens had better get their arse on the bus sharpish as their captain was rather keen to take off.

Maybe my emotions were Heineken-enhanced, but the cloud disappeared as we jetted south-east, and the beauty of the Adriatic coastline followed by the sun-kissed Greek islands lying in the now azure, now turquoise, now wine-dark Aegean was just breathtaking. The light is special. It is sharp, translucent, transcendental. You gaze down, almost god-like from your airborne Mount Olympus, and you can see those skeleton types from Jason and the Astronauts giving it six-nowt against the Spartans. Not Blyth Spartans, the other ones. Okay, so my Greek mythology is a bit iffy, who gives a monkey's bum? Then there was that scene where Jason, or somebody, wins a bet by hoyin' a discus from one island and hitting the next one – a seemingly impossible feat which he accomplished by skimming the discus across the water (clever shite). But then those Ancient Greeks were sodding clever, weren't they? All that philosophy and algebra and suchlike. And they had it all sussed hundreds of years before the Romans even got going. In fact, the Greeks had a thriving civilisation, complete with an early form of democracy, while the Romans, in a manner of speaking, were still plodgin aroond in the clarts to no particular effect.

Between those sand-rimmed islands in the midst of the sun-sparkling sea, you could imagine Poseidon, in the same film, gradually emerging from the deep and generally wreaking havoc amongst Jason's Argonaut fleet, hurling his trident at anybody working their ticket. By the way, does anyone actually know what an Argonaut is? Sounds like something out of Doctor Who, though but!

As the plane begins its descent towards Athens, the city unfolds before your eyes. More low- than high-rise, it seems to be spread out over several gently rolling hills, a vast metropolis and one of the worst-polluted cities in the world. So much so that apparently they try to reduce the traffic by letting in cars with plates ending in an even number one day, odd numbers the next. But of course, nobody pays a ha'p'orth of notice. For they are an anarchic bunch, the Greeks, as we were later to find out. That's democracy for you!

My flight landed about four, and after collecting my oversize suitcase (didn't have time to pack less), I gathered that there was a flight due in from London at half past five. The name on the flip-board kept changing from English to Greek, back and forth, which was a bit frustrating. The flipping thing is flipping over and moving on all the time as each flight gets in, and by the time you get to the English one you are looking for, it changes back to Greek and you start all over again, a line or two higher up. The Greek may well have specified Heathrow or Gatwick (buggered if I know), but the English certainly just said London, so maybe I'd be meeting Don or Chris and Sarah – or none of the three – on the half past five arrival. Their respective mobiles were on answer phone only, suggesting they were all still *en route*.

There was still some time to spare, of course, so what better way to spend that time than to sample some of the local culture by having a couple of local beers at one of the airport bars? Mind, Mythos is a steady drop, but you do get some funny looks changing into your Toon top in the middle of the airport. There was a good chance there'd be none of our lot on that flight, in which case the very next metro into Athens city centre would be essential. For that was a good forty km away and time was ticking by towards the thankfully late kick-off. Five thirty came along in due course, as five thirty always does, and a quarter of an hour later Don appeared out of the arrivals area. We breathed a collective sigh of relief, no doubt both with breath that was strongly suggestive of the cares of office, and hastily if uncertainly did we tappy-lappy across the taxi and bus lanes. We were just about bowled over by the heat as we went, for this was a trip back in time to the summer we had said farewell to a couple of months earlier. It must have been at least twenty-five degrees. Over a pedestrian bridge we went to the metro station – where, to our horror, we had a full half hour to wait for the next metro. But Fortuna was clearly smiling upon us. (Okay, so that's a Roman god, but let's not quibble, I'm from Waalsend, Segedunum, remember? They didn't do Greek gods in Segedunum.) For lo and behold, there was shown unto us a metro station buffet, replete with copious supplies of Mythos. So we thought we might as well have a swift half before the train. Tried Chris's mobile. Still switched off. Shite. This did not bode well... Managed to get through to Barry, though. Hoo's it gannin?

I'm settled down nicely here, Pete, out on my hotel balcony. What a day for a strike! Typical! You should see this view over the Acropolis in the middle distance and beyond to Piraeus and the Saronic Gulf. By the way, I've just had a text message from back home saying that the authors' copies of our *Toon Tales* book have arrived. Missed by one day, otherwise we'd have been able to bring them with us.

I can see right over to Nea Smyrni, where we're playing Panionios, and Egaleo is just a bit further across on the right. The Boro fans should be starting to gather for their match soon. Hold on, that gives me an idea, Pete... If you're not going to be here for another couple of hours... I think I'll go and have a look at the Egaleo stadium and catch some of the pre-match atmosphere before heading for Panionios. The

Boro match starts at a quarter past seven, and ours doesn't begin till half past nine, so there's plenty of time.

Half past nine? I thought it was nine! Well, mind how you go, Barry. But don't get too interested in the Boro game! Give us a bell when you're getting near the ground and we can meet up over there instead!

Our metro was due to leave the airport station at half past six, so down the escalator we duly went. All the signs and adverts were of course in, er, Greek! Though most signs helpfully also gave an English translation, albeit sometimes a bit iffy. None of our party this time had even a smattering of the local lingo, so we were well and truly snookerated. Mind, that is not strictly true, as Kristos and I (Petros) in our frantic pre-match e-mails had taken to beginning with *'kalimera'*, which we reckoned meant 'hello', or 'good morning', or something of that ilk. Unfortunately, that quickly degenerated into *'calimares'*, which almost definitely means 'squid' in Spanish.

No sooner were Don and I safely ensconced in the metro than Kristos rang on the mobile: *'Calimares*, Petros' – *'Calimares*, Kristos'. Then we cunningly switched to Geordie, just to confuse any spies and add to our general air of international mystique, cunning linguists that we are! 'What's gannin' on, bonny lad?' Their flight had landed about ten minutes earlier; they were through customs and running like mad to catch our metro... those bloody air traffic controllers. The race against time was on...

Chris and Sarah came hurtling down the escalator just as the metro pulled away. Looks of disbelief all round. Five minutes later another call on the mobile. They were in a taxi – no doubt they'd be overtaking us soon on the motorway running exactly parallel to the metro line. We'd meet at the St. George Hotel.

Don and I were beginning to notice an acute lack of beer. Difficult to take when you've been getting refills all day long. What were we supposed to do? Don had arrived at Gatwick at half five for his six thirty flight, only to be told that it wouldn't leave for another five hours, maybe. Nothing for it but to tuck into a hearty breakfast pint – remember, you should never eat on an empty stomach. And I had no choice at Bergamo but to have a couple. And another in the plane, at the airport, at the metro station – and then that heat...

Now Don still had those two spare tickets. He spotted a likely couple of backpackers who would surely be interested. Turned out they were two Australians, Bruce and Sheila. Okay, they were Ryan and Sarah really, but we christened them Bruce and Sheila, and those were the names they answered to all evening. They had been to Rome for a few days and were gobsmacked and awe-struck. And now they were going to be in Athens for a few days for more of the same, only older. Turns out that Bruce is a semi-professional cricketer who has made Yorkshire's second team in the county championship. And of course all Aussies are mad on all sports all of the time, and so they bought the tickets (at face value, it goes without saying). Their planned romantic candlelit supper in a Greek taverna was off. But hey, an evening as part of the Toon Army was definitely on!

We all got out at Omonia station, as Bruce and Sheila's hotel and Don's Hotel Amaryllis were apparently just around the corner. The last few metro stations into the centre of the city were more like museums than stations – statues, urns, jewellery on display all over the place, and on display pretty close to where they were found during the construction of the metro for the Olympic Games.

So here was our first impression of an Athens street when we emerged from the metro: utter chaos – horns honking like crazy amid a rush-hour swirl bathed in the early evening neon lights. And everybody, but everybody, seemed to be smoking, just to keep the pollution levels up to the statutory minimum. Plenty coughing to be heard too. And no English at all on these signs. This was abroad with a capital Alpha. Time was not on our side and we were going to be pretty well dependent on the locals' good will and on their being able to understand English. We had a city street map but were not proving very adept at using it, so resorted to asking the way at just about every corner. 'Is this the way to Amaryllis?' we sang, Peter Kay style. Everyone wanted to be helpful, it has to be said. It's just that they weren't, as each successive Greek seemed to contradict his or her predecessor. Take Nick just outside the station, for example:

'You must cross here, I suppose,' he supposed, 'and be going along that street over there for some hundreds of metres.'

At the end of that street, Stavros sent us half way back, at which point we should turn right, he supposed. All this supposing must have something to do with Greek philosophical suppositions, we supposed, logically. Nick the polis wasn't much better, either. He wanted us to go back to the metro station. To start again, we supposed.

As it was getting ever later, Donos came up with the sensible suggestion that he continue the search for his hotel on his own and that I hop in a taxi and make my way to the rendezvous with Kristos and Sarah.

Anyhow, I started walking in what I reckoned had to be the general direction of the St. George and tried to hail a passing taxi. Several occupied ones passed and a few empties just kept going. Then one stopped. I told him where I wanted to go and he nodded ever so slightly and set off – without me. This was strange – but then it dawned on me. The Greeks, like the Bulgarians, nod to say no and shake their heads when they mean yes. The Greeks do just a very slight nod or shake, whereas with the Bulgarians both are much more pronounced. I had been in Sofia (the capital) in the summer and, even after about three weeks, hadn't got used to this. A couple of times I had opened a taxi's front passenger door, asked '*Svobodno li e?*' (Are you free?), and on getting a shake of the head by way of reply, closed the door again and walked away. But here in the congested Athens rush hour it was nods all round, only they meant no.

At about the tenth time of asking, I finally saw the shake of the head I had been waiting for (confusing, isn't it?). So once I was safely inside the clapped-out heap of rust and my oversized suitcase was squeezed (squozen?) into the boot which wouldn't close, I asked the driver – Nick, I think his name was – why the others had not wanted my fare. 'No speak English,' came the reply. Of course! It should have been so obvious to me: none of them had been able to speak English and so didn't want a Geordie passenger. So I told Nick how thankful I was that he spoke English and then, enunciating my words in that familiar exaggerated way we do when we think life or death (or getting to the match on time) could depend on us being understood by a foreigner, I told him 'it – is – getting- very – late. We – must- get- to – the - hotel - and – pick – up - my – friends – and – then – please – drive – like mad – to – Pa-ni-o-ni-os.' To which Nick very reasonably replied: 'No speak English'!

'Oh bugger,' thought I. Not that it would have made any difference anyway. The traffic was just horrendous, and we seemed to be in a maze of one-way streets. The St. George is half-way up the hill and so we had to wind our way up there, going in one direction and then another, and then in yet another. And the streets up the hill are not wide. Everyone was tooting their horn. Taxis were stopping to let old dears out with their shopping as they looked for the right change while holding up the rest of the city on its way home from work, or on its way to the frigging match! Get a move on, for Kristos' sake! Every now and then, you'd catch a glimpse of some floodlit ruins which would be very impressive any other time but now. It was already eight and I was getting worried. If this was how long it took Nick the driver to crawl up the Lycabettus hill to the St. George, how long would it take him to get to the stadium, which according to my map was somewhere down by the docks, a million mazes of back streets away. I needn't have worried. We had already been travelling for about twenty-five minutes when we pulled up in front of the hotel, so I had reached the point where you feel it is time to look at the meter and check your wallet just in case, but all it said was four euros – amazing! We weren't the only taxi pulling up at that very posh hotel, so it wasn't easy to see who was where, but there indeed were Kristos and Saronica, somehow managing to keep their cool despite the heat of the balmy Athens evening and the fast-approaching kick-off time. I jumped out of the car while they dived in the back. Dumped my case at reception with a quickly muttered explanation and then dived back in. Off Nick drove with a smile on his face. He obviously thought it was great fun.

What goes up must come down. (Was it a Greek philosopher who came up with that? Dabizas perhaps? Thinking of leaping to defend a corner in a crowded penalty area?) So down the hill we went and became immersed in the traffic *maelström*. But the Greek gods were with us and there were no major hold-ups. Twenty minutes later, we got out ahead of the police lines around the Panionios stadium in what appeared to be a pretty quiet residential suburb. That two-legged, forty-five-minute, capital-city taxi ride had cost all of seven and a half euros, and Nick the driver seemed dead chuffed with his euro-and-a-half tip to boot. And to think, a Greek colleague (not from Athens, so probably feels towards that city the way we feel towards the smoke) had told me to beware of Athenian taxi drivers. 'Beware of Athenian taxi drivers,' he had said, ominously.

Feeling slightly peckish (not to mention thirsty) by now, Kristos, Saronica and I, Petros, approached a nearby sausage-selling stand where Eumaeus the sausage seller was selling sickly sausage rolls. Strangely, when we greeted him in our fluent Greek, he informed us there was a fish restaurant just around the corner. Funny, that! Next to Eumaeus was Stavros the purveyor of beers. So all was soon hunky dory. We crossed the street, past mounted and on-foot police, to the stadium. Loads of locals came up to us for a bit crack and the first few photos of the evening were taken. Somebody said that Nikos Dabizas came from just around the corner. More and more Toon wallahs appeared and we all naturally formed a cluster that soon found its singing voice. All the favourites got an airing, and the locals, including the polisses, seemed to be lapping it up.

Now pick up the remote and rewind by a couple of hours, back to Barry at the hotel we had just left...

'How do I get to Egaleo?' I ask the concierge.

'What on earth do you want to go there for?' A discerning football fan, I note.

'Just to have a look at what it's like before our match starts.'

'There'll be no one there! They've switched the match to the Apollon club's George Kamaras Stadium in Rizoupoli. It's where Olympiakos played while they built their new ground in Piraeus. It takes about eleven thousand fans, far bigger than Egaleo's own ground. Do you want to go? We'll get you a taxi. It shouldn't be much more than ten euros.'

'Lucky I asked! Great, I'll be back in a couple of minutes.'

I quickly change into an undercover tee shirt less likely to raise the hackles of any over-sensitive Boro fans, stuff my Toon top and banners into a Plaka bag, and jump into the taxi.

By the way, why do they shorten Middlesbrough to Boro? To the confusion of many, there's only one 'o' in Middlesbrough. Like there's only one c*** in Scunthorpe. So its short name should be Bro, surely? As in 'Hey, Bro, how ya doing?' Very rap. As in Bro, the team that put the 'c' in rap.

The rush-hour traffic is grinding along. That's a contradiction in terms, isn't it? You can't rush anywhere in the rush hour. Day turns to night in the good three quarters of an hour it takes us to reach a flyover from where we can see straight into the floodlit stadium to our left. There is already a sprinkling of Boro fans in the white-painted stand. I ask the taxi driver how I can get back to Panionios from here. And now he tells me that in actual fact there's a metro line from just along from the flyover which will take me nearly all the way to Panionios and that I should be able to make it in about half an hour.

As I make my way down to the ground, I bump into the same UK-based scarf-sellers that we've met many times before. They've got a big wad of scarves, half red for Boro, half light-blue for Egaleo.

'How much this time, lads?'

'Five euros.'

'That's not bad. If you've got a Toon one, I'll take one of each. Here's ten euros.'

'We'll fetch you one from the car, but that'll make it fifteen euros, all told.'

'Eh?'

'Yeah, we can't get anyone to buy these Boro ones, and there's only half an hour to go. But you Geordies are good customers. We're heading over to your game as soon as they kick off here.'

Somehow it seemed strangely fitting. The Toon are worth twice as much as the Boro in all respects, even scarves.

The atmosphere outside the ground is friendly and relaxed. Supporters of both sides are mixing together, having a chat while queueing for kebabs and hot dogs. Then I see that they're still selling tickets and the queue is pretty short and moving rapidly. Well, now I am here, it seems a pity not to go in and have a look. The thing is, will they let me in to the home supporters end? If I buy a ticket for the away section, I don't want to take the risk of not being allowed out until half an hour after their game's finished! Which would be half-way through our match! While I'm queueing, I calculate that I can watch the whole of the first half and still be able to get to our match with plenty of time to enjoy the pre-match build-up. Just in case they're not keen on selling home tickets to away supporters, I ask the man in front and he says it probably will be alright. With a friendly smile, he kindly offers to buy one for me at the same time. And for the price of one Toon and three Boro scarves, I find myself sitting up in the back rows of the stand opposite the Boro fans, in line with the goal they are going to be attacking in the first half. I put on the cheap scarf and try to blend in with the locals.

Aside from pre-season tournaments, I think this must be the first time I am going to see two matches on the same day. It's also going to be one of those rare occasions when I'm at a match with no Newcastle shirts in sight. Except the one in my bag. I toy with the idea of putting it on, but decide that discretion is the better part of valour on this occasion – after all, don't PAOK Thessaloniki play in black and white stripes, too? I don't want to be mistaken for one of their supporters and get ejected or, worse still, detained!

Watching a game when you really don't care who wins, in other words watching a game when the Toon aren't playing, is a strange experience. You just want to see something happen. A few goals, a bit of controversy, something to talk about, something to remember. Well, I'm not getting any of those watching the first half of Egaleo v Boro. Though truth to tell, I hope Boro win. It's hard going for them, with neither side having many chances, and Egaleo if anything slightly ahead on points. Zenden, or is it Mendieta, – they both look pretty similar with their floppy blond hair - is fairly active in his new role in the centre, while Viduka is even tubbier-looking than ever and waddling around to little effect. The black left back of Egaleo is doing really well with some good tackles, interceptions and searching forward passes, and looks a good player. I wouldn't be surprised if Egaleo go ahead. The maybe three hundred and fifty or so Boro fans are having a good time over on the other side of the pitch, but they're very isolated with wide open terraces either side of them, so there's not much scope for banter with the home supporters. And even the home supporters don't feel at home because they're not at their own ground; in fact they're at the old ground of one of their biggest rivals. It would be exactly like Boro having to play the second leg at joker park, if it hadn't been razed to the ground. Shame about that, though but...

The half-time whistle blows and the Boro players start to troop off towards us. This is my cue to get up and go. The police guarding the gate wonder why I want to leave, and one of them says something. I was hoping to get out without having to say anything, but I have to admit that I don't understand, so I say that I came just to see what it was like and that their team have played very well and deserve to be edging it at the moment. They let me through and wish me a good evening: 'Kalispera'. Yes please, with red sauce.

I make my way at a good pace to the metro station and, for the very reasonable sum of about forty pence, I buy a ticket to ride the very smart and clean metro tram to the Nea Smyrni district on the other side of town. Once there, I ask a passer-by which street leads towards the ground, and I jump in a taxi, but the traffic's still as bad as it was before the Egaleo match and we crawl along a main shopping street. On the way, there are four Toon fans looking for a ride and the driver asks if we can take them and of course I agree. In fact it's quite normal in Athens for taxis to pick up other fares along the way – they run their taxis more like buses. You all pay your own fare, not a share of the total price, so people can get in and be dropped off along the way. It seems a pretty good idea to me. Anyway, they pile in the back and start on how they've been held up in the airport most of the day and have only just made it in time. One of them was based in Norwich and the others in deepest Durham, and they'd travelled via Gatwick.

It takes quite a while to get to the ground, what with all the traffic, but we can hear match commentary in Greek from the Boro game and can make out a few names of Boro players now and then. Then there's a bit of a roar and we learn from the driver (Nick) that Boro have scored what later proved to be the only goal of the match. We pile out of the taxi, give him our individual fares, and I turn round and there's Pete, Sarah and Chris and a whole load of Toon fans standing outside the away entrance. Then Don appears, proudly bearing a huge great Panionios flag on a six-foot pole which he begins waving, continental fashion. Don collects flags. We take a few pictures with our *Toon Tales* banners and promotional tee shirts and give out plenty of flyers and then head for the turnstiles. Don's pole is long enough to arouse the suspicions of the ground staff (oo-err, missus), who confiscate the flagstaff despite Don's protestations that it's only a little stick, not an Olympic javelin.

The crack among the Toon Army is all about their various adventures and near-misses getting here. Apparently, the Toon Travel flight full of Newcastle lads and lasses has been diverted to the island of Rhodes. Not a hundred per cent sure where that is, actually, but clearly those concerned would have to content themselves with watching the match on the telly. Only about a quarter of an hour to go to kick-off now, so it's high time we get our arses into the ground.

This heat is really something. It's late October and yet it's like a sultry summer evening. And the one thing you need on a sultry summer evening is beer. And UEFA rules notwithstanding, they're selling cans of the cool Heineken, the proper stuff, that is. Beer cans in hand, we can have a proper look around us, so we can.

The stadium is a modest affair, really. Just a basic oval with a bit of a running track and enough terracing around three quarters of the ground for about fifteen thousand. We at least had converted Mickey Mouse bench-type seating in our bit (sort of the old paddock in front of the old stand towards the Gallowgate End), and the main stand was on our left. It's got a bit of the horse-shoe look of the old Olympic Stadium at the moment, because the fourth side behind the far goal just isn't there, though the presence of building site cranes and portakabins indicates this might well be just a temporary situation until a new stand is built. And to our right the U end of the horse-shoe which is still there looks as if it may not be there for too much longer either, as it's cordoned off and empty - and looking very ramshackle. Loads of medium-rise flats overlook the whole affair in the late-autumn-evening Saronic-Aegean light.

We start distributing flyers for *Toon Tales*, and just about everybody thinks it's a brilliant idea (couldn't agree more). Except, that is, for this rather burly baldy lad and his marra, who aren't too keen on the idea at all, for reasons best known to themselves.

'Come here! So what's this all about?' asks the baldy lad in a polis's voice. Mevvies he was a polis, aah divenaa. 'Hev'n seen yees it any games!' Now that's a friggin' joke – I must have spent the equivalent of Andorra's gross domestic product on watching the Toon over the years. And between us, Barry, Chris, Sarah, Don and I have barely missed a single European away game over the last decade. And if we want to write books about the Toon at our own expense and with little prospect of even breaking even, 'coz we love the Toon, then we are going to, and we'll forget the killjoys.

A couple of lads I give flyers to are particularly interesting Toon wallahs. Sunburnt as they are, they obviously left Tyneside a while back. Turns out one of them had been in *Deutschland* for a good bit, and his brilliant German bears witness to that alright. But now the pair of them have some kind of market stall in a Greek village on the coast somewhere. And they have both started learning Greek. There's nee keeping the Geordies doon – best of luck to them!

Panionios beat the much more familiar name of Udinese in the qualifying round, so they're not going to be push-overs. Their team is made up of eight different nationalities - a bit like ours! The easiest to pronounce is their Australian defender called Dodd. Their lone forward, Breska, is Panionios's equivalent to Bellamy and looks fairly useful with his pace and mobility, which get him a pretty good heading chance early on.

Robert is obviously heeding his new manager's warnings that he has to be more involved when we're not in possession and he gets in a very good clearance from back in our own penalty area. He's putting himself about a fair bit, though sometimes giving away free kicks. One's too near our penalty area, from where the Greeks have a good chance with a header. His colleague on the left side, Bernard, makes some good solid tackles and is neat and tidy throughout the half. Just after half-way through the first period, Robert slams a free kick from just outside the penalty area against the wall. From the rebound, which comes nicely back out into his stride, he drives a hard daisy-cutter which the goalkeeper just manages to parry when it looks as if it's heading inside the far post. Robbie Elliott does very well with some long, raking passes, one of which Bellamy just fails to control as he races through into the penalty area. Overall though, a lot of passes are going astray, and there are very few good sequences. One exception sees Milner break down the right then cleverly leave the ball to Carr, who centres to Robert on the edge of the penalty area. He cushions a header to Shearer, who should perhaps have slid it back to Robert who was poised to shoot, but instead pushes it nicely back into the path of Jenas whose perfectly met rising shot unfortunately is aimed straight at their goalkeeper. And just before the half-time whistle, Jenas has probably the best chance of the half when he sidesteps a mass of bodies in the penalty area, but having done the harder part then manages to scoop the ball over the bar.

There's a strange atmosphere to the place tonight. It isn't the usual hundred per cent Geordie *bonhomie*. For instance, some cretinous young turd is prancing around half-cut or half-stoned, getting on everyone's nerves. He and his mate have been spending too much of the day killing time in some airport lounge. While we're getting in a round of drinks at the back of the terraces opposite the netties (and they really are just like the old-fashioned back-yard variety), he's up threatening people and generally being a total prat. At one stage, he clocks his own mate one. They're dragged away by their mates to opposite sides of the enclosure, and it looks as if things have settled down. But then he has a go at the cockney scarf-seller who's made it over from Egaleo, protesting that, after all, he is English as well. The cockney lad is doing no harm and this pissed-up Geordie moron is right out of order, as they say. Anyway, ten minutes or so further into the plot and while we're intently watching what's going on down on the pitch (generally, it's a pretty poor match), we hear this sickening, squelching thud, the kind of sound you imagine an over-ripe melon might make if hoyed with gusto directly against a concrete stair. The lad's completely motionless, with his neck lolling nastily back over the edge of one of the steps, and everyone thinks he's deed. People go looking for stewards but no one appears, so I go up to the drinks stand and ask them to call the Red Cross, but they're much more interested in selling beers and they make as if they don't understand.

You would have expected his previous antics to have attracted the attention of the local law. And indeed they have. But the local law is clearly not interested. Whereas in Geordieland and many other countries the polisses would have stamped on him immediately, the Greek police seem to be taking the view that 'as long as they're fighting among themselves, let them get on with it'. And now that he appears to be at least in danger of bleeding to death, they obviously feel that as long as it stays *entre nous* it's okay. It takes an age before ambulance men eventually turn up and tend to him. We're all genuinely relieved when he finally comes around, because a lot of us had really believed he was a goner. But at the same time, we all hope he'll suffer enormously the next day, because that is exactly what he deserves for being a mindless cretin that has no business among Newcastle United supporters. You're not welcome, bonny lad.

But there's more to come. Somebody's daughter had been to the netty and some lad had joined her there to make sure she was okay. Dad had got wind of that and was not best pleased. Someone appeared shortly afterwards holding a blood-stained rag to his nose. The family drama unfolded before the eyes of the Toon Army. What can Bruce and Sheila be making of all this? The thing is, this kind of trouble really is so unusual nowadays, thank God, and that's why it made such an impression on everyone.

Some tired-looking fans stroll in at half time – the ones who'd been on the Toon Travel plane that had been diverted to Rhodes because of the air strike. 'Part time supporters, you're only part-time supporters' rings in their ears. At least they made it in time to see the goal.

Things get a little heated on the field too in the early minutes of the second half with bodies flying in all directions, and at one point, six different players are writhing on the ground at the same time. In the midst of all this, Lee Bowyer gets booked for mistiming one tackle and soon after is very lucky not to receive a second yellow card when he fails to connect with a loose ball and, in his follow-through, lands on the prone body of a Greek defender who himself had already dived in recklessly at the ball. It was unintentional, but the way he landed certainly looked bad. As if on cue, a big black stray dog then makes its entry onto the pitch, and the interruption has the effect of calming things down a bit. Strains of 'Woof, woof, black and white army' recall the infamous Bloater and Gloater interview of yesteryear about North-East women and dogs. And then a great through-ball from Robert almost lets Bellamy in, but the goalkeeper comes out quickly and foils him. The ball is now constantly in or around the Panionios penalty area. Robert sends in a corner from the left and Shearer connects with a good header but it's straight at the goalkeeper. Then Robert takes a good free kick from the other side and Ameobi, who has just come on as a substitute for Milner, is left free at the far post but fails to guide what should have been a fairly easy header into the net. Yet another Robert cross comes over and again it's a Shearer header, but once more it's straight at the keeper.

Now Jenas is teed up by Shearer but he lofts a long-range shot well over the bar. A deftly weighted through-ball from Robert in the centre-circle sets Ameobi free on a breakaway into the penalty area, but he tumbles too easily and half-hearted penalty appeals are waved away. Time's running out. And then it arrives: Jenas threads the ball through to Shola, whose lightning turn leaves his marker for dead and all he can do is clumsily barge Shola down. Cue 'You do the Ameobi and you turn around and that's what it's all about. Oh, Shola Ameobi, oh, Shola Ameobi, SHOLAAAH'. This added, long, raucous SHOLAAAH shout really makes it! Then the chants turn to 'Shearuher, Shearuher' as he blasts in the penalty. The last action of the game sees our hero heading a Panionios free kick clear from our penalty area to just about the half-way line. Success, and mission accomplished.

As I wrote to wor Scon on the postcard I sent the next day: 'Greetings from beautiful Athens, where Newcastle only just managed to beat the local equivalent of Hartlepool United!' Now as I was sending the card from Greece and do not know a single word of the local lingo, I finished off wor Scon's address with the word Angleterre, which of course is the French for England. Why did I do that? Well because French, believe it or not, is the official international postal language. They gave the frogs that much as a kind of consolation prize when their language was relegated to the Third Division (South) not long after the First World War. Nobody ever uses it as the postal language, mind - 'cept me, of course! Now my scrawl isn't too easy to read at the best of times, but after I have had a couple of Greek beers, well... Anyway, wor Scon gives me a bell a month and half later and says,

'Thanks for the card from Athens, it got here via Australia.'

'What?'

'Aye, that's reet, Australia, doon under like.'

'Hadawayanshite!'

'Nah, honest, it says Mis-sorted to Melbourne, Australia.'

Some Greek sorter must have read my Angleterre as Australia. They should get them sorted, those Greek sorters. Mind, having twice worked on the Christmas post in Newcastle back in the seventies, nothing would surprise me. The best fun was to be had sorting parcels. There was this grid in front of you comprising loads of mail bags. One would be marked Hartlepool, another Heddon on the Wall, that sort of thing – you get the picture. So what happened if a parcel addressed to somebody in Warkworth got hoyed into the bag for Waalsend instead? Well, it went to Waalsend to get re-sorted, that's what happened. 'Coz neebody was ganna dive after it into the bag, that's for sure. And guess what happened to anything that looked like a Pirelli calendar? Whoops, I'd forgotten we all signed the Official Secrets Act. Hey, does that mean we were on Her Majesty's Secret Postal Service? Her Majesty, the Queen of Angleterre and Australia, that is! I wonder if in Quebec they speak the Queen's French? Nah, man, she's English. Well if yer ganna be like that, marra, she's Jorman, actually.

So we had won, and our UEFA Cup dream was very much alive. We were kept in detention of course, but we were all in very good humour now that the lunatic element had been removed. Many of our supporters had spent most of their day hanging around waiting, so they were well used to it by now. This time at least the team came across to our corner and acknowledged the cheers, which helped to pass some of the time and we spent the rest giving out some more of our *Toon Tales* flyers and taking down our three strategically placed *Toon Tales* banners. They'd stood up well to the competition to get them stuck up in good spots pitch-side. Thousands' worth of exposure on Greek TV, but only fleeting and distant glimpses on Channel Five, as we learnt later when we watched the video when we got back home.

On the way out, Don reminded the stewards that they had confiscated his Panionios flag on the way in and they duly gave it back to him. Don had pointed out that plenty of Pan fans had flags, and he was right – there is no justice. We spotted the lad who'd banged his head earlier. He was looking very groggy, but at least he was standing up. When we'd heard the sound, we'd feared the worst. Those Geordie melons sure can take some hard knocks.

So now it was time to head back into town for some nosh and a bevy of bevvies. The crowds soon dispersed and we weren't completely sure where we were. We tried asking some passers-by and got some general directions, then Don spotted a car which was slowing down at a junction and popped his head through the window to ask directions, we thought. But no, in fact he was requisitioning the car and its driver. Don and our new Australian friends piled in, as the driver looked on bemused but didn't complain, and as far as everyone could tell he agreed to take them to the city centre.

We carried on and eventually found a taxi and asked him to take us to Kolonaki Square. One of the main problems during the entire Athens trip was that none of us had the faintest clue about the layout of the city or, more importantly, the names of the various districts. Plus, of course, the only Greek word we were sure about was 'calimares', and even that was patently wrong. But never mind. Nihil desperandum, as they didn't say in Ancient Greek.

Then the phone rang and it was Don up ahead on the Greek driver's mobile phone. They were having difficulty getting the message through. It turns out that Nestor the driver could hardly speak a word of English, so God knows how he ever agreed to let three people and a giant flag on a stick pile into his car. Come to think of it, maybe he'd nodded vigorously meaning 'No way, man' in Greek head sign language, and Don had naturally understood this to mean 'Hop in, lads and lasses, where yiz gannin?' That was the problem.

'Where we gannin?' - this from Don.

Barry: 'Kolonaki Square.'

Don: 'Squalacis Stairs? Spell it to Nestor!'

'K _ O _L_O_ N _A_K _I'

'Where?'

Nestor took some persuading, too, because it sounded like he was becoming a bit reluctant in his new role as chauffeur by appointment to the Toon. About three similar mobile calls followed, transmitted from Athens to Brighton, or possibly to Australia, then to Brussels and back to Athens, but eventually we got there. And a jolly nice square it was, only a ten-minute, albeit uphill, walk to the St. George hotel. Probably.

A quick visit to the nearest hole in the wall, where we all wisely opted for the instructions in English for a change, and we were on the lookout for a nice little taverna. For a Thursday evening late on – it was already well past eleven – the place was heavin', and there were scantily-clad Greek goddesses aplenty – unfortunately generally accompanied by some un-godlike git, customarily called either Stavros or Nick.

We settled down in one of the cafés but a snobby-looking waiter came up and told us in no uncertain manner that they were closing. We weren't sure if it was just that he didn't want football fans on his terrace, because there were plenty of other people still sipping their drinks, but his loss was going to be greater than ours, so we shifted five yards across the pavement into the *Café Peros* instead. It had a sign announcing that it was open round the clock, twenty-four hours a day. One of its particular features was that there was a giant plasma screen tuned into Fashion TV, interspersed with short highlights of the night's two matches, and after midnight it seemed to focus on lingerie fashion, so the lads at the table had no complaints. We were as happy as Larry, sitting out in tee shirts in a pavement café till two in the morning, and it was nearly November: this was the life!

It has to be said, mind, that there was a bit of a pen and ink that wafted in our direction now and then, which caused us to begin to worry a little about the locals' personal hygiene. The mystery was to be solved the next evening...

The first waitress who came across wasn't much more welcoming than her competitor opposite and disappeared off without taking an order. Maybe it had something to do with the merry way Don was waving his giant Panionios flag above his head and getting it tangled up in the awnings.

But then a friendlier girl appeared and helped us make our choices. She taught us some Greek too. '*Yassou*' means 'hello' if you are meeting your marra, but it turns into '*yassas*' if youz are meeting your marras. *'Efharisto'* means 'thanks', and *'parakalo'* is please, but it also means 'you're welcome'. *'Ne'* means 'yes', which is quite confusing really when you think of 'nay, nay and thrice nay'. And *'ohi'* means no, which is just as bad if it reminds you of 'oh aye'. *'Kalimera'* is good morning, *'kalispera'* is good evening, and *'kalinichta'* is goodnight.

'Kalispera, and what would you like?'

'Kalispera, six beers and a glass of white wine, please pet, and three portions of stuffed courgettes.'

'I'll have to check whether the kitchen can still do the courgettes, probably they can, but give me a moment, *parakalo.'*

'If they haven't got them, can you ask them if they can give us something else which is real Greek food, *parakalo*?'

She skips off inside, returning to inform us that they can do us toasted ham, cheese and tomato sandwiches.

'Well, I suppose that'll be three Greek toasts, then, *parakalo.'*

'Efharisto.'

'So much for the open twenty-four hours, then!'

No sooner were we quaffing our Mythos than Bruce and Sheila told us they had recently got engaged. What a way to celebrate your engagement – to see the Toon win away in the UEFA Cup! Both from Sydney, they were doing the European grand tour after the end of the Yorkshire semi-pro cricket season. They'd already been to Dublin, Rome, Paris, Headingley, and of course, Newcastle.

Don's flag-waving was worrying our adorable waitress, Retsina, and she looked relieved when he nodded off to sleep. He only managed to eat half of his Greek toast in his sleep. Remembering the snoozing Toon fan in the *Vieux Port* in Marseille, we wished we could find a traffic cone hat for Don too. Then the language barrier briefly reared its ugly head again. We'd initially ordered seven drinks, and as usual the lads drank a bit quicker than the lasses so we soon ordered another five. Retsina nodded and said,

'So I suppose that's twelve you want, *efharisto*?'

'No, just five, *parakalo*.'

'But you've had twelve, then.'

'If you say so, pet, just keep them coming. *Parakalo*.'

I suppose that was right. All very sound. Several rounds later, we'd all had our fill and it was time to take our leave of Bruce and Sheila, who shared a taxi with Don, who had an early flight to catch. The rest of us wandered up the hill and reached the hotel at about two-thirty in the morning.

Now the St. George is a sound hotel, alright. All three of our rooms afforded a magnificent view of the Acropolis in its floodlit splendour. You have this terrific, nay breathtaking, view of the ruins, plus the lights of the entire city spread out before you, and in the background the sea. Steady or what? I couldn't resist a couple of the cool Heineken from the minibar and a bit sit on the balcony, albeit looking sideways onto the Acropolis. What a brilliant end to a brilliant day. Thanks to the Toon, such things are possible. Time for bed now, because I have got to be up and ready for ten o'clock in my jogging gear, 'coz Barry has this crackpot idea...zzz...zz...zzz...

Doing it for Paula

Barry's brilliant idea was that we should complete Paula Radcliffe's marathon for her! That's right: as far as crazy ideas go, they don't come much crazier than that. Who could forget the disappointment of the 2004 Olympics? When just about the whole world was willing the lovable Paula to take gold for the women's marathon on that searing hot August day in Athens.

Yes, Pete, we had an appointment with our Olympic destiny at The Shrine of Our Lady of the Marathon, located outside the Roland music shop on Mesogion Avenue, about six or seven clicks short of the finishing line in the old

Olympic stadium. As you must remember from the blanket television coverage of the Olympics, this is where Paula Radcliffe's marathon challenge staggered to a halt, completely exhausted in the August heat. Handily, she'd stopped outside a shop with an internationally recognisable name in its trademark big orange letters on a dark grey background, otherwise no one would have been able to remember where it had been, unless they were Greek of course. I've got one of their electric pianos, so it stuck in my mind, the thought that is.

Do you remember, Barry, we saw Paula close up at the start of the 2003 Great North Run? We'd climbed over the barrier to have a pee on the right bank of the Central Motorway and decided to wander down through the throng to the front to catch a glimpse of some elite athletes and some of the cast from Emmerdale Farm and the like. And there was Paula, limbering up before the start of the women's race but still finding the time to smile and wave to the fans. And this in stark contrast to the others, who appeared to be totally focused on and immersed in the task ahead. They could all be forgiven for being in a state, mind, but nevertheless Paula's personality shone out brilliantly against such a serious backdrop. She even bent over backwards, or was it forwards, to let us take her picture. And her apparently relaxed attitude was vindicated by the fact that she won the race by a considerable margin and set a new record in the process. What a fantastic occasion the Great North Run is!

I don't know exactly what the temperature was back in August, but on that late October morning after the Toon's victory over Panionios it was climbing steadily towards twenty-eight degrees by the time we climbed into our taxi at about half ten. Dressed in the black and white, we had already attracted quite a bit of attention as we passed through the hotel lobby. And our taxi driver, Nick the other Greek taxi driver, turned out to be very well informed about the Toon, about Shearer and, of course, Gazza in particular. And Dabizas!

Once again, we plunged into the crazy maze of Athens' one-way streets. They're called 'one-way' because the Greeks only know one way to drive – like lunatics. Just about every side road we drove down was stowed out, everybody honking at the obstacle ahead which they couldn't even see – usually a delivery van whose unloading driver was calmness personified in the midst of bedlam. On the way down to the marathon route, we passed right next to Panathinaikos' stadium.

What was it with all these Pans? Panionios? Panathinaikos? We were now keeping a look-out for a glimpse of Pan's People dancing to the music of Pan's pipes! It turns out that 'pan' means something like 'right across', as in the Toon's pan-European adventures, while 'ionios' comes from the Ionian Sea. Which makes sense when you learn that the founders of the club were Greek refugees driven over the sea from Smyrna in Turkey during the war between the two countries back in the twenties. They settled on the edge of Athens in a district which came to be known as Nea Smyrni, or New Smyrna. Similarly, Panathinaikos must mean 'spanning the athinaikos'. It sounds like it could be extremely painful and could rule out your siring children, so be warned. But our Greek friend Demetrios assures us that it really just means 'spanning Athens'.

Nick the taxi driver wasn't sure about the location of the musical instrument shop, though it did sound vaguely familiar to him and he thought it must have been there that he had bought his Pan's pipes, so he took us as close as the one-way system would allow to the blue line that was still to be seen in the middle of the city streets, marking out the route of the marathon.

We got out at a spot where there was a fork in the road (isn't it inconsiderate of those buggers who go around leaving their forks in the middle of the road?), because if Nick had continued along the one-way route, that would have taken us further away from the blue line. So oot we got and crossed over to the marathon side and started to make our way to the spot where Paula had given up. Nick had told us we were probably about five km from the Olympic stadium, so the thing to do was clearly to walk in the opposite direction, hoping we would come to the music shop before too long.

We were wondering whether ordinary shopkeepers and passers-by would understand and speak English, and were truly impressed by just how many of them did so, including a mechanic in a scooter and motorbike repair garage. 'How many mechanics in the Toon would speak Greek?' we asked ourselves. 'How many speak English, for that matter?' our southern friends might ask. Mind, there used to be a Vespa scooter repair shop in Byker (appropriately enough), at the Toon end of Shields Road, in the arches of the old North Tyneside loop, just along from where that car used to stick out of a wall. Just a Byker viaduct away from the Tanner's Arms opposite Saint Doms, in fact. It was Luigi's place. Luigi, appropriately enough, was Italian and he spoke an interesting and probably unique form of Italo-Geordie that only his wife could understand. 'Itza da plooga', he was wont to say. It's funny, but whenever my sometimes trusty Vespa 150 was *kaputt*, it always seemda da needa da newa plooga!

'He meanza da sparkinga plooga,' his wife Signora Luigina would helpfully explain.

So if a couple of Juve fans had passed Luigi's place when looking for a music shop in Byker, they would have been pleasantly surprised when he spoka dair lingo and probably tried to sell them a newa plooga.

It turned out to be a further two km to the music shop, but we whiled away the time by passing back and forward to each other the sparking plug which we had just bought for no apparent reason. Just before the shop, we passed the *Ethniki Anyma* metro station, which is on line three from Syntagma. If we'd known, we could have been here in a quarter of an hour. This October day in Athens was feeling more and more like an August day occasionally feels in our native neck of the woods. We were already sweating like pigs and we hadn't even started our run yet. Plus, I had only just managed to complete the Amsterdam marathon a week earlier and still hadn't recovered from the essential (and essentially Heineken-based) post-run rehydration. But hey, I had the medal in my shorts pocket ready to display it proudly outside the Athens Olympic stadium!

It felt as if we had already completed our mission and found the Holy Grail – but Barry was having none of it: we were going to complete Paula's run for her, and that was that!

Too right, Pete! Our duty was to re-enact the scene, take a few photos, and then 'do it for Paula' – run the last few kilometres for her. GB Olympic pride was at stake, as was that of the North-East, so we'd got our Toon tops, shorts and joggers on. We'd been expecting some kind of plaque or flowers to mark the sight of the Greek tragedy, but there was nothing. This will not do. We needed someone to take the photos, and who better than the owner of the Roland shop himself? No doubt he must have been used by now to a steady stream of pilgrims coming here to worship at probably the most photographed and famous Roland music shop in the world. We were expecting to be met by a resigned look of 'Oh no, not more of these pilgrim runners'. But no, quite the opposite: it turned out we were the first of the faithful. A puzzled expression descended over his features, as we broke into his absorbed listening to guitar jazz-rock music with a respectful request for a little of his time. Nikos was also quite hazy about the details of the great event that had taken place at this very spot. He'd been out of the shop at the fateful moment, so he was disappointingly unable to fill us in with any anecdotes or little-known details. In fact it was almost as if he'd been blissfully unaware of the sad event until we prompted his memory. Maybe it truly had been a vision, a miracle.

Notwithstanding, Nikos was a really good lad and he willingly offered to take our photos as we recreated the Paula-staggering-to-a-halt scene. Taking photos was quite a difficult task for Nikos as he couldn't press the shutter button because of the very long fingernails on his right hand. He needs them for his other role as a jazz-rock guitarist like his hero, Yorkshire-born Allan Holdsworth, whose music was playing in the shop. Nikos eventually waved across a passer-by to take over camera duties while he joined us on the photos. The news that these photos might well feature in a future book, ensuring some more international publicity for his shop, pleased Nikos very much indeed. The promise has been kept.

Photos taken, Nikos and bystanders waved us on our way as we jogged off down the road, carrying Great Britain's (well, Geordieland's) hopes with us as we shooed the spirit of Paula along the pavement in front of us. Come on Paula, chin up, you can do it, there's just a few miles to go. Mind, that lolling of your head from side to side is making me dizzy. Does it really help? And that Robbie Fowler tape on your nose? Howay man, get a move on, woman!

Now, now, Barry, show some respect! When Paula had been running the marathon back in August, she enjoyed one or two advantages compared with us. For a start, she is the consummate athlete, weighing in at not a single gram over her ideal weight. I, by contrast, am a big fat middle-aged Geordie git. She of course is also wonderfully good-looking, and not a bit anorexic like some of those elite athletes she competes against. But to be fair to ourselves, Barry, neither of us had given in to anorexia either! Now that takes an iron will. Another minor point in favour of the Olympic runners was that someone somewhere had thoughtfully closed the roads to traffic for the day. We were shown slightly less consideration – they didn't even close the pavements for us.

Once we got running, we soon realised what poor Paula had been up against. This was nearly November, but the well-nigh thirty degrees heat was stifling, and we began to wilt as our serious night on the Greek beer took its toll. The air was full of dust and exhaust fumes from the dense traffic, but crucially there was less humidity and the temperature was perhaps ten degrees lower than on Paula's day.

Dodging at least a million Athenian pedestrians, getting on their nerves, occasionally incurring their verbal wrath and side-stepping their dogs, we struggled along on the sunny side of the street, waiting for the gap in the traffic that was never going to come this side of the next Athens Olympic Games. Eventually a set of traffic lights got us to the other side, where the Heineken advert on the hoarding next to the park unfortunately poured only its scorn on us, none of the beer which by this time we were ready for again. Instead, we had to content ourselves with a couple of stops at newspaper kiosks for bottles of mineral water and a bit crack.

We were succeeding where Paula had failed. Let's not dwell too much on details – e.g. the fact that we'd not had to run the more than twenty miles from the town of Marathon to get to the Roland shop in the first place, or that Paula walks faster than we run, or that we weren't weighed down by our own hopes of winning a gold medal and the expectations of the British (plus the Geordie) nation. Such thoughts might detract from our achievement. At last, the finishing line shimmered into sight.

Triumph! Honour restored! We'd done it for Paula! We had the satisfaction of finishing the marathon for Paula three months after the event, a feat perhaps never before achieved in the history of the marathon, and perhaps never to be repeated ever again! Unfortunately, the elongated-horseshoe-shaped marble Panathinaiko Stadium, venue for the first modern Olympics and standing on the very site of the games of Ancient Greece, was closed, so we were denied the chance of doing a lap of honour. Just as well, really, 'coz I definitely wouldn't have made it, so cream-crackered was I! It used to be possible for anyone to go along and run around the track, and I actually did it myself a few years ago, but it looks as if they've now started locking the track off from the public since they renovated the marble terraces for the Olympics.

Do they think someone's ganna nick the marble, like that Elgin bugger?

The Panathinaiko Stadium has nothing to do with Panathinaikos football club, by the way. For a start, it's far too narrow to fit a football pitch in, because originally it was cut out of a hillside and there was no space to make it wider. It has admirably stood the test of time since it was first used in the reign of Queen Victoria (Gawd bless her and all who sailed in her) back in 1896.

Why mention the old Vic? Well, how about this for a little known fact? When it was run in Athens in 1896, the marathon distance was more than two kilometres shorter at forty kilometres, but when it came to London in 1908 it was lengthened so that it could stretch from Windsor Castle to the new White City stadium and round to the Royal Box where the Queen Vic's son, 'Fast' Eddie VII, was ensconced. Since then they've become used to ever more disagreeably sweaty foreigners in shorts ending up on their Majesties' doorsteps. And here was a case in point as we pounded into the stadium grounds, carrying our metaphorical torch for Paula and the hopes of the (Geordie) nation.

At the gates of the stadium, we had our photo taken by a couple of young tourists from Munich. And then, like two modern Phidippides, we sought out the two most senior persons present and announced to them the news that the Athenians had defeated the Persians. The bemused silver-haired couple turned out to be American tourists, as if we couldn't guess, and they took this news well, probably thinking it had something to do with Gulf War II. While we exchanged photo-taking duties, we discussed the relative merits of late October in Minnesota in the snow, Newcastle in the wind, and Athens in the sun. Since we were all standing here voluntarily in Athens, it appeared we'd voted fairly convincingly with our feet and our hired wings. The Minnesotans – by the way, that's where the aforementioned Fargo film was set - were intrigued to learn that what we had really been doing was restoring Paula's pride. They were pleased to note that we were not going to complete the re-enactment by flaking out like Phidippides had done two and a half thousand years ago. Mind, he'd run two hundred and eighty miles from Athens to Sparta and back just a matter of days before his Marathon run.

For the record, we made it down to the ancient stadium in forty-five minutes, which would have put us on schedule for about five hours for the whole marathon. Even in the state she'd been in at the Roland shop, we rather suspect Paula would have beaten us comfortably even if she'd been like that from the start. But we had done it for Paula. And if you ever go to Athens, we implore you to do it for Paula too! It should become a tradition, if not a ritual.

Paula, we salute you (or whatever that is in Ancient Greek)!

Time to get back to the hotel for a shower, a quick change and some suitably lubricated lunch, as Barry had to rush off for a mid-afternoon flight. The uphill walk along by the side of the National Park towards Kolonaki was rendered that much easier by the elation of our recent Olympic success. Interestingly enough, it took us past the presidential palace, whose grounds and approaches boasted an impressive police and army presence, complete with what looked like a guard of honour lining the drive. They looked canny, dressed in their funny fez hats, revealing mini-skirts, white tights with garters, pom-pom shoes, and holding their rifles in one hand, if you see what I mean. We wondered whether they belonged to the Greek Gay Gordons regiment, the 3G as they are known in military circles. This was some sight in the brilliant sunshine and against the verdant and shady backdrop of the well-watered presidential park. There were a few more tourists like us hanging around, but they didn't know what was happening, so we asked one of the polisses on our side of the road, and we received the answer that the Chinese president would be appearing in his motorcade any second now.

Further along, there were some dark-suited and sunglassed Greek wannabe CIA men surveying the gathering. They looked unnecessarily self-important and seemed to give off the air that they were invisible to mere mortals and hence unapproachable, obviously because they thought you couldn't see them with those black glasses on. So we went over and struck up a conversation with them.

'So what's going on, like?'

Shrugged shoulders and shifting of feet.

'It must be someone important. Who lives in the big house?'

A grunt by way of response. At this point, the band struck up a strangely familiar, though somehow anachronistic – nice Greek word, that - and out-of-place tune. Nicely out of tune. Living in Belgium as I do, I have unwittingly absorbed the unmemorable strains of their national anthem, a most sorry example. After nearly twenty years, I still can't whistle it... luckily. But there was no denying it, our 'conversation' was being drowned out by the tune.

'Are the Belgians here? Is it the royals?'

'Errm...'

'Or is it the mild-mannered, bespectacled, imbalanced cyclist, Clark Kent look-alike, Prime Minister whatsisname?'

But before they had a chance not to reply, a motorcade departed from what we now knew to be the Greek President's residence, carrying with it the Belgian royals: er... ye knaa... whatsernames... that's it, them, King Jupiler and Queen Stella, in a rather old mid-blue armour-plated Merc with Brussels-sprouting Belgian flags. Another celebrity close encounter to add to our already impressive collection. You can't get away from them, can you? Life is littered with coincidences.

So who've you met then, Barry?

What a relief! It was a long time coming, the penalty and only goal at Panionios.

Our new mates from Oz, Ryan and Sarah, are happy too. What better way to round off your Grand Tour of Europe and celebrate your engagement than a Toon night out in Athens?

That'll be Mythos and Greek toasts all round, Retsina, pet. And mind that flag!

Just enough time to take in half of the Smoggies' match v Egaleo before heading through the crosstown traffic to Panionios.

Book signing session at Sportspages, London. 'Cahm 'n' get your lahvly Toon Tales, here, mite!'

The famous Roland music shop where Paula's marathon staggered to a halt. Shop owner Nikos wishes us luck as we set off to complete Paula's challenge for her.

We did it for Paula! At the gates of the old Olympic Stadium. Horse-shoe shaped, just like the Panionios ground.

Just one of these for the whole Sochaux away end. It couldn't cope with the steady flow of visitors. After you, marra, and mind your shoes! That's European football for you.

Four-nil, coming up! Sochaux's 1001st home match wasn't a happy one (for them). We wore the black and white tonight for once.

That's some big book you've got there, though but.

Family day out at a very accommodating Shepherd's Bush boozer before the Yeading match. The BBC made Crackerjack next door, ye knaa. Crackerjaaaaack!

The Bling 2, the 'Ding 0. A great atmosphere as the Toon crowd gave a warm round of applause to the Yeading players at the end: 'You are top of your league, say you are top of your league!'

This is the ritual you have to go through every time you pass through Terminal A at Brussels Airport. Hang your Toon top over the replica Angel's shoulders, and rub his toes for good luck.

Wheyabuggama, a Byker Barbers in Heerenveen? Yiv gorra be kiddin, man.

Canny boozer, that *'t Skoffeltsje*. But watch your head! Steve, second left, our local Geordie amongst the Cloggies, helped us overcome our ticketlessness.

Heerenveen had us worried for a long time in this one, but we scraped through two-one.

The road back from Heerenveen takes you through some very strange places. How did the Frisians come up with that name for their village? Wonder if it lives up to its name? Give it a try for your next holiday.

And here's another one! Quick, let's get over that dyke, if you'll pardon the expression, and out of here before those sneaky mackems spot us. Note the spelling mistake in makkum: it shouldn't have a capital 'm', of course.

Read the book to find out what happens next! Remember this is Sexbierum and makkum country.

See what we mean?

Well, probably the highest up the scale would be the King of Norway. I've only met one King, and it was him. I shook his hand in Stavanger. Mind, we've both shaken hands with Sir Bobby in Basel, and I shook his hand on his seventieth birthday too in Cologne. I think we've both got to agree that Sir Bobby beats royalty any day.

I can't argue with you on that one, Barry. Mind, have I told you about the time I met the King of Tonga? In Essen, it was. He was on a goodwill tour of Europe, and Tonga's honorary consul in Germany lived near Essen somewhere, so the King was invited to a reception on the top (27th) floor of Essen's *Rathaus*, or civic centre. Yours truly got to interpret for him. My Tongalese not being all that good, we had to settle for a form of English. He was a big lad, mind, the King of Tonga. Wouldn't have looked out of place among the never-miss-a-weekend-session crowd at Percy Main Social Club back in the glorious seventies. And he wore two gold watches, one on local time and the other on Tongalese time. My Mam and Dad were visiting us at the time and also came along to see the Big King. They remembered well that his flamboyantly-dressed and equally big mother, the then Queen of Tonga, had stolen the show at Liz Windsor's coronation back in 1952.

Well, Pete, another couple of royals we keep bumping into in Brussels are the Prince and Princess. You know, whatsernames. We go for lunch in an English-style tea room now and then, and they're there fairly regularly. It's just round the corner from the palace. She's very smart, much better than she looks on the telly.

Aye, she looks canny, Barry. And how about this? There was the time I had a slash standing next to Max Grundig, as in tellies and hi-fi gear. Felt like asking for a discount on a new king-size telly. Any more celebrity tales, Barry?

Who else, then? Let's think... Oh, how about politicians? Ian Paisley, Kilroy-Silk, Neil Kinnock? Do they count as celebrities? Robin Cook? Nearly tripped over him once.

Then a few musicians and the like. Probably the best was John Peel in the seventies at a university Peel Roadshow. Sting, best man at his friend Keith's stag night in the upstairs room of the pub at the bottom end of Shields Road, not far from your Italian scooter repairer. Pete Townsend and Roger Entwistle out of The Who sat beside me having breakfast at a hotel in Glasgow. It wasn't late either. Mark Knopfler at the next table at a restaurant in Barcelona. And of course, he waved back to us at the start of a Great North Run.

And I bumped into Alan Bennett doing his shopping in a French delicatessen in London near the BBC once. Gabrielle Drake, Nick Drake's sister, walking around theatreland. She looked great.

Footballers. Not too many, actually, if you don't count in and around the grounds, 'coz that's too easy. Steve Harper queueing for a bus after the Wimbledon tennis. Really very pleasant, he is. Pav in the Metro Centre. Peter Beardsley in Marks and Spencer – he said hello before I did. Great man. Supermac in the paper shop at the Central Station. Lawrie McMenemy on a train going back to Southampton with one of his players after a disciplinary hearing at the FA up in London. Big Jack in the departure lounge of Newcastle Airport on his way to resign from the Republic of Ireland manager's post. Still, enough of this gratuitous name-dropping and back to the plot. But not before I mention Albert Bennett, who used to live in a club house near the Cuths and signed his autograph next to the bus stop outside the Fox and Hounds.

Having waved the Belgian royals bye-bye, we headed on to the hotel, took our showers and had a nice outdoor Greek *meze* lunch in the park just down from the hotel. Assorted salads, feta and grilled cheeses, chewy squid hoops, olives, gyros, you name it. All in the shade of what possibly was an olive, laurel and cypress grove, accompanied by a couple, or was it a few, bottles of Mythos and polished off with two cool *frappés*. It was soon time for Barry to head for the airport and for me to have a couple of hours' *siesta* (to use the local word) before meeting Chris and Sarah in the lobby at eight to head off for the *très chic* pedestrian zone in the Kolonaki district where we'd been the previous evening after the match.

Once again, the place was a fashion show as the local talent strutted its stuff on the catwalk that is Friday evening out on the town. Just to reinforce the message, there was a giant plasma TV screen in one corner of our outdoor restaurant showing the tastier bits of Fashion TV again. Chris and I were appreciative.

But just as all the senses were being delighted and we were getting stuck into the culinary delights of our moussaka and chips, we began to have our doubts about the personal hygiene of the impeccably-dressed group sitting opposite. There wasn't half a pen and ink wafting over from their general direction. But when we moved on elsewhere for some sherbet-flavoured post-prandial mouthwash, the same fragrance assaulted us. Then we realised, it was the drains... and it hadn't rained for several days, apparently.

Now the Greeks may have got European civilisation started, and the sewers may have been top-of-the-range and state-of-the-(f)art when they built them a few thousand years ago, but it would appear that they haven't made any significant improvements since.

A brilliant day in Athens drew to a close as we sipped our nightcap on the hotel-room balcony gazing in awe across the city rooftops to the Acropolis perched on the opposite hill. There it stood as time stood still, bathed in the changing tones of its floodlights, appropriately reminiscent of the Toon's floodlit victory twenty-four hours earlier - mackems eat your hearts out. Needless to say, the Acropolis was top of the list of the next day's must-sees!

The next morning duly arrived, as next mornings have a reliable habit of doing, and Sarah, Chris and I approached one of the taxis outside the hotel. Another hot, sunny day was clearly in the making. We took the precaution of asking today's Nick, Our Big Fat Greek Taxi Driver, how much the trip down the dip, through the city chaos and up the other side to the Acropolis was going to cost – an incredible bargain-basement price of only three euros for the taxi ride through horrible, snarling city traffic. Amazing value! But the hidden price we soon discovered we were going to have to pay was that we had to put up with Nick's nauseating non-stop promotional patter – he would take us here and there to see this or that ruin for a bargain all-day flat rate. He gave us his card with his Internet address on it. A taxi driver with a website! His English, it has to be said, was brilliant (though possibly not as good as the Greek your average Newcastle taxi driver speaks) but it was loud, Greek-style in-your-face loud. After the taxi had made the climb up the Acropolis hill, we were glad to get out, and out of earshot of Nick the Big Mouth Fat Greek Taxi Driver.

You cannot help but be impressed by the Acropolis. Apparently, the word literally means 'city at the top', but not just in Athens. It was the name given to the towering, central defensive district in all Ancient Greek cities. So it was only natural that Nikos Dabizas, whose surname is uncannily similar to Acropolis (in that it too is Greek and contains the vowels 'a', 'o' and 'i', as well as the consonant 's') should have come to Newcastle as a towering central defender. Unlike the Athenian Acropolis, however, Dabizas is not two and a half thousand years old. But who put the ball in the mackems' net?

Yes, this place was built in the second half of the fifth century BC – at least that's what it said in the guidebook. Ancient Rome hadn't even got going yet, and the Greeks were building kit like this! In Wallsend, the local Celts would have been living in their mud-brick hovels while their pigeons of course had luxury crees in the allotments! Who says education is a cost, not an investment?

This Acropolis place was built as the home of Athena, the patron goddess of the city, and the most striking of the surviving structures is of course the famous Parthenon, which to me looked remarkably like Penshaw Monument. Now although Penshaw Monument is basically on the fringe of mackem territory, I personally have a soft spot for it. That is because throughout my youth, and on visits back home, I could see it from my bedroom window on the north bank of the Tyne in Howdon. And it looked great lit up at night. Ever since then, when I first see Penshaw Monument driving north on the A1 (me driving, that is, not the Monument), I know I'm home. Then the great dilemma begins in the depths of my soul. Do I keep on heading for the Toon and have the pleasure of crossing over the Tyne Bridge. Or do I fork off (careful with your language, Pete) towards the A19 and go through the Tyne Tunnel to emerge into Howdon on the other side? Both these options are my idea of the perfect way of arriving on Tyneside, which doesn't make the choice an easy one. Mind you, on recent trips home when I have opted to continue on to Newcastle, I have managed not to find the road to the Tyne Bridge, and ended up going across the Redheugh instead. And the thing is, I can never work out how I have done it. Right up to the last moment, I have been convinced I would be crossing the Tyne Bridge, only to find that structure way off to the right. I'll just have to make do with crossing it during the Great North Run. It was particularly brilliant last year when the Red Arrows flew over just as we were on the Bridge of Bridges!

I don't know about Penshaw hill, but the hill atop of which the Athenian Acropolis is perched is imbued with natural mysteries – caves, springs, copses and glens – denoting the presence of the gods. And you can feel that presence, plus the presence of thousands of sweaty tourists, just like us. The place is just awesome, and you can't help wondering how they built all this tackle without the assistance of modern cranes and the like. But I suppose they did have plentiful supplies of cheap (i.e. slave) labour. You can just picture the poor sods hauling great slabs of rock up that hill and then there was the actual building work itself – two and a half thousand years ago! Off to one side is a very impressive amphitheatre, the Roman-built Herodeion (whence our Pilgrim Street Odeon got its name), whose design was blended and tucked into the natural contours of the hill. There is a wonderful museum at the top of the hill just in front of the Parthenon, and the marble sculptures on display are just breathtakingly beautiful. How did the ancients achieve such perfection when basically all they had were a hammer and chisel apiece?

This took us on to the somewhat touchy subject of the Elgin marbles. That is to say, the marbles which one Thomas Bruce, the Seventh Lord Elgin, nicked. Kristos explained to me that these were small round things used in games of childhood. Ah, says I, penkers! Yes, that was them, the Elgin, nay Elswick, penkers. Mind, there was always the danger that, had Lord Elswick left them in Greece, they might have ended up down an Athenian cundy. And, as we had established only the previous evening, an Athenian cundy is not the kind of place you would really like to end up in, judging by the smell after several rainless days.

The collection of Ancient Greek sculptures and architectural details which Elgin-features purloined are of course in the British Museum. The Greeks are, understandably, none too happy about that and drop a few gentle hints here and there in the Acropolis museum. And frankly, they are sodding well right. Just who the hell did that 'aristocratic' git think he was? If you ask me, the Brits have a solemn duty to return the penkers to where they belong. In fact everything in the whole wide world should be given back to whoever had it first. That's going to see some changes not only for the Athenians, but also for the Red Indians, the Incas, and the Aztecs, and everybody, really. Come to think of it, maybe we should just hang on to them a while longer...

All this culture was getting a bit much by the time the sun had reached its zenith, and in the true tradition of Ancient Greek mythology we decided it was time for a pint. So we started wandering back down the hill to the site of what apparently had been an Ancient Greek fish market. Unfortunately, we were sidetracked by the allures of a thoroughly modern Greek taverna and duly set about quenching our well-earned thirst. Rather than go indoors, we sat in a kind of pavilion. The menu included 'meat balls from east', but Kristos took a lot of persuading that they really were from the orient as he reckoned he had detected a decidedly occidental flavour.

A trifle steamed from our liquid noonday solace, we kind of staggered on down the hill into the more modern part of Plaka, where we parted company to do a spot of souvenir buying. The district is a veritable bazaar of a place, a labyrinth of side streets thankfully featuring lots of awnings giving some welcome shade. By no means all the goods on offer in Plaka were made of placka, though the worry beads I couldn't resist purchasing (after a bit haggle, of course) may well have been hand-crafted from that very material. But the Panathinaikos shirts with Greek lettering on the back which I bought for Stephie and Tina definitely weren't plastic!

The taxi from Plaka back to the hotel (about half the distance our three euros had taken us that morning) cost a staggering twenty-four euros, and that is also what it said on the meter! An expensive ride, but an invaluable lesson: beware of Greeks driving taxis, especially in Athens. Always negotiate the fare before you get in. But in fareness (ha, ha) the previous Nicks definitely had not ripped us off.

After the obligatory *siesta* (you see how our knowledge of Greek was improving all the time?), the plan was to have pre-prandial tinctures on Chris and Sarah's balcony, which afforded a mesmerising square-on view of the Acropolis. So there we installed ourselves, cracked open the cool Heineken and soaked up the unique splendour of the Athens sunset, once again gazing out all-agog towards the Acropolis and the glistening Saronic Gulf beyond. Bang on cue, just as the sun was setting, an owl darted out from a copse somewhere below us to the right. Especially for us, he performed his owlian aerobatics, and Kristos quickly reached the conclusion, Ancient-Greek-Philosopher-style, that here was an owl out on the pull. Let's hope he managed to sum up the square of his romantic hypotenuse on that sultry Athenian night. The three of us headed back to the Kolonaki district for a farewell-to-Athens, we-might-be-back-in-a-later-round meal. Didn't stop up too late, as Chris and Sarah had to be up and away at the crack of dawn to catch their flight.

I had the luxury of a lie-in, as the Athens-Bergamo-Luxembourg flight didn't leave till mid-afternoon. And I remembered to do a deal with the taxi driver before getting in the car. He didn't even bother to switch the meter on, and charged me the twenty-five euros we had agreed for the forty minute or so ride (just one euro more than I had paid for the mini-ride the previous day). While supping a pint at the airport, I checked my change and noticed that the Greek national symbol on the one-euro coin is an owl! The plot thickened immediately in my head, as I know that the German expression for 'Coals to Newcastle' is *'Eulen nach Athen'* (owls to Athens). Actually, our *sauerkraut*-eating cousins have a couple of other expressions with the same underlying meaning. One is *'Schnecken nach Metz'*, which literally means 'Snails to Metz' – that's pretty steady, because the pace of the game that time in Metz had been painfully slow. And another is *'Bier nach Dortmund'*, literally meaning 'Beer to Dortmund'. That is also good, as beer is something that is inherently good, even without a direct Toon connection. But hey, we brew great beer, so there is a connection there too. But this was spooky – owls to Athens, indeed! This had to be a sign. Surely this was Greek mythology for 'Newcastle are going to win the UEFA Cup'! Though perhaps a winged swine would have been more appropriate.

It was Tina's half term, so I took the opportunity to blast over to Geordieland for the week.

The atmosphere inside SJP was weird. Because it didn't feel like a European night in the old sense of the term. For a start, it had been a doddle getting a ticket. Just turned up at the box office in the middle of the afternoon, after first having had a leisurely pint in the Strawberry, sitting strategically next to the window so as to be able to gaze out onto the holy of holies. By the way, did you know that it's called the Strawberry after the strawberry fields that used to be cultivated by the local nuns around the SJP area in the eighteenth century? Yeah, you probably did, 'coz there's a plaque on the outer wall facing the Metro station that tells you just that. But have you ever read it?

Well, I haven't, Pete, but it reminds me that when I was a little lad my Dad used to take me and my brother to watch the N's playing up on Nun's Moor. Our strawberry fields didn't last forever, unlike Liverpool's. By the way, did you know that John Lennon lived on Newcastle Road near Strawberry Fields, which rather squares the circle, does it not?

I reckon it does, Barry. And I certainly didn't know that. But back to the plot: the place was only about half full, and the atmosphere ten minutes before the kick-off was, well, just flat. The crowd was a mere 27,218 – the lowest home attendance of the season. It was even lower than the crowd figures for the 2001 Intertoto games against Lokeren, 1860 Munich and Troyes had been! But the weirdest thing of all was that there wasn't a single Tbilisi fan in the away fans' enclosure. Not one. Just empty seats. The poor buggers - a trip to Newcastle from their neck of the back of beyond would have set them back a lifetime's salary, plus a bit more. Instead, there were a couple of dozen officials and footballers' wives just to the right of my seat in the 1892 Club section.

On the pitch, they really didn't put up that much resistance. But despite the Toon's absolute dominance we had to wait a frustrating thirty-eight minutes for Alan Shearer to blast home beautifully from just within the box at the Leazes End. Beardo came onto the pitch at half time to rapturous applause, and for me that was the highlight of the night, obviously. On fifty-six minutes, Bellamy volleyed in a nice one from twelve yards out to seal a two-nil victory. Souness said afterwards that he thought the only thing missing was clinical finishing. He had a point. And we had taken three points on the night.

So far, Sochaux

'Who?' I hear you ask, and 'Where?' And the answer to both questions was 'Sochaux'. Which reminds me: whenever sending cards back to Geordieland on your travels, be sure always to write 'Tyne and Where?' - none of this Tyne and wear shite. It says Wallsend, Northumberland, on my birth certificate. And I've never heard of a Count of Tyne and wear, so how can it be a County? Not that I am what you might call a big fan of aristocracy or royalty, mind.

It was funny to be going to another game in the UEFA Cup that wasn't one round nearer the Final. The idea of a group stage still requires some considerable getting used to, I'm afraid. It kind of drags on, and nothing seems to be all that decisive. The pressure is off and you will always have another chance.

Call me a dyed-in-the-wool traditionalist, but for me a cup competition should always be a sudden-death affair. That's what makes it so exciting. And that's why it doesn't matter at all if we are drawn against total shite opposition. It's eleven against eleven, and anything can happen. And sooner or later, there has to be a result. Give me the true knock-out cup atmosphere any day. That's what cup competitions are all about. And the attendances at SJP against Tbilisi and Sporting Lisbon would appear to bear me out on this!

You see, I have a problem with all rule changes. I tend to think that tried and tested rules should stay the way they are. After all, who would suddenly lop an inch off a twelve-inch rule in the name of progress? Only a raving metric loony, that's who! I felt the same way back in the 1995/96 season when they introduced that rule change that cost us the championship:

Rule 13z: 'In any game involving Manchester United, the standard ninety-minute period of play shall, where appropriate, be extended indefinitely until such time as the aforesaid club has secured at least one point.'

What a bummer that was! And people had been arranging the championship parties at the turn of the year. Just as well the championship parties didn't actually take place at the turn of the year, the way the promotion parties had a few short seasons earlier. No, what am I saying? It's a pity they weren't held then, because it was our sodding championship! It is certainly the nearest I have been to a Toon championship. I don't suppose I'll get any nearer in my lifetime. Or to an FA Cup Final victory, either. Here's an interesting statistic: I was born on the seventh of February 1956. We last won the FA Cup on the seventh of May 1955. Work it out for yourself. If that is not having the Toon in your blood, I don't know what is. Very impressive, Pete! And I was born ten days before on the twenty-seventh of April, and Cup Final day was the day I came home from the hospital!

Anyway, where were we before we set off on these blissful meanderings? Ah yes, *en route pour Sochaux, mes amis!*

I had occasionally heard Sochaux mentioned on the froggie telly and radio, but had never actually consulted a map to find out exactly where it was. Now was the time to sit up and take notice, as we were going to play against them next. And the fact was not lost on any of us that, prior to that encounter, they had strung together a very impressive unbeaten run, including an eyebrow-raising away win at Champignons League contenders Monaco the weekend before.

As to the geography, well you head south from Luxembourg, bending off eastwards to skirt around the Vosges mountains. You can go through them if you like, but it will take forever. Then you turn sharp right just before you hit the Swiss border and end up in Basel (again) by mistake. Now that would have been fawlty, and would have cost an extra twenty-five Swiss francs for the privilege of using about twenty km of their poxy motorway. Head west for another half an hour and you're in Sochaux-Montbéliard. These two towns are as close as Newcastle-Gateshead, except there's no river in between. In fact, it's difficult to see why they're not just one town. The club's called Sochaux but the stadium's in Montbéliard, next door to the giant Peugeot factory. To be sure, that Peugeot plant accounts for the lion's share (get it?) of Sochaux' and Montbéliard's fame and income.

Getting tickets had proved a little difficult this time as our own application through our season tickets was rejected. Luckily, we managed to get some from a friend through our belt-and-braces application techniques. Chris, Sarah and Don had managed to get tickets too – so it remained only to sort out the logistics and the accommodation. Sound familiar?

Don got onto the Internet and hit upon the Hotel Kyriad in Montbéliard, which the website said was five minutes' walking distance from the Stade Auguste Bonal and five minutes from the centre of Sochaux in the other direction. It sounded ideal, but the online booking system said it was full. I picked up the phone and got through to Andrée-Anne and Stéphanie, the very friendly and helpful staff. They explained that there are usually still a few rooms left when the Internet says they're full, so it's always best to phone. They were pleased to take our booking for four rooms at the very reasonable rate of fifty-nine euros for a single and sixty-six euros for a double.

Kyriad is one of a bunch of French hotel chains that offer outstanding value for money. Others are Campanile, Etap, Formule 1, Ibis and, a notch or two up-market from them, Novotel. The Montbéliard Kyriad offers truly excellent value for modest prices. It is unpretentious but gives you all you need for a very reasonable price. When next you are looking for budget accommodation in France, check out www.envergure.fr/kyriadfr.html and you won't be disappointed.

On the transport front, Chris and Sarah were flying from Heathrow to Luxembourg, arriving in the Grand Duchy at a quarter past ten. This was perfect, as it comfortably allowed me to drive Tina to school for her Thursday morning late start of nine thirty and then double back from the Kirchberg to the airport at Findel in time for a late breakfast before the flight from the smoke arrived. Once again, the cosiness of Luxembourg airport came into its own. Parking is a complete doddle, and there is a nice quiet buffet place for a leisurely breakie and a quick read of l'Équipe to see what the froggie media made of *le Toon's* visit. It was all pretty complimentary, with the focus squarely on the expected performance of Robert and Bernard, as you would expect. 'Beware of Robert's set-pieces,' came the dire warning. How right they were to be. Chris and Sarah's flight was bang on time, and all it took was a quick blast along five km or so of Grand Ducal motorway and a bit city traffic to reach the station car park, where Barry was waiting. How's your trip been, Barry?

Well, it's been a perfect winter's morning with frosty fields and forests flashing by my window under a cloudless blue sky. I've been travelling since seven thirty when I caught the local train to the Gare de Luxembourg, which is in Brussels, just to confuse everybody. There I swapped platforms to catch the train to the other Gare de Luxembourg, in Luxembourg. There's one in Paris, too. I suppose it's a bit like having a Waterloo Station in London, and one in Waterloo, Belgium, as well.

The Belgians have a very good system for pricing tickets in direct proportion to your virility or fertility, depending on how you look at it. Anyone who has three or more kids, a *famille nombreuse*, gets tickets on the buses and trains for nearly half price. A just reward, if you ask me. So I treated myself to a first-class seat so I could sit with all the old biddies in fur coats going to visit their money in secret bank accounts in the fiscal paradise island that is the Grand Duchy of Luxembourg. The old dear in front must have been Flemish, as she spent the whole trip absorbed in the financial pages of the *Achter Krant* paper. It's just a short step from *Krant* to Courant, as in Hexham Courant, which nicely demonstrates how close Dutch is to English. Never mind that *Courant* is actually French. Just goes to show what a big happy European family we all are now!

Did you know, Barry, that travelling by rail from Brussels to Luxembourg takes just about as long these days as it did one hundred years ago? In this age of high-speed trains that go 'whoosh', this particular link across the Ardennes would appear to have simply been forgotten. It just continues to go 'clickety-click, clunk, clickety-click' instead of 'whoosh'. On a brighter note, Brussels-to-Newcastle rail journey times look set to be shortened considerably when Britain finally gets its act together and completes the Chunnel link to Saint Pancras in 2007. Then you'll be able to get from Brussels *Midi* 'mid-day' station to the pancreatic bit of the smoke in two hours and ten minutes, walk the couple of hundred yards to the Cross – or carrying the cross if you prefer – and then hopefully hop on the Toon-bound express that is standing waiting just for you. The bottom line is that it should be feasible (if a trifle expensive) to leave Brussels early on a Saturday morning, reach the Toon in time for couple of pre-match bevvies in Bar Oz, watch the match, go for the post-mortem pint, head doon to Tynemouth for an Indian in the Gate, doss, get up and head back to the continent in time for work on the Monday morning. Canny weekend, though but!

The first chunk of the journey to Sochaux followed exactly the same route as for Basel well-nigh a year earlier – down the A 31, past grotty Thionville (or Diedenhofen, if you prefer), and then past Metz and on into the rolling countryside of Alsace. Being creatures of habit (I once ran the Great North Run in a monk's habit, honest!), we decided to head for exactly the same restaurant as we had for the Basel trip. It was, as regular readers will recall, *La Couronne* (the Crown) in that picturesque and quintessentially Alsatian village with the disappointingly French name of Marmoutier. And would you Adam and Eve it, the landlady remembered us! This was truly amazing, nay, *véritablement étonnant* – after all, surely most of her *clientèle* came into the place dressed in Toon shirts. The scran was first class, and they wished us well again - they didn't like Sochaux any better than Basel.

After our repast, we were back on the road headed for the Basel-bound motorway. Shortly before Basel, we duly turned off to the right and, before you could say Franco-Prussian War of 1870/71, we had left Alsace behind and were in the Doubs region – well, shooby dooby doobs. And shortly thereafter, we crossed the watershed – from hereon in, all the rivers (and presumably everybody's pee) ends up in the Med, as opposed to the North Sea. So what about the Atlantic, we were asking ourselves? We failed to sort that one, so if anyone has any ideas... Does that mean there's another watershed as you get near the west coast of France? Suppose it does. And so how, exactly, do the rivers know which way to go? It's amazing, the heavily philosophical questions you can get seriously into on your way to the match!

As we pulled up at one of the *péage* motorway tollbooths, we noticed that by the side of the road they had big adverts showing a father and son driving along and the slogan 'Use the motorway'. In other words, if you've nothing better to do, why not spend some time aimlessly driving around, adding to the pollution? At Christmas time, they could make it more seasonal with a slogan saying 'Lost for a Christmas gift idea? Buy a *télépéage* motorway pass for your nearest and dearest.'

In this neck of the woods, there are lots of *ballons*. Now *ballon* means 'ball' or even 'balloon' in *français*, so you probably think we are talking a load of balls here, but in fact that's what they call their very-rounded-indeed hills. A few balls later and we were just about in Montbéliard. So far, so good, Sochaux. Our route planner had said it would take about four and half hours from Luxembourg, and deducting the lunch break that was just about right. As we veered off onto the slip road on the right, we could see the floodlights of a stadium to our left, but it turned out that wasn't the right one. About five minutes and a few froggie roondaboots later, a wrong right turn took us straight into the car park of the proper stadium this time, where a few Toon wallahs were already millin' aboot – well at least we were now sure where it was! About turn, and the hotel was only a couple of streets away. Great stuff! So we parks up in the Kyriad's own car park and checks in. Only a smallish, three-floor, two-star sort of place, but dead canny like. And the equally dead canny lassie at reception made it, well, a warm reception, made all the warmer by the fact that there was a dozen-strong Toon contingent already firmly ensconced in the bar just aroond the corner from *la réception*, reinforced by about the same number of froggie lads and lasses. Great crack! The arrival of four more black and white shirts naturally triggered a round of 'Toon, Toon, black and white army', or was it *'Ville, ville, armée noire et blanche'*?

This was followed by a round of Fischer Pils, a very steady little Alsatian brew. Now it is no coincidence that the very best French beers are from Alsace. That is because Alsace beers basically aren't French at all. Howay man, bonny lad, look at the names – Kanterbräu, Kronenbourg, Fischer, they're about as French as cricket itself. The pils came in those old-fashioned bottles with an even quainter rubber-lined ceramic stopper on a metal hinge (ideal for keeping Holy Watter in). It even turned out that the Frenchies in the bar worked for that particular brewery – they were in Sochaux-Montbéliard for some kind of conference entitled 'How to get pissed on beer more cost-effectively – drink it quicker'. So to make sure they got into the swing of things, they had decided to sample plenty of the company's products in their own time. Taak aboot devotion to duty – count me in! I finally understood the concept of a busman's holiday – which is fine, provided you aren't driving the sodding bus.

There was a group of five or six Toon fans from Hartlepool and environs in the bar, and they had a great story to tell about their remarkable journey.

'I'm dead, me,' said one.

'Aye, and we're going to his funeral after the match.'

'You what?'

Then they explained.

'As soon as the draw was made, we checked up on the map to find Sochaux and spotted that the neighbouring town was Montbéliard, which sounded familiar.'

'And then this one here, the twat, chimed in. Tell them what you said.'

'Nah, you tell them!'

'Well, what he said was "Why man, of course, that's where Laurent Robert used to play in France. His brother's still there now. I'm sure we can get cheap flights going there." Then he told us that he'd get onto it straight away and book our seats before the prices went up. So within a couple of hours he'd booked us all a seat on a plane going to Montpellier.'

'Of course I found out the next day what I'd done. Montpellier's nearly as far away from Sochaux as Newcastle is. So I bought everyone tickets to Saint Étienne instead. It was the closest airport to Sochaux I could find with budget flights.'

'But it doesn't end there. We were booked to fly out yesterday, but half of us missed the plane, including me. The airport staff told us "Sorry, but there's nothing we can do, there isn't another plane". It was like they enjoyed not being helpful.'

'So we said we'd go on the plane to Montpellier instead.'

'They didn't like that at all and said, "You can't do that. Your tickets don't count to go to another destination."'

'It was great then, because we said "Ah, but you see, these ones do," producing our Montpellier tickets from our wallets. They had no answer to that.'

'Meantime, the rest of us who'd caught the plane to Saint Etienne had to cancel one of the hire cars we'd booked, 'coz this lot weren't going to need it. But the hire car people said we'd lose their booking fee.'

'That's when I had the idea and said that he'd died, and that the others had gone to his funeral!'

'So that's how I'm dead!'

Our *patronnes* André-Anne and Stéphanie looked on, delighted and bemused in equal measure. Little did they know that they were soon to be on BBC Radio Newcastle.

We had in fact arrived at this hotel just in time, i.e. just before half past six. This was not just in time for the match, of course, which didn't start until a quarter to nine. *La télévision oblige, n'est-ce pas?* But it was also just in time for our interview with, wait for it, BBC Radio Newcastle. We had set this up by contacting Jon Harle (canny lad!) and telling him all about *Toon Tales* and the trip to France. Jon had been looking for Geordie ex-pats with a tale or two to tell a few years earlier and, as a result, almost interviewed me just before the start of my first Great North Run in 2000. But I got to the Town Moor by Claremont Road so early that the equipment hadn't been set up yet. Whey howay man, aa didn't wanna be late! And hey, aa was in canny fettle that day – managed to get to Sooth Shields in two hours eleven minutes, and if you make allowance for the pathetic, mickey moose timing on the GNR that was under two hours.

That particular day I inaugurated what was to become my standard routine for the Run. I doss at wor Mick's at Tynemouth. But hang on, rewind a bit. Leave Luxembourg airport at seven for Paris Charles de Gaulle. Have breakie there, get into the Toon airport just before twelve. Blast doon the coast with Mick, see me Ma, blast back up the Toon on the Metro. Couple of pints in Bar Oz with Chris, Sarah and Barry, not too many, mind – we're running a half-marathon tomorrow! 'Whey the beer it flowed like watta, sae they drunk aal they cud staand!' Anyway, Jon gave Pete a mention during the running GNR commentary, with greetings to Mam and Dad, so that was also dead canny, wasn't it? Cheers, Jon!

But back to the hotel bar in Sochaux-Montbéliard. Couple of calls on my mobile, but the Beeb in the Toon weren't happy with the quality (of the line, not our patter, I hope), so they tried to call the hotel on a land line but couldn't get through. Panic stations! Never mind, they called the mobile again, and that would have to do!

This was it. The real thing. A live radio interview. Actually that was a bit of a porky. It was supposed to be a live interview originally, right enough – but for some technical reason they were recording it and were then going to pretend it was live. Who cares? We were nervous as shite anyway – so live or not, it didn't really matter. When Jon asked us what the atmosphere was like, we were able to give the folks back home a true sample by holding the phone out and asking everyone – Geordies and froggies alike – to oblige by bawling back and singing a bar or two. They duly obliged, of course! Jon asked us the perennial question about the reputation of English football fans abroad, so I gave my by now standard answer to the effect that you have to draw a massive distinction between English fans (south of Nottinghamshire) on the one hand and Geordie fans (plus Scousers and a few other sound specimens) on the other. At all events, nobody was going to confuse the Geordies with the less savoury fans of this world. The general consensus was that the Geordies had by now gained something of a reputation in Europe. And that reputation was, ahem, rather good!

The interview over, everyone, especially yours truly, was once again in thirst-quenching mode. Well, what are you supposed to do with a thirst? And so we happily got stuck into downing the Fischers. À propos of nothing, Germany's long-standing foreign minister is also called Fischer! Now he strikes me as a canny lad. In the seventies, he was an out-and-out rebel, but - as so often happens - he mellowed out as he grew older and became part of the establishment. Lost weight, ran marathons, and has now become a big fat git again, just like me!

Presently a roar went up, and rightly so, to greet Don who had completed his arduous journey from Brighton to London, then Paris by Eurostar, Besançon by TGV, and finally local train to Sochaux-Montbéliard. And he had had to cope with striking railway workers in Paris. Yet another strike to hamper the Toon Army on its travels – shades of Athens all over again! We all hoped the result would be similar. Not that we are knocking the French and their right to strike, mind. It's just we would prefer it if they wouldn't strike when the Toon were in the country! No, I truly admire the French revolutionary spirit – they really have a lot in common with the people of North Shields and of Tyneside in general. Remember that business with the Panda cars in the seventies? Well there you go! And wasn't there that guy who was active in the French Revolution of 1789 and who previously had drunk in the Bigg Market? So you see, the French Revolution actually started in the Toon! What was his name, again? Jean something... Hmm, do you mean Geordie Jeans and French Connection, Pete? Quite possibly, Barry!

Some other lads wanted to ask at reception about the location of pubs and restaurants, and we were of course happy to help them out with an on-the-spot, though maybe less than spot-on translation. We weren't so happy to help, however, when they wanted the lass at reception to recommend a good bordello! Apparently, they had a perfect record of visiting the local knocking shop on every Toon trip to Europe since and including Antwerp. Now there's dedication for you! So admittedly, it would have been a great pity not to collect the full set. Let's hope that was all they collected, though but.

Our happy little gang left the hotel and set off into the dark, crisp November evening in search of a watering hole or two. We walked down the Avenue Maréchal Joffre in the direction of the railway station, which was only about half a kilometre away and behind which stood the medieval *château*, quite majestically illuminated by floodlights and the bright and frosty full moon. As our pace quickened in anticipation of more ale, we crossed the path of a suitably attired Toon lad walking in the opposite direction, presumably already stadium-bound. A few yards later, Sarah said 'That looked a bit like Clive.' And sure enough, he must have been thinking at the same time 'That looked a bit like

Sarah and Chris.' So he quickly retraced his last few steps and joined us as we crossed the road for a pint in the local boozer, which might well have been called '*Les Jardins*', and which was bursting at the seams with the Toon Army. Steady little boozer, mind, and some of the lads and lasses were ordering food. Nothing unusual about that, you might think, but the system here was a little bit different in that you selected your pizza from the pub's own menu, and then the barmaid ordered in turn from a pizza delivery service. And your grub then turned up twenty minutes later on the back of a scooter. And why not?

Just a couple of bevvies there, and then we headed for the railway underpass (underpants?) and past the foot of the *château* into the pedestrian precinct of the town proper. There we steamed into a snack-bar-cum-boozer that was likewise heaving with Toon wallahs and wallah-esses. The highlight was meeting the genial Biffa of nufc.com fame, with whom we enjoyed a couple of pints and a canny bit crack. Biffa goes to just about every single match that the first team and even the reserves and juniors play. Niall and Biffa were running a competition on their website with three copies of our book as the prize. The entry deadline was kick-off time at Sochaux. Biffa told us that there'd been loads of entries and the results would be announced in the next few days. It was a pleasure to meet the man who does so much to keep Toon fans all around the world up to date and well-informed, and does it in great style.

It was now time to head back to the Stade Auguste Bonal. It is named after the club president who led them to two pre-war championships. The club began in the twenties as the Peugeot factory team before becoming the first professional team in France, and they had played their two thousandth game just a couple of weeks before meeting us. Their manager Guy Lacombe, a cheerful-looking man with a big moustache, apparently was responsible for discovering Zidane and Vieira. We hoped he hadn't discovered another for this game.

Once again, it has to be said that the police presence in and around the ground was definitely over the top and a bit heavy-handed. It is a good modern stadium, but like Basel it suffered the same lack of lavatory facilities for away supporters. The one French hole-in-the-floor toilet and a sink, which was used as a urinal for two, were no match for the steady flow of customers. That's the modern world for you, isn't it? Sharing 'hot', as in scarce, facilities is efficient and saves you money. As well as hot dogs, they had 'hot bogs' here, like you've got 'hot desking' in offices, 'hot bunking' in navy ships working shifts, and, allegedly, 'hot bonking' for some NUFC players. And they didn't bother to supply bog paper either, so it was no place to get caught short. You've heard of the paperless office, well here they had the paperless toilet. That's fine, but first you need a new design of electric dryer with a three-way flip nozzle: as well as the usual two-way flip for 'face' and 'hands', you need an extra one labelled 'bum'. It would be great for saving the environment.

The stadium is very compact, no running track for a change, so we were right on top of the action in one corner of the ground behind a corner flag. Our section was covered by netting, a bit like at PSV, which made you wonder if we were going to be in for some missile attacks. It was the first time in a long while that Newcastle had worn their black and white stripes in Europe. Tonight there was no choice because Sochaux play in yellow shirts, the same colour as our current European away shirt. Great! At last we could see the true colours!

It was a really cold night and the smoke from the flares set off by the Sochaux fans at the far end drifted out across the whole pitch, giving the same cold and misty look that we'd witnessed in Basel last year. The tense changes as the whistle blows.

We have a not wholly familiar-looking team out tonight: Given in goal, Bernard, Bramble, Elliott and Hughes in defence, a midfield of Bowyer, Butt, Ambrose and Milner, and Bellamy and Ameobi in attack. Alan Shearer's injured, and Robert, Dyer and Kluivert are all amongst the substitutes. We're attacking the far end in the first half. In the early exchanges, Elliott makes a tackle over on the far side of the pitch that incenses the crowd. It looks as if Lonfat is stretching for the ball and going to ground when Elliott steams in from behind. Their legs tangle, and Lonfat's knee gets twisted.

Sochaux have most of the play in the first twenty minutes. The seventeen-year-old Jeremie Menez takes a curling free kick from the left of the penalty area but it's tipped around his right-hand post by Shay Given. Then Oruma and Ilan both have good opportunities when our defence seems to part before them as they make long unchallenged runs into our penalty area. Luckily, last-minute tackles remove the danger when it looks easier to score than miss. Nevertheless, Bramble is looking good and hasn't put a foot wrong. But Bowyer gets booked for a tough tackle.

Milner's persistence down the left sees him get in a low cross to Bellamy but he scoops his snap shot over the bar. We're coming back into it as Sochaux start to misplace their passes and Bellamy nearly finds another opening as he chases down a ball intended for their goalkeeper. And just a few moments later, Bowyer scores, having started the move himself in his own half by lofting a loose ball up to the right-hand corner of the penalty box where Ameobi wins out over Paisley. The ball then breaks free off Paisley into space on the edge of the box and Bowyer arrives at speed and, without breaking stride, slams a low shot through a tangle of Sochaux legs into the corner of the net.

There then follows an eventful couple of minutes when both sides could have scored. From a Newcastle corner taken short by Milner to Bernard, the ball is cleared out into the Newcastle half towards young Menez, but Given races out to near the half-way line to control the ball like Franz Beckenbauer and make a long, curving, accurate pass up into the path of Craig Bellamy out on the right of the penalty box. His excellent cross comes across at waist height to Milner in front of the goal. He leaps to try to stab it in, but sends it over the bar instead. It could have been goal of the season.

From the goal kick, a ricochet off a Sochaux player from a Bramble pass takes the ball to Menez whose nicely weighted pass drops into the path of Ilan. He looks clean through on goal but Given makes another great save, this time with his outstretched right foot, to thwart the Sochaux attacker. Every time Sochaux take a corner, they insist on placing the ball just outside of the quadrant. We're right on top of this with a perfect view and we jeer and whistle to the ref and assistant, but they never do anything about it.

Chants of 'Ketsbaia my lord, Ketsbaia' and monkey noises 'Ooh, Ooh, black and white army' greet a shaven-headed but particularly-hairy-all-over Toon fan who takes his top off and starts to swing like a monkey on top of the safety fence. It's just a few days after the monkey taunts directed at England players in Madrid which created such a furore. This has got nothing to do with racism, but it's clearly in everyone's thoughts as we join in a kind of ironic protest.

Then a great Sochaux pass slices through our defence to their captain Isabey on the left edge of the penalty area. He lofts it above Shay, but somehow Shay flips the ball away to Bramble with his fingertips as he falls to the ground. There's just ten minutes to go to half time and this is a period of sustained Sochaux pressure with a couple of corners and Isabey having a series of headers and shots, and Menez going just wide. Just before half time, Bernard receives a yellow card for a sliding tackle on Ilan, and Mathieu takes the free kick from Robert range but slices it over the bar. Then Ambrose rides three tackles in midfield, breaks forward to the right-hand edge of the penalty box and sends over a cross to Milner on the opposite side, who cushions a header back but it doesn't quite reach Ameobi. The whistle blows for half time and we can be happy with one-nil to the Toon – we've done well to take the lead, but we've ridden our luck a little.

We don't have to wait long for some more goal action. From the re-start, we attack down the left wing and Bernard puts in a low, hard cross which deflects off a Sochaux defender. It's Paisley again, who'd been muscled out by Ameobi for the first goal. His intervention wrong-foots the goalkeeper and the ball comes across the face of the goal where Ameobi, coming in from the right, does well under pressure to side-foot in from a tight angle at the far post. Watching it later, it was a much harder chance than it looked in the heat of the moment. Two-nil and 'You do the Ameobi and you turn around and that's what it's all about. Oh Shola Ameobi, oh Shola Ameobi, SHOLAAAA!' Sochaux really fall flat for a good while after that. There's no spring in their steps, their legs are sluggish and their chins nestle into the logos on their shirts. Still, they keep up their neat passing. Menez goes off to be replaced by Santos, a Brazilian-born Tunisian international, would you believe it, who straight away latches onto a long ball into the right of the penalty area but shoots weakly across the goal. Then we make a change and Bowyer goes off to sustained applause as Kieron Dyer comes on.

A Sochaux attack is cleared off the line but play is halted as the ref's assistant flags for something neither the referee nor just about anyone else had seen. Apparently Bernard had tugged Isabey's shirt to impede his run into the area and then Isabey had taken a tumble. A little harsh, but I suppose it was a penalty in the strict application of the rules. What do you know, Mathieu scuffs a weak left-footed shot along the ground and wide of the right post with the goal at his mercy, Shay having dived the other way. You would think this would knock the stuffing completely out of their players, but no, they stiffen their resolve and come back at us. Santos tries another long-range shot but it sails over the bar and Oruma attempts a flying scissor kick which goes just wide of the right-hand post, with Given seemingly beaten.

A neat sequence sees a forward run by Butt beat three players before he passes to Bernard on the left, who moves it to Milner. He flicks it into the path of Ameobi, who strides into the penalty area and lays it off to Ambrose. But it just doesn't match his stride, otherwise it could have been the third. Then a long Sochaux clearance comes to Bramble, who cushions it imperiously on his chest – just another example of his great performance tonight.

With a quarter of an hour to go, a Sochaux attack is thwarted by an Elliott header on the left edge of the penalty area. Bernard controls the ball and moves it on to Butt, then Ambrose, who lays it off for Dyer. He races into space in the centre circle and beautifully times a pass into the path of Hughes who dribbles to the edge of the penalty area before slotting the ball through the last two defenders into the path of Bellamy, who side-foots it into the goal. Three-nil. 'Craig, Craig Bellamy, tra la la, la la' and 'Let's dance, in the East of France', to the Pet Shop boys' 'Go West' tune. He went to Saint Cuthbert's too, didn't he, Neil Tennant out of the Pet Shop Boys? Wonderful diction. So did the Dec half of Ant'n'Dec, both Toon fans too. What talent the Cuths has produced! Don't forget Sting. And certainly don't forget Lawrie McMenemy, who kindly launched the mackems on their way down into the third division. Nice one, Lawrie!

This heralds the entry of Laurent Robert, whose track-suited appearance on the touchline to warm up is greeted with much cheering. A quarter of an hour left, and Sochaux are wilting – 'Are you sunderland in disguise?' sing the Toon fans. Robert's first three touches end up at the feet of Sochaux players, and then there's another hair-raising moment as he receives the ball in our penalty area and dribbles it out to the goal line under pressure from two attackers before bouncing it off one of them into touch. Then comes his big moment. Ameobi is fouled by Mathieu in Robert country, five yards out from the right-hand corner of the penalty box. Robert steps up and flights the ball over the wall into the top right corner and beyond the hopeless leap of Richert, the Sochaux goalkeeper. Four-nil and 'Laurent, Laurent Robert, everyone knows his name' rings out as he skips over to the dug-out where Kluivert feigns the role of shoe-shine boy for Robert's white boots. Cue Steven Taylor to come on as substitute for

Darren Ambrose, his second Euro appearance after Real Mallorca in the spring. Cue also to the froggie fans to start leaving in their droves as we spoke to their souls in their own tongue with our massive chant of '*Au revoir, au revoir*'.

Barely a minute later, Bellamy races clear onto a long through-ball but instead of side-footing it in, he passes to Ameobi whose shot is well saved by Richert. It should definitely have been five-nil. A few seconds later and it's Robert intercepting a Sochaux pass and racing through on goal to shoot from a tight angle, but it's saved again with Hughes looking on and Bellamy letting rip his frustration, though not really justified, because a Sochaux defender was blocking the pass. So it could have ended six-nil, but four-nil would do very nicely, especially given that Sochaux had beaten Champignons League finalists Monaco away at the weekend. Plenty of reason to 'Let's dance in the East of France, let's dance in the East of France' with Robert and Bernard, who stayed out on the pitch for a long time at the end of the match, doing interviews for French television, and jigging from side to side to the tune of the Toon Army choir. What a cracking match! One of the best of this season, that's for sure.

After the match and our usual detention were over, we naturally headed back into town through the now very cold night in search of scran. And we happened upon a splendid pizzeria right next to the *château*. The Toon was well represented and there was plenty of good-natured banter with Sochaux fans who were drowning their sorrows while stuffing their faces, like us, with authentic French pizza aplenty. Sarah swapped scarves with one of them. Then we headed back to the hotel for a nightcap (or maybe two), feeling jolly pleased with ourselves.

Surprisingly, the Kyriad offers each of its guests a book, which they are free to take with them. Makes a change from the Gideons Bible – open at page one. In my room, I found Jules Verne's 'Around the world in eighty days'. Personally, I would settle for 'Around Europe in fifteen games of the UEFA Cup, including the Final'.

Breakfast the next morning was spot-on; a nice buffet where everything was as it should be – even the scrambled eggs tasted like scrambled eggs, and not like scrambled cardboard as they do at some places. So once again, well done Kyriad, you have won over some new and satisfied customers. Of course, our upbeat morning-after-the-victorious-night-before mood may have coloured our judgment in a slightly favourable light. Who knows? Who cares? There were four or five local and national papers available in the breakfast room, so we duly ploughed our way through the match reports – much to the bewilderment of the hotel staff: they had probably expected something different when they heard that British football fans would be staying. So Geordieland won a few more friends. Though we maybe didn't get all the subtleties of the reporting, the general message came through loud and clear: Newcastle had deservedly won. And we even found ourselves on a big crowd picture taken just after one of the goals had gone in.

I ventured to say that there would be no point in consulting that quality daily *Le Monde*, as it didn't go in much for news as such, as far as I could make out, and was more into your background and in-depth analysis, *à la* British Sunday newspapers. In fact, I'll never forget that on the day after the Twin Towers attack, *Le Monde* was the only paper I came across that had no news of that rather important event. It obviously gets put to bed a lot earlier than the others and nobody dares to disturb its beauty sleep. Just to be sure, we did in fact consult it after all – and sure enough, no report on our match: instead, only the results of the matches that had taken place on Wednesday evening! Don took his leave straight after breakfast to catch his train. He had to be back for Brighton's match v. Ipswich on Saturday! Likes his football, does *notre ami* Don.

The staff at the Hotel Kyriad had really been very friendly and made us very welcome. They thought it was a great idea when we got them to join us on a couple of team photos. We bade them farewell and hoped that some time we might be back again. After the draw for the next rounds, it looked as if it might be sooner than anyone imagined.

The four of us set off for the return journey to Luxembourg, where Barry would be catching the train back to Brussels. Then it would be on to Trier, where Chris and Sarah would be staying till Sunday. We took basically the same route back, except that instead of taking that country road past our Alsatian local *La Couronne*, we decided it might after all be a wee bit quicker if we stayed on the motorway the whole way. It probably was, even though we were slowed down considerably when the motorway took us smack bang right through what appeared to be virtually the centre of Strasbourg. However, we were justly rewarded with a view of *la cathédrale de Strasbourg* (ding dong, ding dong) and, even more impressively, of the Kronenbourg brewery. Sarah pointed out that it can be frustrating when you order a Kronenbourg in France, because the froggies normally refer to it by the number 1664. You see it on the bottles, but it never really registers on the British side of the Channel.

Then comes the tricky bit about French numbers and dates again. I for one always end up tongue-tied when trying to get the dates right, and I would stutter on trying to say *mille six cent soixante-quatre* and trying not to give away that I had already had a couple, but in fact – as Sarah pointed out – they just say *seize soixante-quatre*. Wouldn't you think *une Kronenbourg* would be easier to say, though, even for the French? But such are the great mysteries of life. Another great mystery about Kronenbourg that had me puzzled for years and years was the little slogan that used to feature in the beer's 'coat of arms' on both the bottles and the glasses. It read *'Hatt brasseurs depuis 1664'*. *Brasseurs* means 'brewers' and *depuis* means 'since', but what on earth was *Hatt*? I even had to borrow a Kronenbourg pint glass from the Turk's Head in Tynemouth back in the seventies so that I could ponder the question at home at my leisure. I found that it was actually easier to ponder if the glass contained beer. Surely they couldn't brew hats, could they? No, that would be *brasseurs de chapeaux*! Ah well, better pour in another bottle's worth and think again. It wasn't till years later that I found out (or at least I think I did) that *Hatt* was the name of the brewers concerned, and that a comma or a dash after the name would have helped. On second thoughts, not a dash – it would be a pity to dilute that beer in any way. If the name sounds German, that's because it is. But as we discussed in *Toon Tales*, all the best French beers have the bite of an Alsatian and so were originally German – but let's not mention the war(s).

Once Strasbourg's sprawl was behind us, we were out on the open road. Just right for some music. It was a case of ladies first, of course, and Sarah's rather excellent choice was Fog (not frog) on the Tyne. I don't suppose I'm the only one who has spent a lot of time since the advent of the compact disc recompiling their record collection of the seventies, and Fog on the Tyne has a special place in every Geordie heart. And when you are blasting through the French countryside on your way home after a victory in Europe, those songs are sure to create a warm glow as you create a little bit of Geordieland right there in your car. 'Wheyabuggama, the fog on the Tyne is all mine, all mine.' That's the thing: you can wrap yourself in a little cocoon, i.e. your car, make it into a time and space machine and take Geordieland along with you!

And with the right music – Lindisfarne, Focus, Jethro, etc. – you can take yourself back to the golden seventies at the same time with the sounds you used to hear aboot the Toon in the Durham Ox and the Printer's Pie of a Friday and maybe the Geordie Pride, the Barrel Bar (that was kind of integrated into the Station Hotel in the Central, do you remember?) and the Man in the Moon of a Saturday. Not forgetting the Grape Vaults, of course. I had forgotten the exact location, to be honest, but recently happened upon it again when going to the bog of the café that is attached to the

Theatre Royal. Had to just stand there next to where the juke box (Witch's Promise) used to stand. There you would take your lass, listen to the music, drink the Younger's Tartan pop – in the days when people weren't yet ready to admit they preferred lager and didn't dare order a bottle of Dog for fear of gettin hyem totally palatic and gettin a reet pastin off tha da.

We got to Luxembourg only just in time for Barry to catch his train, but the excitement was all the greater because I inexplicably took a wrong turning at the last minute and we ended up on the wrong side of the station, and Barry leapt out into the middle of the road when some traffic lights were on red.

Yes, Pete, I had to dash for the train like Popeye Doyle in French Connection I. I ran full pelt into what I thought would be the station but turned out to be a goods yard. Had to throw my bag over a fence and then clamber over after it. Then up a spiral staircase, over a footbridge, down into the station, along the length of the platform and onto the train with seconds to spare. This was getting to be a bit of a habit - I'd done exactly the same thing in the Syntagma metro station after the Panionios trip. Luckily, I'd done my marathon training in Athens.

From Luxembourg, it was only an hour's drive to Trier. Sarah and Chris had never been to Trier before, so we planned to have a good look around all the Roman ruins. Maybe some of Chris's ancestors had been stationed there, as he is quarter eye-tie after all. In fact his folks came from the village where Cicero went to school. Trier is very much of a backwater in modern Germany. But it was the biggest place north of the Alps at one time. When the Romans first came here, this neck of the woods was not in Germania at all, but in Gallia. Germanic tribes poured in only as the Roman Empire was collapsing. The city was founded in 16 BC by the Emperor Augustus and was known as Augusta Treverorum, the local Celtic tribe being known to the Romans as the Treveri. For a time, the Roman province of Britannia was administered from Trier, which was the capital of the Western Empire. The town had its own mint, and coins on display at the Segedunum Roman museum in Wallsend include some that were minted there! So back in those days, Britain was in fact already signed up to the single European currency.

So we spent Saturday taking in the Roman remains and generally having a proper look around. Then it was back to Luxembourg on the Sunday. When they had woken up on the Thursday morning, neither Sarah nor Chris had ever before set foot in Luxembourg. But on the Sunday, *en route* for the airport, they were entering that country for the third time in four days! Mind you, it is only a small Grand Duchy. But I can't think of a bigger one.

So that was the Sochaux trip over and we were now assured of a place in the knock-out stage of the competition – and all we needed to ensure first place in the group (and under the weird UEFA Cup rules a lesser opponent in the next round) was a draw against Sporting Lisbon at home.

It's the morning of the sixteenth of December and I'm writing this on the run(a)way bus taking us out to the first SN Brussels Airline plane of the day to Newcastle. We're playing Sporting Lisbon tonight and it's a home game, but for me it's an away trip of almost a thousand kilometres, a Megametre. Travelling time is a good time to write, because it usually involves quite a bit of sitting around waiting for something to happen. But whenever you write something and have it printed, there's always something that slips through all the proofreading. Damn those gremilns!

A good example is Teplice being in the Czech Republic, not in Yugoslavia. This was pointed out by our Czech-born, British citizen, Oslo-based friend Jiri, who helped in the arrangements for our Vålerenga tickets in February 2004 by acting as our local contact for Christian of the Scandinavian Magpies, and who appears with daughter Lilly on the cover of *Toon Tales*. Jiri told us that Teplice is a bit like Newcastle in that it is in the industrial North-East of the country, and like the Toon they challenge for titles and cups but somehow never quite make the final step to success, falling to the 'Hollywood FC' teams such as Sparta Prague or earlier, in the unlamented Communist era, Dukla Prague. Of Half Man Half Biscuit away kit fame.

It's a crazy place, this Brussels Airport. I thought the bus was going to take us out to the plane, but instead it's motored around to one of the other terminals where we've been deposited and now we have to go inside this terminal instead and proceed across the gangway into the plane. Can you believe it? They make us walk about fifteen minutes through one terminal to catch a bus at the far end, and then the bus takes us just about back to where we started from. Why didn't the bus at least start from the near end of the long terminal instead of the far end? There's no reason at all for that, though there is an explanation of sorts for why we went in one terminal but caught the plane from another, and it's called 'Schengen'. Which is not a Flemish word meaning 'piss these foreigners about, it's nearly Christmas.' No, it's the name of a tiny town in Luxembourg which stands at the three-borders point where Luxembourg, Germany and France meet.

As such, it was the symbolic choice of where to sign the EU agreement to throw open most of the borders to allow free movement of people across the length and breadth of Europe. It's only 'most of' because the UK, Denmark and Sweden didn't sign up. It actually has had a big effect on football too, because it's part of the wider scheme of opening up the free movement of labour in the EU, which meant it was no longer possible for the football authorities to place restrictions on the number of foreign, as in European, players in teams. You could look upon this performance of marching us recalcitrant Brits up and down airport terminal corridors, in and out of buses, into different terminals, and finally onto planes as another kind of symbol of us being self-imposed Schengen exiles.

I've just settled into seat 7A. There's loads of space to stretch out, with the plane being only a quarter full. So we're playing Sporting Lisbon tonight… distant echoes of 1968/69 and also of this summer's pre-season tournament when they beat us one-nil in a lacklustre kickabout. Both teams have already qualified so that takes away some of the edge, but the question is who will finish in which position in the group? Middlesbrough played last night and headed their group after winning handsomely three goals to nil against Partizan Belgrade. You no doubt ruefully recall them as the team that knocked us out of the Champignons League qualifying round last season when we lost on penalties, as always. Some might say that if it hadn't been for them we might never have gone so far in the UEFA Cup. Others might say that the game was a watershed for the team and the club and that we've never quite been the same since.

I just remembered that I should have had my copy of *Toon Tales* in my hands while I'd been sitting in the airport, but I'd forgotten. An ideal publicity and marketing opportunity missed again! I'd fallen to taking it with me on trips and ostentatiously reading it in cafés, airports and railway stations, planes and trains. You sit yourself in some strategically visible seat and hold the book well up so that the cover's easily visible. Then you smile contentedly and occasionally let out a hearty chuckle. Good marketing.

I'll get it down from the overhead locker in a minute, so that when the lassie comes around with the papers I can say in a distinct voice, 'No thanks, pet, I'd rather get on with reading this here *Toon Tales* book. I can't wait to find out what's going to happen next.'

We took an unusual route to Newcastle today. We crossed pretty smartish over the sea and then flew overland for most of the way. As we got towards the end of the flight, I glanced out of the window and realised we were flying down the course of the River Tyne from somewhere out by Hexham. It was fantastic. The sky was clear, we were already pretty low and I could see everything. We flew right down over the city centre and on to the coast where we made a turn over Whitley Bay and the sea and then came back in right over St. Mary's Island. I think this has to be my best ever flight into Newcastle. It had been a blustery day, and I think this must have had something to do with the unusual flight path. A perfect moment.

The way the schedules of the Champignons League and the UEFA Cup worked out this year, and with the new group stage introduced into the latter, there was scope for a certain amount of tactical thinking on the fifth and final match day. The top three teams out of the five in each group would go into the draw for the next round. There a definite incentive to come top of your group, as that gave you a tie against a lowly third-placed team from another group, whereas ending up second would see you playing one of the eight third-placed Champignons drop-outs. And when you looked at the names of some of those eight teams, who'd played their last games the week before, you really didn't want to be ending up second and risking facing current UEFA Cup champions Valencia or Olympiakos with Rivaldo playing for them, or a nightmare journey to Shakhtar Donetsk. In some ways, it was actually going to be better to finish third rather than second for the same reason, and this was where tactics could possibly have come into play. On the other hand, a trip to Valencia in mid-February would no doubt be a pleasantly warm break, while Moscow, Kiev or Shakhtar Donetsk would be anything but. That's decided it; let's go for first place.

Some teams in second place had the luxury to speculate whether it would be better to win the last game and come out top of their group, or draw and stay second, or lose and end up third. But their nightmare would be to draw or lose and get overtaken by a late runner and end up fourth. The teams which currently occupied one of the top three places but had to sit out the fifth match day, having already played all their games, just had to wait and hope things would pan out and they would not be evicted by a bad combination of results. The endless combinations meant that, for nearly everyone, except the few like us and Boro and our opponents Sporting who had already qualified, there was no real room for tactics and the best plan was to go hell for leather for a win to scrape into the following day's draw for the next two rounds.

As things stood now, I thought we really needed to avoid losing and cement our place as group winners so that we could play a third-placed team. Ironically enough, Boro's win over Partizan Belgrade had left our nemesis of last year in third place in their group, so there was a chance that they might be our next opponents. Quaking in our boots time. We didn't even have Nobby Solano any more to score our solitary goal. The other three teams that had finished third in the group games the night before were rather more attractive in terms of our prospects of beating them, and of their locations: Aachen, Auxerre, who'd knocked out Rangers, and

Graz AK. The three other possible opponents were going to be decided in the Thursday evening matches to be played at the same time as ours. Ones which caught my eye were Club Bruges (though they actually call themselves Club Brugge in Flemish) and Standard Liège in Belgium, two easy places to go, and Hearts, the last Scottish survivors. Basel, our opponent a year ago, was another possibility. Funnily enough, of all of them, only Basel survived the evening's games.

It was a bitterly cold night and some of the Sporting players were wearing gloves and those black tight leg-warmers under their shorts (shades of that home game against another Portuguese side, Vitoria Setubal, some thirty-six or so years earlier). Apparently one of their players might have five whatsits, and he has to have his jockstrap-cum-legwarmers specially made to order: they say they fit like a glove.

There were about a hundred and fifty Sporting supporters up in the normal away section, plus a few more in the posh seats in the West Stand. The mood in the ground was pretty morose. They could have done with the audience of kids who'd been at the afternoon pantomime at the Custom's House down in South Shields, where the atmosphere had been brilliant, as the kids would surely have called it (does nobody say 'geet lush' any more?). Well done to the kids of St. Oswald's Primary and Harton School. The Custom's House panto is definitely always the best, thanks to Ray Spencer, aka Tommy the Trumpeter, and Bob Stott and the rest of the Geordie cast. A local panto for local people (we'll have no trouble here).

Sporting's star player is goalkeeper Ricardo, famous for making the save and then scoring the winning goal for Portugal in the penalty shoot-out against England in last summer's Euro 2004 Championships. Then of course the big connection is that they took back Hugo Viana on a season-long loan, which seems to be working out well as he's been re-gaining his form and fitness and raising not only his profile, but also his sale value in the process. An all-round good outcome for everyone concerned. Unlike Lua Lua's loan to Portsmouth last season, one condition is that he is not allowed to play against us, so he missed out on their one-nil win in the pre-season tournament and he can't play us in the UEFA Cup either.

Again, the attendance was very disappointing, with just 28,017 turning up on a windy night. The Toon got off to a geet lush start against eleven Sporting players who looked as alike as eleven peas in a pod thanks to their awful away strips of various shades of green. Bellamy it was who delighted us by heading home an Ameobi flick-on into the Leazes End goal. But on thirty-three minutes, Given was also beaten by a header, from Sporting's Miguel Custodio. Souness was quoted as saying 'We were the team that needed a draw to get through and win this section, and that's exactly what we have done'. And I suppose there is no arguing with that. Mission accomplished.

After the match, I hung around outside the ground in the icy blasts of the gusting wind in the hope of giving a courtesy copy of our book to Graeme Souness. Quite a few autograph hunters stayed too and they convinced me that he would be coming out, but he never appeared and he must have left by another exit. While I was waiting, I ended up having a chat with a Portuguese fan who, it turned out, was living in Newcastle for a couple of years while he did a course at the University. We wished each other's teams well, in the pious hope that we might meet again at the Final in Lisbon on the eighteenth of May.

So, we had qualified with ten points from three wins and a draw, the highest number of points of any team in the UEFA Cup. If nothing else, these points come in handy to boost our ranking in the seedings for future years. It's hard to believe, but our exploits in last year's UEFA Cup, which had included so many wins rather than just draws or narrow away losses, had seen us end up with a haul of UEFA seedings points bettered only by Valencia and Porto. Amazingly, we even got more points than our vanquishers, Marseille, and the Champignons League runners-up Monaco. It doesn't really seem fair that a UEFA Cup home win against NAC Breda gets you just as many points as an away win against Real Madrid in the latter stages of the Champignons League, but it does. I think we've found our right level, haven't we?

After the results of the Thursday night matches, we were placed in Pot Two for the Friday lunchtime draw along with Boro, Feyenoord, Atletico Bilbao, Dnipro, AZ Alkmaar, Stuttgart, and Lille. We would be drawn against one of the third-placed teams who were all in Pot One, which meant we could be facing either Alemannia Aachen, Heerenveen, Basel, Parma, Graz AK, Austria Wien or Partizan Belgrade, but not Sporting Lisbon. I've listed them in my order of preference for the draw. Boro faced the same choice, except they couldn't draw Partizan again. I certainly didn't want to end up playing Belgrade. The eight Champignons League drop-outs were in Pot Three, comprising Olympiakos, Dynamo Kiev, Ajax, Fenerbahce, Panathinaikos, Shakhtar Donetsk, Valencia and CSKA Moscow. Making up the final eight in Pot Four were Schalke, Steaua Bucharest, Zaragoza, Sochaux, Villarreal, Auxerre, Benfica, and Sevilla. Just think: on the eighteenth of May, one of those teams was destined to win the Cup.

When the draw came out from UEFA HQ in Nyon at a quarter to two, I was pretty pleased that we ended up with my second choice of Heerenveen in the north of Holland, a three and a half hour drive from Brussels, and the team that sold us Jon Dahl Tomasson. Boro and Graz AK were the first teams drawn out of the hat, while our game was drawn out second, so there was no time for suspense and speculation for the North-East teams. I think we both came out of it pretty well. They also drew out the matches for the subsequent round, and if we got past Heerenveen, we were going to be up against either Olympiakos or, coincidentally, Sochaux again. Whichever way it turned out, therefore, success against Heerenveen would see us retracing our steps from the previous round, either to Athens or to Sochaux.

After the Sporting game, I stayed on for the weekend. I'd never been to Tyne Tees TV before and I'd never been to the BBC either, and now I went to both within the space of an hour. I had to take a copy of *Toon Tales* to Tyne Tees, and on Saturday morning while I was having a spot of breakfast I switched on Radio Newcastle. They said they were giving away first come, first served tickets to go to the opening of the Sage Music Centre. Do you remember when they used to have Harvey Smith on 'Wednesday Sportsnight with Coleman' once a year doing showjumping somewhere indoors, maybe at Olympia, was it? What I remember very well was that there was a horse called 'Sanyo Music Centre', which I always felt was a mighty fine name. I think there was another one called 'Everest Double Glazing', but 'Sanyo Music Centre' was best. I've got no idea if the horse was good, or what colour it was, but its name was too good to forget. Well, every time I hear about the Sage Music Centre, I think about showjumping. A very unfortunate word association.

They said they didn't have many tickets left so I downed my tea, jumped into the car and raced off down to the BBC, which is out on the edge of the Town Moor on Barrack Road. There was a steady stream of people going in for tickets but I managed to get three for brother Ian, niece Sophie and myself. I then headed through the crosstown traffic (thanks, Jimi) to Tyne Tees TV on City Road. With it being early Saturday morning, it seemed very quiet. To get in, you walk up the Tube that used to feature in the early-eighties Jools Holland and Paula Yates show called 'The Tube', coincidentally. Just after the glass doors at the end of the Tube, there's a security guard at a reception desk. He checked, but there was no one around to whom I could hand over the book personally, so I left it with him to give to the sports desk producers for the Mike Neville Show. And that was that - in and out in a minute. Then it was straight over to the other side of the river, where I found a place to park outside Barry's Tyres, and then into 'The Sage', as I think they like you to call it. Personally, I prefer 'the slug' or 'the whale', and I like 'the egg-slicer' for the new bridge next to it. The tickets were for the morning tour, so there was no time to lose. It was a really lucky coincidence that the Sage opening was on this weekend.

I hope it does well. It has everything you could want if you like any kind of music. On that first morning, all the staff and all the visitors were oozing so much enthusiasm. I really hope it's sustained on all sides. What I especially liked were the twenty-five or so practice rooms on the bottom floor. They're of different sizes to take any size of group or band or ensemble or choir, from one person to maybe twenty or thirty, and they all seem to be soundproofed. Maybe it was only on this opening day, but you could just walk in, sit down at one of the beautiful baby grand Yamaha pianos and bash out the intro to 'All the way from Memphis'. At least that's what I did, and no one complained. If it stays like that, they've definitely got my vote.

A festive Arsenal and Birmingham

Didn't expect to be home during the 2004/5 festive season, but Mam wasn't feeling up to a trip over to Deutschland, so we went over to Geordieland instead. Left Germany the day after Boxing Day, returned second of January. Equals two possible home games, Arsenal and Birmingham City. Got on the blower to the box office, but even with the special priority given to Club Membership holders (my arse), there were no tickets left for the game against the smoke's arse. Plenty left for the Birmingham game, however, so there was something to look forward to that would go nicely with the New Year's Day hangover. Bit of a long-haul trip back home this time, as wor lass not only can't fly, won't fly, but also can't drive an overnight ferry, so won't sleep on one either. Only leaves the Chunnel or the short-hop ferries. Now the Channel Tunnel is great for speed, alright – as in mevvies popping over to the big fat city for an away game against some bunch of cockneys. But when you've driven from Deutschland and you're homeward-bound, then you need a break. So the Calais-Dover ferry it was. Now here's a little tip: when crossing the Channel by ferry, choose the Seafrance boat. That way you won't have to put up with listening to quite so many southern accents around you! Here's another tip in the same vein: whenever you are sent on a business trip to sunderland, just don't go – tell you're boss to piss off, and get the sack instead.

There was clearly no chance whatsoever of getting hold of a ticket for the game against Arsy Whinger's side, but there was still Bar Oz and its giant-screen Sky coverage to look forward to. We'd arranged to meet up with Chris and Sarah there for pre-match tinctures and the post-mortem drowning of sorrows as usual. They were up from the smoke for a breath of fresh Tyneside air over Yuletide. Hey, isn't it amazing how many different ways we have of saying Christmas? There's Christmas (not unlike the Dutch *kerstmis*),

Noel (not a million miles away from the French *noël*), and of course Yule (from the Scandinavian *jul*). But there I go, digressing again. Not that the timing of Christmas has anything at all to do with the actual date of Christ's birth, of course. From time immemorial, as far as I can remember, the solstice has always been an excuse for eating and drinking to excess. The Church just latched on to a convenient occasion and harnessed it to its own needs while ensuring it would meet the least possible resistance from the so-called pagans, who didn't give a toss either way as to why they were having a good time, as long as they could simply go on having it. And mind, up our way you have got to have some excuse at that time of year, haven't you? By mid-December it's getting dark on a cloudy day not long after three in the afternoon, and stays that way till about half past eight the next morning. So you have to do something to blot it all out. What must it be like in the north of Sweden, or in Iceland? No wonder they like their drink too.

But back to the exciting scene developing in Bar Oz. My whole clan (Iris, Tina, Stephs and her lad Dominik) and I had decided to watch the match there, but on the way in I decided on the off chance to ask Barry the Baaldy Booncer (a true gentleman, and surely the most genuinely-liked booncer in the Toon) if he'd heard of any spares going. He shook his head knowingly, but suggested I have a word with Graham behind the bar (a Ketsbaia lookalike). So I had a word with the Graham the Baaldy Barman and he promised he would keep his eyes and ears open and get back to Barry the Baaldy Booncer if the unexpected happened. At least I had the satisfaction of having left no sturn untoned, as usual.

Immersed in my third pint of Kronenbourg, the genial crack and the generally electric pre-match atmosphere unique to Newcastle pubs, my mind had no sooner drifted away from the subject of an elusive match ticket than into our little group pops Barry the Booncer, a Cheshire cat smile on his baaldy face, asking:

'Still lukkin' forra ticket like?'

'Aye.'

'Well here ye gan.'

And standing behind him was a guy holding out the ticket from a season ticket book.

'How much ye askin'?' ventures I.

'Nowt, it's Christmas.'

'Ya kiddin' – howay man, av gorra gi ye summik.'

'Nar, ya aalreet.'

'Well leruz get ye a pint.'

But he was having none of it. And when I tried to press a tenner into Barry the Baaldy Booncer's hand for his trouble, I thought he was going to chin me. By the way, have you noticed how all the booncers on Tyneside are baaldy?

The lad with the spare ticket was Colin from Cullercoats (alright, Whitley Bay, really, but there's no alliteration to be had there), who explained that his mate Davie (not from Denton, unfortunately, but Tynemouth) wasn't feeling too grand and his match ticket was looking for a good, deserving home. Wheyabuggama, there I was: a good and deserving home.

So let it be said and writ large at this modest juncture that the Barry the Baaldy Booncers and Cullercoats Colins of this world are the salt of the earth – soond-as-a-pund Geordies and fantastic people. I mean, can you imagine a similar scene being played out in some cockney boozer?

Ticket tout: 'ere you gow, mite, come dahn the frog and towd for a point of pig's ear? Well all you need do is put your end in your sky rocket and pull aht a pony, init, and you've got yourself a ticket for the big gime, eh, cam on Arsenal, eh? Know wot I mean, do me a favour, leave it out, knock it on the 'ead, eh, eh?'

Ticketless Geordie: 'Piss off, you cockney tout twat. Aa divvenaa wat ya gannin' on aboot.'

To which Eric Cantona might add: 'A ship is safe in the harbour, but that's not what ships are built for. And it takes iron men to build wooden ships.' Ahem.

So I got to the Arsenal game after all, and what a cracker. I reckon it was the Toon's best performance of the season so far, including the four-nil win at Sochaux. We were so desperately unlucky to lose to that jammy deflection in the time added mysteriously on to the first half. And didn't lucky Arsenal get up to their usual tricks? 'Same old Ars'nal, always cheating.' And 'one-nil to the referee.' The atmosphere in the ground was just brilliant that evening, and what a joy to be part of it in the Gallowgate towards the Popular corner, level with the highest seats in the East Stand. So thanks again, Colin and Davie. Glad I could at least give you a lift to the Toon and back on New Year's Day.

The programme for that New Year's Day match against the Brummies contained the usual 'fan of the day' feature. It's actually my favourite bit of the programme, as it is always liable to throw up something slightly surreal. What particularly grabbed my attention this time was Fan of the Day Allan Scorer's answer to the question: 'What is the funniest or strangest thing you have seen while following United?' His reply was as follows:

'It has to be the Pope smoking a huge Havana cigar accompanied by his four cardinals blessing the crowd while walking around the cinder track before one of the games in King Kev's reign as a player, I think it was in 1983/84.'

Now there may have been several possible motives for Allan saying that. One is that the Pope actually did come to the Toon, had a smoke and a stroll around St. James's Park and blessed the crowd. And I for one am not saying he did not.

Alternatively, this may have been a vision sent to Allan by the surely soon-to-be-beatified and then sainted Cardinal Basil Hume, Wor Baz. The symbolism is of course crystal clear. One of the cardinals in the vision was Wor Saint Baz himself. The proximity to the Pope represents the fact that he himself was short-listed for popehood by the pundits and his prime papal priority was to bless the crowd in the Gallowgate Coliseum, which in a further image was his gateway to greater things, transcending even the spirituality of the Toon with its saintly array of heavenly pubs.

On the other hand, Allan may just have been winding up any Toon wallahs with a secondary affiliation to Rangers (apparently there are some) and taking the piss out of the nuggets who publish the programme and will believe anything you tell them and don't have the nous to check things. Either way, it was a nice one.

Now I must go away and think about the funniest or strangest thing I have ever seen while following United... hmmm...

As the tube train approached our Shepherd's Bush destination, a funny farty smell filled the carriage and got stronger and stronger as we drew nearer. It wasn't us. I don't know what they do after lunch on a Sunday afternoon in Shepherd's Bush, but whatever they do, they certainly make a smell while they are at it.

We all met up outside a place that used to be called Edward's Bar, on the corner of Wood Lane and Shepherd's Bush Green, just up the road from the tube station. It had to be outside because they wouldn't let kids in and we had plenty with us! There was Olivia aged four and Edward aged six with Don; Sarah and Brian aged eight and twelve with me; and Penny aged ten, daughter of Don's friend Alan. Sarah and Chris were of course there too. With Chris working just around the corner at the BBC Television Centre, he knows all the pubs around here, and he recommended that we try O'Neill's down by the side of the Green, on the corner next door to the Shepherd's Bush Theatre. As we passed by the rather run-down red-brick theatre, a dim and distant memory interrupted my step:

'Chris, is this where they made Crackerjack?'

'Crackerjaaaaaaack!'

'Peter Glaze and Leslie Crowther, piling up cabbages in your arms if you guessed wrong in the quiz. But you always got a Crackerjack... '

'Crackerjaaaaaaack!'

'... pencil.'

'Well, actually, I think you may be right. Either here or just down the road at Lime Grove. The BBC has had four or five places dotted all over around here. They made the Old Grey Whistle Test here too.'

O'Neill's was very welcoming, especially to kids, so we settled them down at a couple of tables beside the giant screen showing Rangers versus Celtic in the Scottish Cup (shouldn't that be Celtic versus Rangers, Barry?). Celtic scored and looked the better side, but I wonder whether they could do with another speedy little forward to replace the now-departed Henrik Larsson? We bumped into Chris's BBC colleague Clive, who'd been working the morning shift, and lots of familiar faces including members of the London NUFC Supporters Club, and Brian, The Mag columnist who seems to be at every single match, and whom we'd met with his pal Biffa, just about the most famous ever-present of all, in Sochaux.

Going to QPR's ground at Loftus Road brought it home to us how far we've progressed in the last fifteen years in terms of our ground, and how clubs like QPR have been left miles behind. You could even buy away tickets at the turnstiles, just like the good old days. And to think that not too long ago, we were playing them in the League. Do you remember that time when we were four-nil up against QPR at half time in the smoke and the final result was fours apiece? What was that about a curse, Mr Gullit? The ground's fully equipped with seats, but they still have old-fashioned stands where your view is partially obscured by the pillars holding up the roof. And going out at half time behind the stands really did take you back to the world of a good old-fashioned ground with hot dog stalls in huts out in the open. Someone saw me carrying Sarah on my shoulders when we went to queue up for a cup of tea, and he must have recognised us off our book cover. He'd got the book at Christmas from The Back Page, and had just begun reading it. Fortunately, I managed to convince him that he would have to contact the publishers if he ever decided that he wanted his money back.

By rights, we should of course have been at Yeading's own ground near Hayes. Home to a regular fan base of between one hundred and fifty, and four hundred, depending on which report you believe. And whose turf had been graced by the silky skin, if not skills, of Keira Knightley in 'Bend it Like Beckham'. There must have been a long queue of volunteers to be the physio for that match: 'Need your thighs massaging, pet?'

Typical foot-in-mouth timing a couple of weeks earlier had seen Chairman Fred pronouncing at a Dubai conference on football that he didn't care one *iota* - can't stop using it now! - for lower league teams as long as his team was doing alright: 'There's no sympathy here.'

Not the most diplomatic thing to say at any time, but guaranteed to turn the whole country against us when it was raked up again when the inevitable happened and we got drawn against non-league Yeading FC, the lowest-ranked team in the Third Round of the FA Cup. Errol Telemaque, one of Yeading's forwards, said of Shepherd: 'People like that don't care about the game - they're not looking at the big picture.' Now I wonder who's right?

One interesting comparison - the average wage of Yeading's part-time players is sixty pounds a week, a thousand times less than the Toon's top earners. For this one match, they were all earning a thousand pounds each, only sixty times less. And they earned it with a very creditable performance, especially in the first half when they held the score goalless. They billed it as the Bling versus the 'Ding, which just about sums it up.

We started off in the third row for the first half, but moved down to the front row for the second when some kind souls offered to swap seats when they saw that Sarah wasn't getting much of a view. There was only a couple of yards between us and the pitch, which was great for the atmosphere. To add to it, we stuck our spare Toon tops where advertising hoardings normally should be. The velcro provided was a very convenient way of hanging them up.

This match saw the débuts of Boumsong and Babayaro (the French accent in 'débuts' is in their honour). Both looked pretty good, except for one or two disconcerting lapses from Boumsong when he lost his player. In the second half, when he was running up and down the left wing right in front of us, Babayaro showed some excellent close control and made a good few probing passes. We'd gained two more B's which would allow us to have a defence solely made up of B's: Bernard, Bramble, Boumsong and Babayaro. This of course didn't last for long, because we lost two B's by the end of the month. Bernard's departure, which everyone had seen coming with his failure to agree his contract renewal and the arrival of Babayaro, and then the sudden and unexpected exit of Craig Bellamy on the last day of the January sales. Celtic's Larsson replacement. While she rested her elbows over the advertising hoarding, little Sarah announced:

'Number ten's my favourite. What's he called again?'

'That's Craig Bellamy.'

'Yes, he's my favourite 'coz he runs around a lot and he scored a goal.'

'Me too.'

In the middle of the second half when everyone was happy and relieved that we'd scored twice, someone started up a chant, 'Souness, Souness, give us a wave, Souness, give us a wave.' And he did. Then 'Saunders, Saunders' and he did too. Then someone started up 'Shearer, Shearer', but I don't know where he was and I don't know if he waved. When we got back home, I saw he'd been one of the BBC pundits so I suppose he must have been hidden away in a TV studio box somewhere in the corner of the ground. Then it was the turn of the old favourite, 'Yeading, Yeading give us a song. Ssshhhhh!' Then there were lots of attempts to encourage 'Boumsong, Boumsong (to) give us a wave' because he was closest to us, but he was concentrating on the game. Either that, or he's hard of hearing. In which case, it's a good job he's the talker at the heart of our defence, not one of the listeners.

Some Yeading fans started throwing a big buff blow-up doll around in the end behind our goal in the second half. I wonder whether the fans had managed to get it through the turnstiles full size and ready for action, or whether they'd hidden it up their jumpers and blown it up at half time. It must take some big puffs to do that. As Brian Ferry might say, 'In every dream home there's a heartache'. It brought back memories of the rubber-chicken-hoying session at Real Mallorca last year. Eventually it landed up on the pitch behind Steve Harper, who took occasional wary looks at it, no doubt hoping that nobody would take a picture of him in a compromising position if he had to dive over in her direction. Eventually a steward reluctantly came across and gingerly picked it up at arm's length and dragged it away by one of its feet, trying to ignore the catcalls from the crowd.

Yeading had played really well and they deserved the nil-two result that they got. A higher score would not have reflected their good contribution to the match. The players paraded around the ground to celebrate their excellent achievements this year and the Toon struck up with 'You are top of your league, say, you are top of your league.' Which was true as they were running away with the Ryman League and heading for the Conference. Good luck to manager Johnson Hippolyte and his players.

We hung around after the game as I was determined to get our complimentary copy of *Toon Tales* to Graeme Souness (if you can't sell 'em, give 'em away!). I'd failed to see him at St. James's after the Sporting Lisbon match three weeks before, and he proved equally elusive this time too. Then Brian had a brainwave:

'Give it to that man there packing the kit into the coach.'

'Good idea... excuse me, this is a delayed Christmas present for Graeme Souness. It's just a book. Could you pass it on to him, please?'

'Yes, of course, no problem.'

'Thanks very much, err ... could I have your name?'

'It's John.'

'Well thanks very much, John. Good luck.'

Sarah and Emilie had wrapped it up like a Christmas present, and if we'd waited any longer to get it to him, we would have had to put it in Easter wrapping instead. Or

Valentine's. Though maybe that might have been going a bit too far.

We stayed for the weekend at the St. Pancr(e)as Youth Hostel on Euston Road, right opposite the new British Library. We went in to see if we could ask them to bring our book up from the vaults, but when they heard that it had only been deposited two months ago, they said we'd come a few months or even years too early. They're so deluged in books and periodicals arriving every day that they're between four months and even four years behind, depending on the kind of book. The shelves are growing at a rate of twelve kilometres a year! It must be a huge place, with most of it hidden underground. While we were there, we looked around the 'treasures room', which is absolutely fascinating. You can see the only surviving piece of script written in Shakespeare's own hand, the Magna Carta (this is a list, not a subordinate clause, in case you're wondering), a report written by a survivor of the Charge of the Light Brigade, and letters by Winston Churchill. The log of Lord Nelson's flagship HMS Victory from the Battle of Trafalgar describes how he slipped away in the knowledge that the battle was won, but there's no mention of 'Kiss me Hardy'. I suppose that was a southern 'me' as in 'myself', not a Geordie 'me' as in 'my'. But let's not forget that it was actually a Geordie lad, Lord Collingwood of mouth-of-Tyne-statue fame, who won the battle after one-eyed jack had snuffed it. Luckily, it wasn't him listening to Nelson's last words, otherwise there could have been an embarrassing incident. And don't forget either that the 'ogre' Napoleon was finally taken to St. Helena by the HMS Northumberland – Geordieland rules the waves alright! There is also a very interesting display case of Beatles lyrics including 'Yesterday' alongside their original record sleeves. One of the lyrics is written on the back of a kid's birthday card with a big red bus and balloons on! I think it was 'Ticket to Ride', but I can't be sure.

On Sunday, the twenty-third of January, we lost one-nil at Highbury. Not really such a bad result against the arse, you might think on the face of it. But hang on, we were absolutely destroyed before the TV eyes of millions, and had it not been for Shay Given's heroics, the gooners could easily have gone into double figures. Some of Shay's saves were thoroughly world class and speculation that he could be seeking pastures new will now no doubt come to the boil. But given the outfield team's performance, who could blame him? Why do we simply give the ball away to opponents so bloody often? We didn't get a corner till about the eighty-fifth minute, and we really only had two half-chances over the full ninety minutes, both of them in the second half of the second half, when Bowyer looked as if he could be through. And if we're honest, Shearer's header from ten yards was never really going anywhere, was it?

So we remain firmly ensconced in the wrong half of the table at the time of writing. This coming Saturday sees us at home to Coventry in the fourth round of the Cup. Surely we will beat them. Won't we? But the main cause of all the fuss these past few days has, of course, been a former Coventry player, Craig Bellamy. He wasn't even on the bench on Sunday, and Souness told Sky that was because of pulling a hamstring in training on Friday. Then out come all sorts of conflicting stories, and the bottom line – allegedly – is that he feigned injury to avoid having to play out of position.

The Times wrote this morning that it is the supporters who suffer most in all this, and that newspaper is dead right. I really just don't know what to think.

On the one hand, Bellamy is one of the greatest talents ever to have come to Newcastle. He is dead exciting to watch and when played in a forward role is always going to make and score goals. Never mind that he blasts three quarters of his opportunities wide or over the bar. The other quarter find the back of the net, thank you very much. And because his pace brings him four times as many chances as other players, that works out to be a hundred per cent effectiveness in our book. And this is our book, after all!

On the same hand, I have not yet fully taken to Souness. That incident at Anfield where he stretched up and lovingly touched their crest above the players' tunnel as we were running out really pissed me off. You can perfectly understand that the 'Pool means a lot to him, and rightly so, but he shouldn't have done it on camera. And quite frankly, I think he really has been playing Bellamy in the wrong positions.

But on the other hand, he IS the manager and Bellamy should be proud to don the black and white even if he were told to play at full back. *You just do not refuse to play for Newcastle United, Bellamy, you just do not*. And if you haven't managed to take that concept on board, well good riddance to you. Consider once again the money that these little brats are on. Again, The Times writes today that he will be fined two weeks' wages, which equals eighty thousand pounds! Excuse me? He gets paid forty grand a week (not even a month, but a week) and he refuses to go out and play for Newcastle United? Just which planet do these obscenely overpaid brats think they are on? In the real world, as opposed to the decidedly makie-on world of professional football, faking an injury constitutes grounds for constructive dismissal, as Don so rightly pointed out.

One positive note for me was that Bellamy has clearly been influenced by Wor Sir Uncle Bobby at the linguistic level, because he is reported as having said that Souness had gone behind his back right in front of his face! Now that is priceless. By the way, can't wait to hear Sir Bobby speak at this year's Saint Cuthbert's reunion piss-up – sorry, I meant to say Gala Dinner - scheduled for 15 April!

But before that, Tina and I, plus Tina's Luxembourg-born German friend Kathrin were off to Geordieland for the week-long half-term holiday, which included Pancake Tuesday and Ash Wednesday and so offered yet another chance to lay off the demon drink for Lent. How long would it last, though? With the prospect of a six-week dry period looming large, the thing to do, of course, is to get as much doon ya neck as possible over the few remaining days. So the gi-huge Rotterdam to Hull ferry with its numerous bars, including a kind of floating Irish Pub, offered the ideal venue for some pre-Lentern over-indulgence.

Suitably hung over, I managed the short hop from Hull to Geordieland in the customary three and a bit hours, which included the for me equally customary trip around York's very interesting one-way system, as I had as usual missed the turn-off for the outer ring road. Mind, it's hardly surprising, because the signposting is just crap. I reckon it's because York Council wants to lure as many tourists as possible into the city to spend their money. Much the same reasoning lies behind the, for non-Geordies, equally crap signposting when you drive off the Amsterdam ferry (well, Ijmuiden ferry, really) at North Shields (well, Percy Main, really). Small wonder that on any given morning in the summer months you can spot any number of cloggie and kraut cars and motor bikes meandering seemingly aimlessly around the streets of Shiels and Waalsend and gannin' roond and roond the roondaboot ower the Tyne Tunnel approach road because they cannot find any signs for Scotland. Quite right, too – they should spend their hols in Geordieland and Northumberland!

Time to pop in to see Mam in Tynemouth and unload the car at the brilliant holiday flat with a view of Cullercoats Bay before blasting straight up the Toon for the Charlton game. Rendezvous'd with Chris and Sarah, who had just blasted up from the smoke, in Bar Oz (where else?) and had a bit crack with Barry the Baaldy Booncer and with Colin (of Arsenal home game ticket fame) and his marras in the far corner. This time my club membership had secured me a ticket in the Gallowgate End, though it took a while to work that one out, as on the ticket itself it said Newcastle Brown Stand. Come on, I ask you! Gallowgate End it always was, Gallowgate End it always will be – when will the club ever get real? Answer: never! Colin asked where my seat was and I told him the crap designation just mentioned. At first, neither he nor his marras had a clue where a 'Newcastle Brown' stand might be. But then Davie said 'Hang on a minute, I think that's what it says on our season tickets as well'. And sure enough, their Gallowgate End season tickets strangely also bore the words 'Newcastle Brown'. And as it turned out, my seat was about three rows in front of theirs, just in from the corner flag on the Popular side, about level with the top of the East stand. Perfect!

If the view was perfect, the match was complete shite. That sinking feeling when the ball bobbled off Andy O'Brien to Rommedahl, who ran across the width of the penalty area before firing low past Shay Given to equalise. How come Newcastle just cannot hold on to a lead? We are always at our most vulnerable just after we have scored a goal. It is absolutely crazy. We were totally bereft of breadth in the form of wingers and the whole thing looked completely shapeless. All around, there were people shouting 'Souness Oot!' or, to be more accurate, 'Souness, Souness, oot on your arse!' When chants of 'Craig, Craig Bellamy' went up in some quarters, including not a million miles away from where I was sitting/standing, I was firmly on the fence - the consummate mugwump indulging in consummate mugwumpery. The Bellamy nostalgia was quickly stifled by the boos of others, and civil war was narrowly averted. Well at least he went to Celtic and not Rangers, I thought. And he'll probably net a hat-full if they play Berwick in the cup next year.

But then I reasoned to myself that Souness really had no choice once the situation had arisen. I mean, what do you do with super-brats who are so deeply in thrall to the luxury life that goes with forty grand a week as to be completely beyond remedy? Try saying those words out loud, very, very slowly: forty grand a week. Is that obscene, or what? On reflection, I reckon this was the season at its nadir. Even worse than when Sir Bobby was sacked without having anyone lined up to replace him. Even worse than when Woodgate was sold and we supposedly were going to be 'pleasantly surprised' that the money was going to be spent, not on a defender, but on Rooney. As if! The transfer deadline week had been allowed to degenerate into a 'This town ain't big enough for the both of us' showdown between Bellamy and Souness, and no one had known what to do. If those two other low-points hadn't occurred, the situation would not, or at least might not, have come about at all! But it was all academic now. Bellamy was past tense and he clearly was not going to play for the Toon again. So in the minds of much of the crowd, there was nothing for it but to move on. Move on to shouting for the manager's heed, that is!

In the wake of the Charlton *débacle* (the French accent here is in honour of no one in particular), the Chronicle ran a five-day fans' forum to gather their views on what was now a manifest crisis – dire straits already! The likes of you and me were invited to e-mail, fax, phone, telex, shout or smoke-signal in our opinions, and I am pretty sure I read every single contribution. So I think it is fair to say that the majority of people – a good three-quarters by my estimate – were of the 'Souness Oot!' faction.

A couple of other interesting events occurred at about that time. One was the Labour Party Spring Conference, though spring definitely hadn't yet sprung, which took place at the Sage (whale or slug or 'neigh', take your pick) a week after the Charlton game while the lads were having a well-deserved break (hmm) in Dubai. Plus, the engagement was announced of His Royal Highness the Prince of Wales (used to be a canny pub!) to Mrs Camilla Parker Bowles (what, all three of them?). How unkind of some to call her Camella Porker Bowels. Someone asked, most irreverently: 'Is she pregnant?' Only to be 'corrected' by one wag who suggested the more precise term was 'in foal'. This sort of thing truly is awful. It was just as bad when that picture of Prince Harry wearing a Nazi uniform appeared and some not very loyal person said 'What do you expect? Maybe he found it in the cupboard? After all, Adolf might have presented it as a keepsake to Harry's great uncle, the old Prince of Wales, after one of his visits in the thirties.'

In a clear sign of socio-political solidarity with us lesser mortals, the Chronicle, which clearly knows which side its bread is buttered on, gave far more prominence all week long to the sorry Souness-Bellamy saga than to either of those somewhat lesser occurrences. To be sure, its interview with Mr Blair on the Thursday or Friday included the subject we were all most interested in. Tony boxed clever, however, and refused to back Souness or denounce him. He probably just wanted to say nothing at all about NUFC, lest he put his foot right in it once again. Maybe he thought Souness was a member of our 1955 Cup winning team! Souness/Scoular – it's pretty close!

Our next destination was Heerenveen in Friesland in the North of the Netherlands. The first leg was over there on Thursday, the seventeenth of February. So, as they might say in Dutch: *Waar gaan wij heen? Naar Heerenveen!*

On the face of it, not a bad draw from our point of view. Not many people had even heard of Heerenveen, though at the time of the draw they were something like fifth in the cloggie league. Straight onto their website, of course, only to find out that theirs is a pretty tiny ground. Up in Friesland, or Frisia, they speak Frisian, which is a dialect of Dutch and even closer to English and to Geordie than Dutch itself.

Appropriately enough, Newcastle's twin town in Friesland is Groningen, not a million miles away from Heerenveen. Come to think of it, me and wor Mick bumped into a bunch of lads and lasses from Groningen Council in Moscow back in 1987. Some nice lass came up to us on Red Square, asking the way in German, but with a strong cloggie accent. So we quickly got cracking. Turned out the whole bunch of them were staying at the same hotel as we were, Hotel International, which offers a great view of Red Square and of Lenin's Mausoleum. We actually wanted to see Lenin, but the queue was from approximately Wallsend East End Club to Percy Main, so we went instead to the Lenin museum opposite, where amongst other things his 'property-is-theft, all-men-are-equal, exploitation-of-the-workers, capitalist symbol' Rolls Royce is on display.

Anyway, we met up with those Frisian cloggies in the hotel bar that evening, where appropriately enough the cool Heineken was a'flowing. Learned a rude Dutch song from them, which went something like this. The lads would sing *'Wij zijn de jongens van de landbouwschool – wij willen zaaien'* (We are the lads from agricultural school – we want to go a'sowing). To which the lasses sang: *'Wij zijn de meisjes van de landbouwschool – wij willen naaien'* (We are the lasses from agricultural school – we want to go a'sewing). Now it has to be pointed out that while the Dutch verb *naaien* does indeed mean 'sew', it also has another, somewhat ruder meaning. I'll let you guess what: *honi soit qui mal y pense*. When they interview Frisians on cloggie telly, they actually show subtitles, in the same way they do on German telly when interviewing 'German'-speaking Swiss.

With the Heerenveen fixture, there were shades of Vålerenga in that we just didn't have any clarity. Remember: at various times, that game was going to be played in Oslo, Trondheim, or maybe even exotic Middlesbrough! This time it wasn't the venue that was unclear, it was the date: either Wednesday the sixteenth or Thursday the seventeenth of February! Now this really is not on. If you consulted the official NUFC website in the early days of 2005 you'll have read that it was Wednesday, while the cloggie site said Thursday.

The only thing for it was to book a hotel for both nights. Easier said than done. There are two Jahe Hotels in Heerenveen and both told me they were fully booked up for that week because of the skaters. Now I could only assume, and it's a fair assumption, that Heerenveen was one of the main places for the famous *zevenstedentocht* – the skating tour of seven towns, when any number of cloggies dressed in all-body condoms go skating down the frozen canals, swaying their arms furiously from side to side, presumably in a bid to stay warm. I've tried to imitate that style on an ice rink, and I find it is only possible if you have had a couple of the cool Heineken first. But I was wrong; Heerenveen was in fact staging indoor skating championships – European ones, I think.

Anyway, there was no room at the inn (not even the Holiday Inn) in Heerenveen, so I took the Jahe receptionist's advice and tried the Bastion Hotel in Leeuwarden instead. The guy on reception was very understanding and agreed to take a reservation for three rooms for the two nights, on the understanding that one of them would be cancelled once we knew for sure when the game would take place. Eventually, on the sixth of February, Sarah was first to find out that the game would be on the seventeenth, so I was able the same day to finally sort out the hotel reservation.

Once again, it has to be said that this is no way to run a brothel. People have to be able to plan their trips, to arrange to take time off work, etc. Come on UEFA, get your act together!

Against the already quite depressing background of the Charlton draw and the Bellamy controversy, we were concerned, nay consumed, by other pressing matters, principal among them being how to get hold of tickets. The Abe Lenstra Stadion only holds about nineteen thousand, or at least that was the limit that UEFA had imposed for our match there, and the Toon contingent of tickets numbered all of seven hundred. That is not what you might call a lot, especially for a place that was so easy to reach, by plane to Amsterdam or by DFDS ferry from Shields to Ijmuiden.

The season ticket holders amongst us did not have a lot of luck, despite the incontrovertible fact that they rank without the merest shadow of a doubt amongst the most loyal of the Toon's followers. Barry and Ian's application drew a blank, as did Chris and Sarah's, but they were coming anyway on the grounds that they were bound to get a ticket somehow – that's the spirit! What was it General Melchet said in 'Blackadder goes Forth'? 'If all else fails, a pig-headed refusal to look facts in the face will see us through.' But after the Marseille experience, their optimism was pretty well-founded, really. Don managed to get one, but he himself was prevented from attending this particular outing by a now urgent need to gain a few domestic brownie points in the shape of a new bathroom suite. We've all been there, haven't we? So he sent Barry his ticket. One down, three to go.

By mysterious means that certainly won't be divulged here, the telephone numbers of two of NUFC's high-ups found their way into our sphere of knowledge and we duly got in touch. But alas, both led to a dead end. Barry also got the phone number of the Heerenveen chairman, Mr Riemer van de Velde. It's such a nice club, they helpfully supply such numbers on their website! Taak aboot freedom of information, like! You don't get that on the official NUFC website, do you? We thought we had nothing to lose, so in the late afternoon Barry gave the Heerenveen Chairman a ring. Tell us about it, Barry.

Yes, I tried the number and it turned out to be his mobile phone. I found myself talking to his very friendly wife as she sat out on her sun terrace in Spain where they were enjoying a winter break. I explained that we were writing a book and that it would leave a bit of a hole in the narrative if we couldn't actually see the match, and she was very sympathetic and helpful. Mrs van de Velde explained that they had never had such interest in any of their matches ever before and they were really looking forward to a memorable evening. She advised me to contact the Chairman's Assistant the next morning because by now she would have left to pick up her children from school. Somehow, I couldn't imagine having the same conversation with our chairman or his wife. What a good club Heerenveen must be if their Chairman and his wife were anything to go by. This was a club in the true meaning of the word. Which made me remember that if you look on the NUFC letterhead, the 'C' now stands for Company, not Club. That says it all, doesn't it? The next day, I had another very nice telephone conversation with the Chairman's Assistant this time, but the outcome was still that we had no more tickets. They'd been inundated with phone calls, but UEFA rules meant that they would have been in big trouble if they'd sold tickets to Newcastle supporters.

We were resigning ourselves to going along ticketless, until at the last moment along came our saviour. For years, Barry has been a contributor to the UNUFC BBS Toon Internet forum on www.notbbc.net/unufc and has come to know, at least in an ethereal, unworldly kind of way, Toon fans all over the world, including Stevo in Holland. Stevo, or Steve in the real world, reported that a Dutch e-Bay-type set-up called '*marktplaats*' was offering a ray of hope in the shape of cloggies who had snapped up tickets and were now out to make a killing. He had agreed to buy one for himself and a spare from a Heer de Boer of Heerenveen, who promised to post them to Stevo as soon as a deposit was placed in his account. They came at triple the twenty-five euros face value, and so was anyone interested in the other? Barry instantly replied in the affirmative, and that was me fixed up with a seat among the Heerenveen supporters. Well, what are you supposed to do? It was already the Monday, three days before the match! We had been under cover in the Netherlands before, and I had nee qualms at aal aboot gannin' Dutch yit igen!

That still meant that we needed three tickets for Sarah, Chris and Brian, and things weren't looking good with only a couple of days to go. In the end, Brian and Barry decided that there was too big a risk of ending up stuck watching the game on a bar television in Friesland. It wasn't a very attractive prospect after a long journey, so they decided that discretion was the better part of valour and so Brian would stay at home this time. In any case, it would have been a very late night, with a dash back to school very early the next morning.

So that was how things stood – we just had the two tickets and had to get another two for Chris and Sarah. The plan was for me to pick up Chris and Sarah at Schiphol (Amsterdam's gi-huge, size-of-a-small-town airport) and for us then to drive up to Heerenveen and meet up with Barry early evening. He would be working in the morning and leaving Brussels at lunchtime. Brian would be watching it on the telly.

Now Netherlands-based Steve lives in Leiden but works in Scheveningen (on the coast, next door to the Hague, so as not to be vague), and he was also working that morning but could get to Schiphol by train for about one to one thirty. Chris and Sarah's flight from Heathrow got in at ten thirty, and I had to take Tina to school in Luxembourg before blasting up to Holland. So we got into a fast and furious

The omen, just like in The Odyssey: two elusive magpies at the Temple of the Olympian Zeus (apparently modelled on Penshaw Monument), down by Hadrian's Gate, so elusive you can't even see them.

The red raucous rabble let rip in Piraeus. The Panathinaikos fans call Olympiakos the stinking little fish, the *Gavri*. We'd never experienced an atmosphere like this. Stand and salute Alan Shearer for the way he took the penalty down at that far end.

The Toon looks on as the Olympiakos fans start a riot down below us.

The only thing separating us from the *Gavri* was a thin olive line.

They bring the Broon in to Athens in tankers.

Book signing at The Back Page in Newcastle. Now, what would you like me to put?

Now, sonny, what would you like me to put?

There's only one Sir Bobby Robson. And only one Chris, too, of course

Lisbon street scene:
'Can aa gi' ye a hand with that mop, hinny?'
'O Qué?'

Nearing the end of the Odyssey. For the team at least.

The highlight of the home match v Palace was the dart throwing competition. It just about sums it up: all we had to show by the end of the season was this.

'Wisht lads, haad yer gobs and aa'll tell ye 'boot the Cup!' Clive in fine voice.

Well, there's still a match to win in Cardiff on Sunday…

Stuck inside of Swindon with the Cardiff blues again. 'This wagon train ain't going nowheres until some of you Geordies get off. This here's a local train for local people – we don't want no trouble round here.'

What makes it all worthwhile. Forget what was happening on the pitch in Cardiff. Look at the sheer quality of the black and white crowd all around you.

Made you proud to be a Geordie. The Byker Wall of Sound grew to a crescendo the longer the game went on. 'Four-one and ye still can't sing.'

UEFA Cup Final day and the CSKA fans were getting into the spirit, most literally.

Not all the green and white hoops were for Celtic, but plenty were.

Quite a few Toon fans were around too. One had come all of the way from South Africa, the others from Consett. It's probably about the same distance both ways!

And this is what we'd come for: the 2005 UEFA Cup Final in Lisbon. Just a pity the team couldn't have been there with us! The pilgrims' trail was clearly marked.

CSKA fans celebrate with their team, and they deserve it, out-numbered nearly twenty-five to one in a Final played at their opponent's home ground. Next year, could it be us…?

exchange of e-mails and settled on meeting up at Schiphol at half past one. Not really a problem for Chris and Sarah to kill the time, as there are plenty of shops, restaurants and bars, etc.

Perhaps even James Bond would have been proud of our level of organisation. Steve kindly e-mailed us a map of Schiphol's layout, which includes a designated meeting point in the Schiphol Plaza. The Schiphol Plaza (isn't it a crime that they pulled the Tynemouth one down?) is a huge great concourse on the arrivals level. It is just in front of the main entrance and right next to the integrated rail station. All around the edges are shops and eateries. In the middle are ticket machines and a great big cube comprising red and white squares. That was the meeting point – pity about the colour scheme, though but. Could they not have chosen black and white? Steve also mailed a photo of himself, and I sent him one of Barry, Chris and Sarah outside *La Couronne* restaurant in Alsace *en route* for Sochaux. And of course, we all had each other's mobile numbers. I'd say the Toon Army is pretty well organised, wouldn't you?

Hey, getting back to the Plaza at Tynemouth, it struck me during my week back home after the Charlton match just how much the face of Tyneside really has changed over recent years (for recent, read the quarter of a century or so during which I have not lived there). I have always been back four or five times a year of course, and so changes have taken place gradually for me too, but sometimes when you walk through the Toon from one beloved watering hole to the next, you kind of take stock and think to yourself: Wheyabuggama. Well you do, don't you?

The most important and obvious transformation is of course that of the Holy of Holies itself. And it has changed entirely beyond recognition compared with the late seventies/early eighties. This in turn is mirrored by the complete makeover of the Quayside. And in both cases, the changes have definitely been for the better. No wonder the Toon is party city number one! But hey, how come people talk about the Gateshead Millennium Bridge? No offence to Gatesheed whatsoever, and call me Mr Thicky, but don't bridges usually go from one bank of a river to the other and therefore comprise two halves? Surely half of the Millennium Bridge is in the Toon? I've heard it was Gateshead Council that masterminded it and did all the wheeler-dealing to get it built. But maybe they could have had the magnanimity to let it be called the Newcastle-Gateshead Millennium Bridge? Even if the Newcastle side doesn't seem to have had all that much to do with getting it in place. Anyway, no one calls it anything but the Millennium Bridge (or the egg-slicer). Personally, I would have called it the Pontoon. The whole word means a bridge, the first half is like *Pont Neuf* in Paris or '*Sur le Pont d'Avignon*' (went there last year on hols), and the second half needs no explanation. Let's build another bridge and call it PonToon!

But what really thrust itself with a vengeance upon the consciousness that week (sign of approaching old age) was the sheer number of Tyneside landmarks – monuments for several generations, including mine – which have disappeared from the face of the earth over recent years. Apart from the Plaza, these notably include Gallowgate bus station, that pub opposite Chirton Garage in Shields whose name escapes me (was it the Collingwood? I am not even sure now), and the Bewicke pub in my native Howdon. And even the Northumberland Arms at the other end of Tynemouth Road before you dip down Rosehill Bank was all boarded up. It's terrible! And at the time of typing this up, St. Aidan's Church in Willington Quay was likewise boarded up, pending demolition. And the old (long since demolished) school's lower sports field had been invaded by bulldozers preparing the ground for another housing estate. Was it Gloria who was sick and couldn't come in on Monday?

Anyway, where were we? Ah yes, the rendezvous at Schiphol had been set up. It would have to be 'Moscow Rules', as we were going in behind enemy lines once again, but at least we could count on the help of the Dutch

Resistance as our last line of defence. They would surely be better than Newcastle's defence had been in recent weeks. There was nothing else for it: we would have to wear clogs and perhaps even a Dutch cap. Never mind coffee and cakes in Berlin, and certainly avoiding Dutch coffee shops and their space cakes. It would be *uitsmijters* and the cool Heineken all round. To blend in completely with the natives, we could even go around singing a song which my brother Mick and I had cunningly devised a good decade and a half earlier while on holiday in Walcheren: '*Oh de PTT en de VVV, en dank U wel voor het Heineken bier!*' The same verse was repeated ad infinitum with only the name of the beer changing so as to display our broad awareness of Dutch culture. From Heineken we switched to Amstel, and then to Domelsch bier, etc. until we finally arrived at Gulpener bier. But we decided in the end to delete the Gulpener verse after gulpin' doon aboot a gallon of the stuff one fateful evening in a boozer known as the *Muizeval* (or mouse-trap) in a lovely little place called Oostkapelle. It was in a rather similar way that deceased Roman emperors whose memory had fallen out of favour under a subsequent regime had their names expunged from milestones, triumphal arches and the like! *Sic transit gloria mundi* indeed.

The day of the Schiphol rendezvous had finally arrived and I dropped Tina off in Luxembourg very early at eight o'clock. Being the wonderful, understanding daughter that she is, she agreed to a very early start and met up with her friend Lynn for a pre-school breakfast in a café in the Auchan shopping centre on the Kirchberg, only a short bus ride from school.

And so I left Luxembourg, heading first for the Belgian border next to Arlon and then along the E411 through the Ardennes towards Brussels. This was Thursday morning, remember, and on Monday, Tuesday and Wednesday there had been snow showers in the Trier/Luxembourg region. But this morning there was only the odd patch of snow on the ground in Luxembourg. Not so by the time I was in the

Ardennes. Some of the time it was snowing, and the whole countryside was covered in a glorious thick blanket of white. It was that wonderful late-February, late-winter almost hazy greying blue light beneath a leaden-grey sky. The kind of bitterly cold outerworld that says to you in the warmth of your stereophonic in-car luxury that you really deserve the breakfast you are going to have at that pyramid-like services place in the middle of the Ardennes.

You can almost taste already the toast, the bacon and the easy-over fried eggs. When travelling along the E411 through the Ardennes I recommend that you stop for a break at what we call the Pyramid (you'll see why) at Wanlin. It is almost exactly half way between Brussels and Luxembourg, so about an hour out of either city. It belongs to the AC chain of restaurants/hotels (but Wanlin is a restaurant only). Stayed at an AC hotel at Zevenum after the Champignons League Eindhoven game and at another one for two Amsterdam marathons (AC Hotel Amsterdam Zuid). Both were great value for money, so the AC chain (throughout Benelux) qualifies for my personal recommendation.

The Ardennes were experiencing a late winter offensive (again, sixty years on), but it was a clean, easy sweep with not a great amount of traffic as far as the Brussels ring. Then it was the usual story past Zaventem airport and on to Antwerp. Between Brussels and Antwerp, you pass places called Duffel and Hulst, which are pretty funny, and I understand that Erps-Kwerps is not far away either. The Antwerp Ring was a bit of a struggle as usual, but I was soon passing the *Sportpaleis*, or Sports Palace, which is a venue for all sorts – tennis matches, rock concerts, maybe even neo-nazi rallies, who knows? It is impressive enough, lying just to the right of the motorway as you follow the signs for Breda. The city itself is off to the left, where you can glance over and glean the odd church spire and what looks like it could be the town hall. And looking ahead and to the left, you can see the cranes that adumbrate the docks. But back to the right and just after the *Sportpaleis*, there used to be a giant advert for

Belga cigarettes. It is no longer there, however, and I suppose that is because cigarette advertising is now banned in Belgium. I am a non-smoker, and I favour a complete ban, but at the same time it is sad that the giant hoarding has gone, because it had class. A silhouette *art nouveau* type of affair, on a par aesthetically with those bull silhouette adverts for Osborne brandy in Spain. They call it Ossubornay!

Anyway, you have already just passed the spot where the sexy Belga advert used to be and now it occurs to you that over to your right, not more than about five km away, is the Royal Antwerp stadium, scene of our glorious five-nil return to Europe in 1994. And then it suddenly dawns on you that the rest of today's itinerary will take you to within five km of Breda's ground (we won one-nil) and then within a similar distance from Feyenoord's stadium in Rotterdam (we won three-two). And countless pre-season drubbings. In other words, we are travelling along a kind of mystical Toon victory corridor in which we put paid to a host of Dutch/Flemish-speaking clubs. This surely meant that we would beat Heerenveen! The only blemish on this hypothesis was that we were beaten at PSV in the Dalglish days! But hey, Eindhoven was nowhere near being within five km of today's trajectory, whereas Heerenveen – by definition – clearly was. So that was sorted, and the vortex was stabilised!

You need to have your wits about you here and get in the right lane for heading on towards Breda and Rotterdam. This is the tail end of the Antwerp Ring and it is seriously Wacky Races. Lorries are tearing along on both sides of you and indicators are going mad all over the shop. The weaver birds are a'weaving here alright. But pretty soon, you've sussed it and you are making a beeline for Breda.

By the way, that wasn't a hundred per cent joke about neo-nazis. The ultra-right *vlaams blok* (they don't deserve capitals) has been particularly successful in Antwerp in recent years and has even had the shout on the city council. This may have something to do with the high percentage of immigrants, particularly moslems, in Antwerp. The same goes, by the way, for Rotterdam. Very recently, the Belgian courts actually banned the *vlaams blok*, declaring it to be openly racist. As was only to be expected, it has reappeared virtually immediately in a 'cuddlier' form known as *vlaams belang* (Flemish interest), but the substance of the beast would appear to be the same.

As you sweep clear of the Antwerp Ring and hit the open road for Breda, you can admire to your left the almost completed Brussels-Amsterdam high-speed train line that will slash the journey time between those two great cities. For a good stretch after Antwerp, it looks like a massively elongated concrete railway carriage with its great big square windows in the side. In a few years' time the trains will be whooshing past you in both directions and you will seriously be asking yourself why you are travelling by car - *Waar zouden wij zijn zonder de trein*? - as they say. Further along towards the Dutch border and then particularly beyond, the line looks slightly less almost-ready, and you see tangles of temporary viaducts, piping, bridging and the like. And the scars still open in the Dutch landscape here and there are suggestive of a country built on sand, an impression often reinforced by the roller-coaster subsidence along the motorways. Which is hardly surprising really, because sand is precisely what much of the Never-never-lands are built on, reclaimed from the seabed - more of which anon.

The traffic in the Netherlands wasn't as heavy as I had expected. This was a very pleasant surprise, as normally the Netherlands for me equate to one long traffic jam. This is especially true of the *Randstad*, of course, that massive conurbation comprising Rotterdam, Amsterdam, Den Haag, Leiden, Scheveningen, etc. It really is a seriously big conurbation, on a par with Germany's *Ruhrgebiet* and the smoke. The traffic is just awful; repeat: just awful. In fact, it's the traffic in that bit of the Netherlands that puts me off driving up to Ijmuiden to get the ferry to Shiels, even though if is, of course, nothing short of magic getting off at Percy Main and being immediately hyem. Plus, the bars and restaurants on the boat are full of beautiful eastern European barmaids and waitresses and it is great to see their reactions when the Geordies order a *duże piwo beczkowe, proszę bardzo*. I don't know offhand what percentage of the overall Dutch population lives in the *Randstad*, but it has to be a considerable chunk. And come to think of it, Schiphol airport must also account for an appreciable proportion of the overall surface area of the Netherlands! Look at a map of the Netherlands and it certainly stands out a lot more than, say, Heathrow does on a map of Britain.

Anyway, I made such good time that I got to Schiphol at about a quarter to one, a good three-quarters of an hour earlier than I had expected. Got parked up, duly noting where I was (that's an aspect that shouldn't be underestimated) and gave Chris a bell while walking along the autowalk. It dawned on me that it was almost exactly a year since I had done the same at Oslo airport. Duly made my way past the Sheraton, sandwich bars and the like, down the escalator, glancing across to the distant Amsterdam skyline obstructed by all the advertising hoardings, into the Schiphol Plaza area. Immediately spotted the horribly mackem-coloured but otherwise tastefully designed giant meeting-point cube, but realised that Chris and Sarah wouldn't be seen dead actually standing next to such an affront to good clean Geordie taste. Duly found them sitting outside the burger-type restaurant directly behind the offending object. Running on the giant plasma TV screen behind them was a rather sexy advert for Pepsi involving female gladiators in the Coliseum. Yes!

First rendezvous completed. Chris had rung Steve and he was due to arrive any minute, so we were in fact ahead of the game. Couple of mins later and Steve appears next to the mackem monstrosity. We recognise him immediately from the photo, as he does us likewise, and it is very much a case of 'well met, fellow, hail'. While Steve subsequently grabs a burger at the burger place (they can't touch you for it), Chris, Sarah and I approach three or four suitably attired and thus easily identifiable Toon wallahs, but still no joy on the ticket front!

Never mind – off we tappy-lappies to my motor. When we get there, I realise I should have paid the parking fee at one of the pay stations nearer the main concourse. Back along the autowalk, put the money in the machine, back to the car park – such is life, but hey, we've got stacks of time. Come to think of it, I am pretty sure the same thing happened when I picked up my cousin Steve at Schiphol for the Amsterdam marathon in October 2004. That was just a week before the Athens game, so I could not possibly have been focused. As a result, I achieved a less than Olympic finishing time of five minutes short of a quarter of a day. But hey, I finished, and that's not bad for a big fat Geordie git in the middle of a mid-life crisis. An' wor Steve (bags of swagger, and quite right!) did it in less than four and a half. It was great to stagger back to the sports hall where the changing room had been, and which now featured a bar. I spotted wor Steve, proudly held up my medal and sang 'Two-nil to the Geordie lads'. Seeing I was completely cream-crackered and out of it, he gans te the bar and brings back two cool Heinekens each. First one didn't touch my lips. Priceless. Magic. Canny neet oot in Amsterdam an' aal, aa can tell ye. And bumped into quite a few Geordies, of course.

Right, so we're leaving Schiphol and gradually we get clear of Amsterdam. We could either go left around the Ijsselmeer up to the *Afsluitdijk* (the enclosure dam) or to the right past Almere and Lelystad. As the enclosure dam is basically a geet long causeway gannin' oot across the sea, we reckoned there could be problemos if a lorry broke doon or jack-knifed or if any of a million things happened – there would be no alternative route, like. So we decided te gan the uther way roond. To welcome Chris and Sarah properly to Holland – in other words, to say *'van haarte welkom in Nederland'*, I had bought 'Best of Focus' one week earlier at Windows in the Central Arcade. Where else? It includes what else but - *hoe had het ook anders kunnen zijn?* - a mind-bendingly fantastic rendition of *Hocus Pocus*. The great thing is, it starts off with an arty-farty flute solo of Baroque music which then bursts orgasmically into *Hocus Pocus* and becomes, whether you like it or not, a Wayne's World-like heed-banging experience. You get into the mad headlong rush of organ, electric guitar and flute, with Thijs van Leer racing up and down the octaves and reaching heights that surely only eunuchs can reach, and only then with the aid of a Heineken or seven.

The trouble is that when listening to *Hocus Pocus* and driving a car at the same time, it is rather difficult to stick to the speed limit. But don't worry, because such is the iconic status of Thijs van Leer and Focus in the Netherlands that, under the jurisprudence of the highest courts of the land, listening to *Hocus Pocus* (and possibly also *House of the King*) is accepted as a legitimate excuse for speeding. Honestly, it's known as Dutch Justice, but to believe that you probably need a bit of Dutch courage. Hey, don't the Dutch get a rough deal when it comes to such phrases as Dutch courage, Dutch uncle, Dutch cap and going Dutch? I think we should write a French letter and request French leave of such expressions.

That took us as far as Almere. Steve told us that it was the Netherlands' newest town, a sort of a Milton Keynes (let's not wish the Wombles upon the good *burghers* of Almere), and it was rapidly absorbing a massive overspill of people who could no longer afford the horrendous prices in Amsterdam, whither most of them commute every working day. The town had only got started in the thirties. Indeed, prior to that, the site had been a bit wet. That was because it was in the sea, the Ijsselmeer to be precise. The Dutch are hydraulic engineers *par excellence* and no stretch of water with real-estate potential ever lasts long when they get their hands on it. To reclaim the land on which Almere and its environs now stand, they first had to build the *Afsluitdijk*. That was no mean feat, and we just had to go there on the morrow. Remember how difficult it was to keep the water out of your sandcastles on Tynemouth Long Sands? Well that's precisely what they were doing on a massive scale. When the enclosure dam was complete, they were able to fill in the bits they wanted to reclaim. Presumably they got all the kids in the Netherlands to come along with their buckets and spades and start hoyin' sand in. Yes, that's how they must have done it!

Steve was an absolute mine of information. He came to the Netherlands only eight years ago and didn't speak a word of Dutch when he got off the boat. Now he is megablastically fluent and works as a social worker, presumably also dealing with some dodgy situations, and all in his new language! Respect! It's amazing how many cunning linguists there are in the ranks of the Toon Army. He also told us, as we got further north and there were more and more open spaces and less and less traffic (thank goodness), that their lass had once remarked on the difference in the scenery in the north of the country. Now all that you and I see is one very flat landscape dotted with windmills here and there. But the Dutch themselves notice that this part of the country has quite a few more water features, geet big seawater lakes. Again, we have to remember that so much land has been reclaimed from the North Sea. In fact, if the Dutch keep on going at this rate, their coast will only be seven miles off Tynemouth by the year 3000. One slightly worrying thought for the Dutch, however, is that a lot of their country is below sea level, so their sea defences, including big sand dunes along much of the coast, are absolutely essential items. Remember the story about the lad who saved Holland from flooding by putting his finger in the hole in the dyke?

The estimate of an hour and half's run from Schiphol to Heerenveen was about right, so we were level with the town at about three o'clock. It clearly was a small place. Steve reckoned it had about thirty-five thousand inhabitants, which is about ten thousand fewer than Waalsend. So the club was very much a regional thing and people would come from all around the surrounding area to support the team. But remember, the stadium only holds about nineteen thousand.

We could see the floodlights away to our right. We now timed exactly how long it would take to get to our hotel in Leeuwarden. The reception lassie's twenty-minute estimate proved to be spot on. The Bastion Hotel in Leeuwarden looked absolutely fine, and so it proved. It thoroughly deserves its three stars and was very reasonably priced at eighty-nine euros for my single and a hundred euros for Chris and Sarah's double. The price included a very acceptable breakfast buffet in a most pleasant restaurant area complete with a biggish plasma TV on which we were to watch the highlights three times over the next morning. There is also a pool room, which in the end we didn't get around to using. When next you are in Leeuwarden or touring this part of the world, don't forget it comes with our *Toon Tales/Odyssey* recommendation. Check out the site: http://www.bastionhotel.nl/

There was a bit confusion at reception when I was told I had already checked in! Lo and behold, there was another Cain in our Leeuwarden hotel that day. At first, I reckoned it must be wor Mick playing silly buggers on one of his train blasts, but no, it really was someone else. Spooky!

The big question was of course, 'How long will the bar stay open tonight?' The answer was, 'Till midnight', unless the barmaid was in a particularly good mood. Was she a Heerenveen supporter, we wondered? But then maybe she supported Leeuwarden, currently a second division outfit. Apparently they are Heerenveen's big rivals, so maybe we would be in luck and she would be on the Toon's side tonight.

Meanwhile Chris was on the mobile to Eric, who had rung earlier when Chris's phone had been in his coat in the back of the car and nobody'd heard it. The voice mail message was that at three o'clock Eric had the chance to buy two tickets in their kop-type end for fifty euros each. Should he buy them? When Chris got through to him, Eric gave him the mobile number of the lad selling them. He had sold one and had one left. Okay, Chris asked him to expect us in half an hour. This was a Geordie lad who had bought them off a Dutch fan but then found out that his mate had already bought two as well. That's the sort of thing that can happen in the frenzied haste to get hold of tickets for Toon games, as well we know. Anyway, we needed to know exactly where he was and he had difficulty getting his tongue around the name. It sounded like 'scoffles' and turned out in the end to be *'t Skoffeltsje* and he said it was pretty central, next to Café Connect and opposite the Friesland Bank.

We blasted back down the motorway, or *autosnelweg*, and wanted to park right in the shadow of the ground, with a view to a quick getaway back to the Bastion bar straight after the match. The ground sort of stands on its own on the edge of a housing estate with a lot of empty terrain around it. But it is only a quarter of an hour's walk from the town centre. When we turned into the car park adjacent to the *Abe Lenstra Stadion*, the steward saw we were in a German-registered car, though he probably didn't notice the registration number included NV 92 – it was supposed to be NU 92, but I just pretend it's a Roman U. It's funny how things like that will go slightly wrong – wor lass's car has got TR NU 91, just one year out! So the steward wise-cracked *'Ah, Deutschland über alles'*, to which of course the reply is *'Nein, Deutschland unter anderem* (amongst others)'. Anyway, he was bemused to find Toon supporters in a German car and even more bemused to find that two of them spoke Dutch. So just to be sure, he asked *'Zijn jullie engels?'* to which I replied *'Nee, wij zijn Geordies'*. He looked puzzled, so I asked if he was Dutch or Frisian. Frisian, of course, was the reply. 'Well, there you are,' I said, 'that's how it is with us, too, we're not really English, we're Geordies.' So there was a good bond already.

There is a sign when you enter Friesland that reads 'Frislân', as opposed to the Dutch 'Friesland'. And there is a local radio station that broadcasts in their dialect. So we really do have a lot in common. And if Dutch is the foreign language that is closest to English, then its Frisian dialect is even closer to Geordie, if you see what I mean.

Anyhow, despite all this brotherliness, the steward said we couldn't park there, so we had to cross back over the road and park in what looked like a building site but was signposted as a medical centre car park. Then we started a brisk walk into town, following instructions via mobile from the Geordie lad with the tickets in the pub who had done the walk himself. Straight ahead and cross over the canal, then right into the pedestrian zone. There we asked a passer-by where the Café Connect was, but he had never heard of it. The Geordie lad had said there were only three pubs open, so we reckoned they must be dead central ones, and as Steve needed to know exactly where the station was for his getaway to catch the last train at eleven o'clock, we asked the way there instead, thinking we'd be killing two birds with one stone. We were pointed right into the pedestrian zone and, sure enough, we could see several pubs that were closed. Why was this? Surely by now the Toon Army's excellent and outstanding reputation must be well known in the Netherlands! We had taken nothing but friendly good will to Eindhoven twice, Feyenoord, Breda and countless little pre-season grounds! A very positive aspect was that the police were keeping a very low-key presence. You would see the odd patrol car, but there was nothing over the top. Maybe at least they had heard about our reputation after all. And maybe the top-heavy presence in Rotterdam had been more because of the Feyenoord supporters, who also came along to spoil the party in Breda, if you remember.

Be that as it may, we asked a few more people the way, including those wearing the Heerenveen blue and white, to whom we wished the best of luck and who wished us the same. As directed, we walked the few yards down the Nieuwstraat, and sure enough, next door to the *Café Kannet*, not 'Connect' after all, and directly opposite the Friesland Bank, was *'t Skoffeltsje*. Now the apostrophe in that name signifies that *'t* is a shortened form of *het*, which means 'the'. A bit like tha sez 't in 't Yorkshire dialect. And the *'je'* on the end of any Dutch word denotes a diminutive (like *–chen* in

German). So far, so good. We could be absolutely sure we were dealing here with the little *skoffel*. Trouble is, we couldn't find that word in our shite dictionary at the time. We scuffled into the little skoffel and were delighted to find that it is a very pleasant little skoffel indeed. Strangely, there were all sorts of implements and other things dangling from the ceiling, suspended on ropes. For example, a spade and a pitch fork on the implements side. And the other things included a small, but potentially lethal, concrete block, which I for one was certainly not going to stand under! The whole pub was a kind of oblong shape with a standing area as you went in and quite a long bar half way down the oblong with an accordingly narrow standing area in front of it and another more square standing area with dart board behind it in front of the bogs. If you'd like to know more about this steady little boozer, check out the website: http://www.skoffeltsje.nl. Another mobile call by Chris, who because of the music had to go outside to make the call, and we learned our ticket contact was in the darts area. That deal was quickly concluded, and so we only needed one more ticket now. We just started asking around.

One Dutch lad sitting at the bar had a spare ticket but he wanted a hundred euros. We were a bit shocked by this, as Chris had just paid fifty euros. I even got a bit angry and suggested to him that he would be lucky to get thirty nearer kick-off. But my first impressions had been totally wrong, as we later found out. Chris rang Eric to see if maybe he had found another ticket, but no joy. He was at his hotel at Sneek (pronounced very like the way we say 'snake'), a short drive away from Heerenveen, like our hotel in Leeuwarden. And he had met up with someone who knew me. It's Alan from Gateshead, Chris informed me, adding 'Who's that, like?' 'Oh,' I replied, 'that'll be Alan from Gateshead'. And sure enough, it was. Readers of *Toon Tales* will know that we bumped into Alan in Zurich, where that international café-chair-moving incident had to be defused, again in Rome in a boozer near the Coliseum and again in the ground, and again in Basel. That's the great thing about the Toon Army, isn't it?

Anyway, there was no joy ticket-wise in Sneek, so Chris made the eminently sensible decision to go for the hundred euro ticket after all, though with a ninety euro bid. And you know what, the guy really was sound after all. The ticket was for a really plush, club-type part of the ground and included a half-time drink. We all convinced ourselves that that was well worth the money. But hey, wouldn't it have been awful to come all this way and then not get into the ground? It turned out that the ticket had been for the lad's eighty-five year-old dad, who never missed a home game. It was just that this particular home game started at a quarter to nine, which was really a bit late for an eighty-five year-old on a potentially very chilly mid-February evening. So that was it, we were all sorted on the ticket front. The question was who would now go where? Sarah understandably didn't fancy the idea of going into their kop end on her own, so we decided she would take my ticket and sit next to Steve and I would go in the kop. Sarah insisted on refunding me twenty-five euros, which was very nice of her but not necessary! And Chris would be sitting next to his new Dutch marra.

We gave Barry a bell to see how he was getting on and to give him directions down to *'t Skoffeltsje* to meet us. Why, here he is now:

Hello one and all. I've been struggling with some kind of flu all week and it was only the magic healing attraction of the Toon that got me up the road to Heerenveen. The newly-built *Abe Lenstra Stadion* is out by the motorway, making it very easy to find. The helpful stewards at the club car park directed me across the road to another parking place just a minute's walk away and in full view of the very impressive ground. And what do you know, I spotted Pete's car there too and parked up right beside it. It was great to meet Stevo from the BBS at last, after years of reading each other's posts. It turns out that we'd been passing within a few steps of each other for years at all the Dutch pre-season tours,

Champignons League and UEFA games. I am sure the locals in 't Skoffeltsje bar were impressed with two Toon fans, Stevo and Pete, chatting away in Dutch.

The old gadgy who sells souvenir scarves at most of the games pitched up, and he gave us a group discount: four scarves for the price of three. We guarded his bags while he went around the bar selling his scarves and badges, and we had a chat when he was done. It was a noisy bar and sometimes hard to make out what he was saying. Gerry Harrison has been a souvenir seller since the sixties. He began his career with the Beatles and was on especially good terms with his namesake, George Harrison. He worked with the Bay City Rollers in the seventies and it sounded like he was with them over in New York at some baseball stadium one time when things got out of hand. Mind, I can't quite work out where there could be enough space for any kind of stadium in New York. Perhaps he was confusing New York with North Shields proper and was thinking of Appleby Park in the old days (now a housing estate, of course). He concentrates on sports events now, and this same week he'd been at the rugby in Dublin and then in Denmark before coming to Holland. A strange way to spend your time, but if you're old enough to be a pensioner, it's a viable alternative, as they say.

Let it be said categorically that all the people we met in and around Heerenveen, including in the ground, were very friendly indeed. There was not even the merest hint of bother. They clearly are great football supporters and have nothing in common whatsoever with the minority scum-of-humanity faction within the Feyenoord following, whom we'd seen running amok in the Rotterdam cafés before we'd knocked them out of the Champignons League a couple of years earlier. Those scum are the lowest of the low. Heerenveen supporters, by contrast, are brilliant. We hoped those travelling to the Toon would have a fantastic time, whatever the result! We talked to quite a few who would be travelling, and the favoured route was the ferry from

Ijmuiden, so the crossings alone would be a guaranteed two good nights out, plus the night in the Toon. Quite a few of the Toon contingent had come over to Holland by the same route. Most would be stopping over in Amsterdam after the match and then catching the Friday evening ferry hyem. I have been on that crossing a few times, and there are so many Geordies on mini-trips to Amsterdam that it is rather like a night out at Percy Main or High Pit Social Club at sea! The crack is magic.

It was time to have a walk around the town and a bite to eat. On the way through the town to meet everyone, Barry had spotted the impressively named *Byker Coiffure* (really!) by the canalside, so we retraced his steps and took a picture there with all of us on. A bit like *Bobby's Bar* in Lokeren, and the *Blue Star* bar at the Leverkusen game. From the Byker Barbers we continued on our way towards what appeared to be the very centre of town, though we didn't come across the kind of central square you always expect to find in Dutch and Belgian towns. But maybe we just missed it and some of youz did find it. We passed a couple of police vans in a street simply called *Dracht*. Again, it was just a low-key, smiling presence – the message must finally have got through about the kind of people who follow the Toon! From there we turned right into a street called *Gedempte Molenwijk*, which sounds like it should mean 'subdued mill district' but surely doesn't, where we happened upon the *Ristorante Pizzeria Italia*.

Now this place qualifies for five stars in the *Toon Tales/Odyssey* eateries guide. It was great! Fantastic food: we had prawns or stracciatella soup for starters, and I think we all had pizzas – mine was a *frutti di mare* and was excellent. Like a chinky, everything had a number and the waiter only took orders as numbers as he didn't know the names. I think there were seventy-three different pizzas, but you couldn't get a sixty-nine. Except if you booked in advance, probably. The wine was great, as was the service. Check out the website http://www.pizzeria-italia.nl/, and if they also deliver, get them to bring some pizzas across to you on the Ijmuiden ferry, they were that good! And very reasonably priced as well, at twenty euros a head for starter, main course and copious drinks! That is real value. Mind, they might charge you extra for delivering across the North Sea, so you should ask first. It was jam-packed, which was making service a bit slow. The clock was ticking and before we knew it, it was a quarter past eight. So we settled the bill, and after a brisk twenty-minute walk we were all approaching the stadium, whose bright lights glowed welcomingly from afar.

The stadium is a five-minute walk from a business park and a residential estate, but is immediately surrounded by wasteland just itching to be converted into a retail mall, while the town council plan to add further sports facilities around it too. Heerenveen is at the centre of ice-skating country and it turns out to be the home of the fastest skating rink in the world, where Dutchmen in skin-tight shiny nylon suits (those all-body condoms) do that strange kind of rhythmic, one-arm-swinging skating that you see on the Winter Olympics once every four years. Situated very much like Breda, the stadium is about fifteen minutes' walk into town. They're currently adding an extra tier to the ground on top of where the Toon Army was billeted, the aim being to arrive at a capacity of twenty-six thousand, which is very close to the population of the town itself! They've specially opened up one part-finished section just for our match to boost the crowd beyond the initially announced fourteen thousand to more like nineteen thousand.

Abe (pronounced like Abba) Lenstra apparently was the fifties equivalent of Johan Cruyff, another universal Dutch hero. Univé, a Dutch insurance company, are the shirt sponsors and I thought they must have something to do with the little red Valentine's hearts dotted over their blue and white stripes. They've got even more little hearts than Portsmouth with their Ty fluffy toys sponsors. It might have been Valentine's Day on Monday, but surely it didn't mean that it was going to be their week. A Heerenveener later told us that the hearts are in fact red lilies, which are the emblem of Friesland, and the football club shirts are exactly the same colours as the Frisian flag. Funny how Friesland has an 'e' but Frisian hasn't, eh?

As we approach the stadium, we split up to our different corners of the ground. If we take the players' tunnel as our reference point and then apply the layout of Saint James's Park *mutatis mutandis*, Barry is in with the Toon in the third of the Leazes next to the Milburn, though their Leazes is not even as big as our old one was. Sarah, Chris and Steve are in the East Stand, more or less level with the eighteen yard box, with Chris perched quite high up, with club-like facilities and what look like corporate boxes behind him, and Pete is in the Gallowgate, half way between the goal and the Milburn stand. We've got the ground covered.

We line up to have our tickets checked and be searched, and one of the police guards picks me out and asks me to say something, anything. He then explains that he thought I didn't look as if I was English. 'You're right, I'm a Geordie.' Maybe I've been away too long. As I climb the steps up to the terracing, I look around and I'm confronted by a sea of flags. Heerenveen's sponsors have given everyone in their ninety-five per cent of the ground a flag on a stick to wave and it's a very impressive, though faintly comical, sight to see.

The Toon end is packed to the rafters. Well into the first half, Toon fans continue to stream in as the police divert them to our section when they spot them trying to get into other parts of the ground with their touted home tickets. We're crammed in, standing in front of the seats with others standing on the seats behind us, and with the single gangway full too. How are you settled, Pete?

I'm sitting/standing in the very first row, although the seat number on the ticket is somewhere completely different. However, the first row is raised up-a-height, so I have a brilliant view – in fact the best I have had at a match in a good while.

The access system was a bit strange, but is the one used at a few grounds in the Netherlands. There are only a couple of main entrances, and then you walk around the pitch, but at a lower level than the pitch and there is a great big barrier so you cannot see any of it as you walk, until you come to your section. Then you climb up some stairs and show your ticket to a steward. So when you are in your seat you look over this kind of walkway moat (only two or three yards wide) onto the pitch. The stadium is packed and you can genuinely sense from the atmosphere that this really is a big one for the Heerenveen fans, and quite rightly so. The little flags they're waving are reminiscent of the scenes you would see in the past in television coverage of Communist rallies in East Germany, the Soviet Union or China. All rather strange to Geordie eyes. Except this time they've been given out by the local sponsors, in the same way that 'papers' such as the Sun give out plastic hats and things to wave at Cup Finals.

I'm no sooner in place than the game kicks off, and both sets of fans are in really excellent voice. The Heerenveen fans are mostly singing the standard songs you hear at Premiership grounds, which is a bit sad really – have they completely lost their own creative spark? But it has the advantage that I can join in and just sing 'Newcastle' when they sing 'Heerenveen'. The guy next to me quickly realises that I'm from the other side and he and his wife think it's brilliant, so at half time I get the chance to tell them what the Toon is aal aboot! Over to you, Barry.

We start the match kicking towards the far end with Shola, Shearer and Kluivert in a triangle up front, supported by Faye, Bowyer, and birthday boy Jermaine Jenas in midfield, and a back four of Carr, Bramble, O'Brien and Babayaro. Harper has chicken pox and got sent home, so Shay is in goal. It could be a difficult evening as Heerenveen are doing well this season and are currently fifth in their admittedly rather weak league, but they've had some decent results against good teams recently. Stevo, who keeps well in touch with Dutch football, told us to watch out for the young centre forward Klaas-Jan Huntelaar, as well as the old hand, Bruggink, and the winger Yildirim. I'd seen highlights on Dutch television of their previous weekend's game when they'd won three-two away at Roda, when one of the goals by Vayrynen was like an action replay of Rommedahl's run across the front of the penalty area and equaliser for Charlton against us in our last league game. It looked as if they could score goals, but also that their defence was well capable of letting a few in. A bit like us, really. And their four-three-three line-up was just like ours tonight.

There are half chances at both ends in the opening minutes, with Bowyer having a header saved and Huntelaar getting into our penalty area but being held at bay by Bramble for what should have been a goal kick but is given as a corner. Yildirim's corner bounces invitingly across the face of the goal but no one can reach it, luckily for us. Hansson's having a hard time staying with Ameobi and gets a yellow card for dragging him back. This is just one of many examples as the Heerenveen defenders are indulging in plenty of holding and tripping on both Shearer and Shola.

Amdy Faye is looking very dependable in midfield and giving confidence to JJ and Bowyer to try their luck going forward. In a couple of attacks, Shearer makes good strong runs down the right and crosses, but no one is there to take the chances. A moment later, Shola collects the ball in the centre circle and sets off on one of his loping dribbles but the defender Hansson does well to force him wide when he could have been through. If only he'd managed to do what Drogba had done to Hughes in a very similar position in the second leg of the Semi-Final in Marseille. Just after, Bowyer slices a shot wide to the left from an Ameobi lay-off. We're doing well and we are on top at the moment, with most of the action up at the far end of the pitch. But now the ball's on the left of our area with Bramble looking as if he should kick it out of danger to the left touchline, but instead he turns in towards Bruggink who takes the ball off him and slots it back to Huntelaar on the edge of the box. He spins round and free of Faye and in a single movement slams a rising shot into the roof of the net. Twenty-four minutes gone, one-nil to Heerenveen and slightly against the run of play. A couple of minutes later from a long, raking cross, Huntelaar nearly heads in a second but he aims it straight at Given. We come back with some pressure, and in the midst of this Bowyer gets booked when he jumps to challenge with his elbow out and contacts the Heerenveen player.

I overhear probably the comment of the night from a couple of lads just behind me. One arrives back from the bogs saying:

'A've just been steppin' in shite. Me boots are covered in it. It's smurred (exact word) aal ower the floor.'

'That's European football for you. Shite on the floor.'

I take careful note of which seat he's standing on and pity the poor soul who might decide to give his feet a rest at half time and have a sit down. You don't get this level of insight into a European away tie when you're sitting in your armchair at home, listening to the Channel Five or ITV commentators.

There's five minutes left of the first half when Bramble feeds a good pass through to Ameobi, whose surprising speed and footwork lose his marker. He puts in a great cross over the face of the goal, but no one manages to reach it. Babayaro's been making some good overlapping runs throughout the half too, but as the half comes to an end we're trailing and not really looking a big threat to Heerenveen's lead. Everyone tries to lift the team with a sustained chant of 'Toon, Toon, Black and White Army.'

Let's ask Pete for his 'Andy Gray' half-time thoughts:

Well, 'Brian', Heerenveen are clearly no mugs, and to be perfectly honest they thoroughly deserve their first-half lead. Even from my 'Gallowgate' perspective I could see that Huntelaar's twenty-fourth minute screamer that went in off the underside of the bar at the 'Leazes' end was an absolute cracker. We haven't really created any proper chances down at my end, and Heerenveen definitely have the edge. On a positive note, Jenas is beavering away creditably and on occasion he's shown an almost 'Brazilian-like touch in laying the ball off', to quote Chris. When they scored, two huge inflatable figures, one at the 'Leazes' end and one at the 'Gallowgate' end were inflated by great big fans (ventilators, not big Frisians) and were waving around like mad. You'll have seen them at all the grounds during coverage of the Belgo-Dutch Euro 2000 Championships. Not the kind of inflatable figures youz had seen at Yeading, I hasten to add! By half time, I was hoping we weren't going to let in a second.

Thank you, Pete. I can see the teams coming out again, so it's back over to our commentary team.

We start the second half at a high tempo and put some pressure on their defence, but then Babayaro gets tackled, injuring his knee, and we play with ten men for a few minutes before he has to be replaced by Hughes. He looks the part, even though he hasn't had a game for a while, and puts in a good tackle to get himself into the match. There's a scramble from a Heerenveen corner with the ball ricocheting everywhere except into our net, luckily. It could easily have been two-nil by now, and a big section of our fans are getting very restless. A few jibes are directed at Graeme Souness, but the 'Souness oot' chants are short-lived, whereas the board and chairman in particular feel the full brunt with loud and repeated calls to 'Sack the board', and 'Shepherd, you're a w***er'. Why's he a wonder? We then get 'Attack, attack... attack, attack, attack,' just like at the Dalglish Cup Final. Then it's 'Laurent, Laurent Robert, everyone knows his name.' It's as if he's become a bit of a martyr and a symbol of the divide in opinion on tactics between the fans and the manager. He certainly is very appreciative of the support he is getting from the fans in his increasingly rare and brief second-half run-outs. He comes out to warm up, but so do two more of our subs just when the Robert chant starts to get really loud. I get the feeling that maybe Souness is going to bring one of them on instead, as they stay out exercising on the touchline much longer.

Bowyer latches on to a Carr layback from the goal line but shoots wide, and, shortly after, a great free kick from Heerenveen bounces into our goal area but none of their players is around to tap it in. Play switches to our end and a good free kick from Faye is headed by Shearer invitingly back across the face of the goal, but Shola manages to miss the chance to duck and head it in. This is the cue for Robert and there's a huge roar as he comes on in place of Shola, who'd done a decent enough job, but our forwards seemed to have been getting in each other's way a lot of the time. There's still half an hour to go, so Robert has got enough time to make his mark. His first touch is a mis-directed pass and his second is a free kick into the goalkeeper's arms, but at least we've got some variety and width in attack now. Hughes links up well with Robert and passes the ball into space for Robert to run onto down in the corner, from whence he puts in a good cross, but it's plucked out of the air by the goalkeeper. All of a sudden (a big black puddin'), things are looking different and we're applying pressure.

Kluivert plays a perfectly placed through ball for Shearer, who takes it on and fires off a fierce shot, but it's blocked and rebounds to Carr who shoots over the bar. Maybe it's just as well, because in any case the ref's assistant says Shearer was offside. The clock is now ticking around to sixty-eight minutes when Robert, in the centre circle, calls for the ball from Jenas. He runs at the defence and passes through to Kluivert, who chooses to slip it back into the path of Shearer rather than to Robert who has accelerated through, looking for a one-two. The decision is more than vindicated as Shearer jinks to the right and fires a powerful rising shot into the right side of the net. One-one, and there's a major fan collapse with bodies toppling down the terrace, but by good fortune, nobody is injured. It took you back thirty years to the big shed of the Leazes End! The voices of dissent are silenced or at least winded for the moment, as we strike up with 'Hey,

Shearer... ooh... aah... I wanna know-oh-oh-oh... how you scored that goal' and 'You're still England's Number One'. Then 'You're not singing any more' and 'You're not winning any more'!

While all the pandemonium is going on in our section, there is more of the same in our penalty area and an involuntary handball by either Jenas or Faye as the ball ricochets between them. The ball rebounds to Huntelaar, but Bramble steams in with a great tackle to redeem himself in part for his first-half error. In quick succession, Bruggink and Huntelaar, the architects of their goal, go off with the former being replaced by Viktor Sikora, a winger who was a rumoured Toon transfer target a couple of years ago while he was still at Ajax. And then Robert picks out Kluivert with a pinpoint cross-field pass just as he runs into the far side of the penalty area. Rather than taking it in his stride and first-touching it towards the goal, it looks as if he's lost his chance as he dallies on the ball, but he manages to get it out from under his feet towards Carr coming in from the right wing. He sends it first time across the mouth of the goal and Bowyer is on hand to side-heel it in, much like Kluivert did back in November against Crystal Palace away, in the game before the Sochaux match.

From our viewpoint behind the goal, it looked more like he'd bundled it in any old how, but it turns out it was a pretty neat touch. Robert is racing in behind Bowyer at the far post and looks delighted as he collects the ball out of the net. It's time for more pandemonium and fans tumbling down the terraces and an ironic new chant of 'Keep the Board' is briefly heard! The mood is broken a couple of minutes later when Bramble makes an even worse mistake than in the first half and presents the ball on a silver platter to Vayrynen. He advances into our penalty area and shoots, but Shay makes a miraculous save and pushes the ball over the bar. This is the kind of moment when having a good goalkeeper is equivalent to having a Shearer at the other end of the pitch.

It's still all go, and the next thing we see is play being stopped over on the far side of the pitch and it's not clear what's happened, but then Bowyer is shown a second yellow card and he's off, head downcast. Apparently, he'd either tried to handle the ball or pull back his opponent by the shoulder. Out in no man's land and with no immediate danger, why do it? We're now faced with having to hang on to our narrow lead for about ten minutes. Shearer passes the captain's armband to JJ and strides off to huge cheers. He's replaced by Taylor, who takes up his place to warm applause. Heerenveen throw everything at us, trying to make the one-man advantage tell, but we forcefully withstand their attacks. *Fortiter defendit triumphans!*

The best example of this is Taylor running down the time by the corner flag with two Heerenveen players just bouncing off him while he's laughing at them. Nineteen and already with such confidence and strength. He's obviously been learning from Alan Shearer. Let's hope he really comes through and fulfils all the promise that he's already showing. The whistle blows and we've survived! The Heerenveen crowd give their team a rousing reception, and it's well deserved. Of our players, Taylor and Robert come right over to thank the fans for their support.

Over to Pete for his post-match analysis:

I have to say that Heerenveen tired somewhat in the second half, and the Toon gradually gained control. And what a cracker that Shearer shot was in the seventieth minute! I didn't get such a good view of Bowyer's flick, and when I finally saw it on the telly the next morning I was suitably impressed. But I did get a superb view of Shay's brilliant save right in front of me late on. We have him to thank for the fact that we went into the second leg actually in the lead. Mind, let it also be said that Heerenveen should definitely have had a penalty in the second half. I think the culprit was Bramble, whom the *Algemeen Dagblad* described as *het eenmandestructiebedrijf*: the one-man demolition operation.

And so we had won, and we could already start counting our chickens and look forward to another trip to Athens or a Dance in the East of France. Olympiakos had only beaten Sochaux one-nil, so that was still up in the air. We all met back at the car park. Barry was giving Steve a lift as far as Utrecht, from where there were all-night trains to Leiden, so he didn't have to run for the eleven o'clock from Heerenveen after all.

Sarah, Chris and I headed back for the hotel. Despite what initially looked like something of a logjam, we were soon on the dark motorway and it only took us thirty-two minutes from the car park to the Bastion, which gave us a good twenty minutes before the bar closed. Plus the barmaid was in a good mood (she must have been a Leeuwarden fan after all) and we were able to sup a few pints before turning in. I had been drinking the non-alcoholic stuff (Amstel Malt, which isn't bad at all, considering), so the first two in the hotel didn't even touch my lips. Before we turned in, three more Toon wallahs came into the bar, and we all agreed it had been a great night up in friendly North-East(ish) Holland.

Next morning, Chris knocked on the door just after nine to say Sarah and he were on their way doon to breakfast. I joined them about twenty past, by which time they had seen the goals twice over on the rolling telly news coverage, but they had no objection whatsoever to watching them again with me while I broke my fast.

Before setting off, we checked the old map again and saw that, for our scenic route back to Schiphol, we needed to head for Haarlingen and from there to the *Afsluitdijk*. The lad at reception said it wouldn't take us more than one and a half hours of solid driving to get to the airport, and who were we to question his local knowledge? Sarah and Chris didn't have to check in until two o'clock and it was only a quarter to ten, so there were no worries (for a change!) about getting to the airport in time. And I didn't have to pick Tina up from her Friday after-school dancing class in Luxembourg until a quarter to seven that evening. Traffic here in the north of the Netherlands (hey, we could shorten that to Northerlands) was just so amazingly light compared with the motorway madness of the *Randstad* - it was bally-well relaxing, so it was!

We stopped for some essence of petroleum spirit and I bought the *Algemeen Dagblad* for the match report. I also asked if there was such a thing as a local paper entirely in Frisian – you know, like you get papers in Catalan as well as Spanish in places like Barcelona. The answer, unfortunately, was *'nee, hoor'*, but apparently the local Leeuwarden paper did include a Frisian column or two. But it was already sold out. Never mind, such is life. The Frisian language will probably have to wait a wee while before I take an interest in it again – which will be the next time we play a club in Friesland.

As we got nearer to the *Afsluitdijk*, the names on the signposts were becoming ever more hilarious. We thought it was just brilliant that there is such a place as Sexbierum. If you wanted sex, beer and rum, that was clearly the place to go! But it got even better. A further six clicks or so along the road and we came across a sign with the two place names Sneek and Makkum. That confirmed what we had always suspected, namely that the only way the mackems would ever get into European football (and experience shit on their shoes) would be by sneaking in and holing up at the sneaky mackem base of Sneek Makkum. Sarah sent the photo off to The Mag and they printed it in the March edition! But of course even in the unlikely event of the mackems actually qualifying for Europe, their fans wouldn't be allowed to travel. Don't forget they are still banned from crossing the sea because of the damage they did to some ships the last time sunderland played in a European competition: apparently they tore down the sails and hoyed all the cannons overboard!

The name game was to reach its climax later after we had crossed the Afsluitdijk, when we saw the sign for Schagen.

Not bad, eh? Imagine asking someone the way from Sexbierum to Schagen! Could you keep a straight face? You're a better man than I am, Gunga Din! Now the Netherlands is a liberal sort of place, as we all know, but this really took the biscuit (or was it space cake?).

But before we even knew about Schagen(!), we had to cross the dyke – if you see what I mean. The *Afsluitdijk* is twenty or so kilometres of enclosure dam and it can't be more than about twenty metres wide. A vast drainage project was begun in 1920 and completed in 1932 with the closure of the dyke, which effectively sealed off the Ijsselmeer. We were a bit confused about it maybe being called the Zuiderzee causeway, and Sarah could remember learning all about it at school. So we decided to delve into it, and for the record: the site of the old Zuiderzee is now split by the dyke into the Ijsselmeer, a freshwater lake fed by the River Ijssel, and the Waddenzee which lies on the seaward side of the dyke and extends to the Frisian Islands.

The dam incorporates a tippy-up bridge not far from the end we were coming from and indeed we had to stop as a ship was being let through. On the dyke itself we had a great view of the Ijsselmeer to the left, but the potential view of the North Sea to the right was blocked by the raised nature of the dam on that side. Half way along there is actually an island, so we thought we should explore. It wasn't really worth the effort, however, as all they have there is a single official-looking building and a caravan park. On balance, I decided it wasn't the sort of place I'd like to spend my hols. So we got back onto the dyke road and decided to stop at the monument café a couple of clicks further along. This was more like it. The car park was slightly raised, and the bridge crossing the road from our side to the monument side afforded a brilliant view of both the North Sea and the Ijsselmeer. Just in front of the bridge, on the side where we parked, is a life-sized metal sculpture of a worker laying stones. It stands in honour of the people who physically built the dyke – and hard labour it must have been! Unfortunately, the figure in question is bending down in a way that just cries out for a rude (or Ruud) pose. Chris duly obliged, and so there is a picture of him being Ruud on the way to Schagen! You could always take the piss out of him for this, if you like. But I wouldn't, if I were you. Chris has a black belt in karate, remember?

The monument itself is, in effect, a small- to medium-sized lighthouse with an integrated café at slightly-less-than-dyke-road level and a kitschy-tat shop at slightly-raised-above-road level. The light is up-a-height, as you would expect. Chris was so impressed by the café that he decided to make it his favourite Dutch local. And quite rightly so: apart from the stunning Ijsselmeer view (which possibly inspired Thijs van Leer to write 'Moving Waves'), it also featured a wide range of stuffed seabirds and various furry little animals. Also included within this posthumous menagerie was a stuffed magpie. Hmm, not sure I like the idea of magpies being stuffed. Black cats, yes, but magpies...?

Once our whole being had been suitably moved to ecstasy by the *ambiance* of the café, the motive behind our impulse was clearly the desire to reach upwards, and so we climbed the few stairs to the kitschy tat shop. On a scale of kitschiness from nought to ten (with ten being utter kitsch), this shop scored a good nine and a half, and there was no way I could resist buying a souvenir miniature monument for the wall unit in the living room. It would look great next to that miniature Eiffel Tower! The kitschy-tat seller recognised our half-Toon/half-Heerenveen scarves, and so we had a bit crack. It probably brightened up his humdrum day of selling, well, kitschy tat.

Now me, I've always fancied consecrating an automotive Temple of Tat. If I'd stayed on the Toon side of the North Sea, the chosen sacred vessel would undoubtedly have been a Ford Cortina Mark Two. But as I had opted to leap sausage-side, it would have to be one of those older, boxier-shaped Mercs. You know, the variety that was much beloved of Beirut bombers in the late seventies and early eighties.

Presumably, they had them nicked to order in Deutschland, the way that some parts of Eastern Europe are alleged to have started doing a decade later. Anyway, I would love to have a field day. For a start, there would be that tinted top bit of the windscreen, with the words Pete on the driver's side and wor lass's name on the other. Suspended from the rear-view mirror you would have to have two furry dice. The driving wheel must be leather-bound, and the seats would have those bead covers. Waving in the wind but attached to the power-extendable aerial would be a fox tail. And on the back shelf, I'd have a crocheted bog-roll concealer. Not forgetting the Churchill nodding dog and a wibbly-wobbly Elvis the Pelvis. Magic! Oh, and the bumper stickers that say 'My other car is a Porsche' and 'My other bumper sticker is funny'.

Not long after we'd reached the other end of the dyke and left the sign for Schagen behind us, the traffic density increased exponentially (what a lovely word that is – think I'll use it again: exponentially). Some spaced-out Rastafarian madman in a clapped-out piece of automotive junk nearly ran into the back of us, overtook, and then for good measure nigh-on clipped us as he cut in again. Welcome to Amsterdam. We successfully negotiated the magical motorway tangle and reached Schiphol about one. The original plan had been to have some bait with Sarah and Chris but I reckoned that I should press on to be on the safe side and allow a bit of leeway in case of hold-ups. Didn't want Tina to be standing around on her own in the caad in Luxembourg. But let it be said in fairness that, though it's true dodgy things can and do happen there too, Luxembourg has to rank as just about the safest 'city' in Europe. And truth to tell, I'd have been far more worried about her standing around on her own in the Toon!

Farewells said, I blasted on doon the motorway, and in spite of the really heavy traffic (permanent normality in that neck of the woods), I made excellent progress as far as the approach to the Antwerp Ring. I was able to admire the

Sportpaleis in a major way, as the traffic had ground to a halt and I was going nowhere less than slowly. The traffic news for the Brussels Ring was equally uninspiring, so when things did get slowly moving again I gradually crossed over a few lanes to the right to get into the one that was heading for Hasselt and Liège (Luik, Lüttich). Time for some scran at that Carestel before the motorway forks off to either Eindhoven or Hasselt, and then a blast all the way through to the Liège ring. This was cutting things fine, and the question was whether to take the shorter route that leads towards Aachen (Aken, Aix-la-Chapelle) and then sweeps down through Verviers and on to St. Vith and into Germany – then turning right at Bitburg and on into Luxembourg - or the longer route right through the middle of the Ardennes back south-west towards the E411 Brussels to Luxembourg *autoroute*. I opted for the latter as I reckoned it should be quicker despite being longer. The route takes you through Liège on an urban freeway and gives you some great views of the Basilica and the valley expanse of this industrial mini-conurbation. Then you go quite a way up into the hills. Before I knew it, I was back in a winter wonderland. The sign said one hundred and thirty-five km to Luxembourg and after a rapid pit stop at the motorway services I calculated that I needed to do a constant one hundred and twenty to get to Luxembourg just in time for Tina. There was no longer any leeway for hold-ups. And you know what? It worked out perfectly. One minute I am still blasting along the Grand Ducal motorway. The next, or so it seems, it's the urban cycle of Luxembourg, and the next after that I'm pulling into the parking space at our usual meeting place next to the Rue Goethe and Tina is coming along from her dancing class. In you get, petal. Have a good day? Perfect timing and a perfect end to a perfect Toon trip.

While I've been writing this up the weekend after, I've taken time out to watch us beating Chelsea one-nil in the FA Cup Fifth Round. Of course, there couldn't have been a better time to play them, with so many second or third-choice players in the team because of the injuries to Robben and Drogba and the suspension of Terry, and with Mourinho worrying about playing Barcelona in the Champignons League in midweek. But using just about the same team as in Heerenveen when Robert came on, we've done it! Hard luck of course for Wayne Bridges and his bad injury, but Mourinho certainly was taking a chance when he brought all of his three substitutes on at half time, and it backfired to our advantage, with us ending up playing against nine men including two walking-wounded by the final whistle. Bramble was a rock, redeeming himself for his Heerenveen blunders, and Robert and Kluivert again combined to give us the goal. What we'd achieved was excellent news not only for us, but also for all the other teams left in the competition. We'd done everyone a big favour.

The next day in the Monday lunchtime draw from Soho Square, we got our just reward for our valiant efforts: another home tie, this time against the winner of the Spurs v Nottingham Forest replay. Who's for another four-three win against Forest, followed by a two-nil victory over Burnley in the Semi-Final, and then a different result in the Final?

The games were coming thick and fast, and on the Thursday of what everyone had been calling the make-or-break week, we had the second leg against Heerenveen in a snowbound Toon. Patrick Kluivert must have been pig sick, missing the return game against his Dutch compatriots with a knee problem, and having just scored a great header against Chelsea, which had found the net, nee problem.

Heerenveen came out to a rousing cheer from their brilliant supporters. Their singing and jumping up and down continued right through the game. Hope they had a great time in the Toon and in Percy Ma(r)in(e) Social Club both ways between Ijmuiden and North Shields! I am sure they must have.

But did you see the state of the Heerenveen away strip of dark blue tops and orange shirts? It must have reminded a lot of people of what was definitely our worst-ever alternative strip, that horrible dark blue, orange and green confection that we had a few years ago. What an abomination that was. It wouldn't have looked out of place in the bargain bin of a toddlers' shop: baby's first sweatshirt. My friend Eric once told me about an old English army officer who wrote in his memoirs that, every morning, he woke up and thanked God he was British. Well we wake up every morning and thank Him we're black and white. And tonight we were resplendent in the true colours.

There were a few changes from the Chelsea game, with Kluivert out, Babayaro having 'flu, and Boumsong cup-tied. So we had Shola and Shearer up front, a midfield of Robert, Faye, Butt, and Dyer, and a back four of Hughes, Bramble, O'Brien, and Carr, and Shay of course in goal. The ground was only half full, but there was plenty of noise coming out of the visitors' Level Seven enclosure. On the previous couple of nights, the Champignons League had started again with knock-out ties replacing the previous second league format, and results had gone badly for Arsenal, Manchester, and Chelsea (again, ha ha ha), but Liverpool had won impressively, three-one. Tonight was our turn, and Middlesbrough's, which was surprising as it had been snowing down south too. We all know that the last remnant of a snow-monkey not quite yet trickled down a Hartlepool gutter was enough to 'force' them to call off our game a couple of years ago. Somehow, they managed to clear the cold white stuff this time and did very well to overcome the Austrians from Graz, with a two-one win tipping the balance after the twos-apiece draw at the Arnold Schwarzenegger Stadium the week before. The Grazers' participation in this year's UEFA Cup was well and truly terminated.

Meanwhile back at St. James's, any worries of an upset were dispelled with less than one third of the game played. Robert had one of his best ever games, especially in the first half. Man of the match for my money. Here, there and everywhere, he was. Hughes played a big part to help Robert, interchanging positions with some strong overlapping runs. The first goal came after less than ten minutes when Robert ran powerfully down the wing and drilled a centre into the goal area where, under pressure from our on-rushing attackers, the unfortunate Breuer could only deflect the ball into his own goal. Another great cross from Robert, just like against Chelski in the FA Cup on the Sunday four days earlier and in Heerenveen the week before. Then, on the half hour, the second goal came from a free kick just outside the penalty area. Robert brushed the ball with the sole of his foot a couple of yards towards the centre and into the path of Shearer. He blasted a low drive straight at Dyer, who was positioned just to the left of the Heerenveen wall, ready to leap up and out of its way. Which he did to great effect, leaving the goalkeeper with no time to recover before the ball ripped into the bottom left corner of the net. What a cracker! Hope he does stay on another season.

There were plenty of other chances in a very one-sided first half in which our passing was both perceptive and accurate. With a little more luck and composure, Ameobi could have had at least two goals. One from a rasping shot from the right corner of the penalty box and another, a towering header which he somehow managed to direct onto the left post rather than into the gaping mouth of the goal.

The second half began in the same vein, but the withdrawal of Shearer after the hour seemed to be taken as a signal from the manager to the team that the game was won, and the pace and levels of concentration dropped. With all the missed chances to go three or four ahead, it was no surprise and typical of our season that Heerenveen should come back into the game through a bit of a daft handball when Ameobi flailed his arms into the air as he rose to defend a cross into our area. Bruggink put it away with ease. At least it made it more exciting for a last few nervous minutes until it became apparent that Heerenveen were not going to be able to do anything to take advantage of their moment of good fortune. So the score stayed at two-one on the night and four-two overall, taking us safely through to the next round.

It had been a good week for the Toon. But if a week is a long time in politics, how much longer must it have been for the Toon Army? Souness had had a good week, no doubt about it. But what had he done? A two-one win away to a Dutch side that would be lucky to hold its own in the Scottish Premiership, followed by an FA Cup victory over a second- or third-choice Chelsea side that had been reduced to seven and two half men for most of the second half, and then a home win against the Dutch again. So where did this leave us?

At the same time, over in 'Let's dance in the East of France' Sochaux, Olympiakos were squeezing through one-nil in both legs, giving us probably a harder task to face in a fortnight's time. I have a couple of Greek friends, Thanos who supports Panathinaikos, and (a different) Christos who supports Olympiakos. It was a perfect night for Christos as not only had his team gone through, but also the bitter enemy had been knocked out at the feet of Sevilla, with two goals in the dying minutes. The good news for Christos was also good news for us, as it meant that we would now play our away game as the first leg. UEFA had decreed at the time of the original draw that if both Athenian teams had survived, then the first legs would have seen Panathinaikos at home and Olympiakos away to avoid a clash of supporters. Back in October, they hadn't done this for the Egaleo and Panionios fans. Maybe they aren't counted as rivals, and there were certainly far fewer of them. The same was in some way true of the Boro and Toon fans who actually travelled to Athens.

Liverpool had edged out Olympiakos from the Champignons League with a late goal from Steven Gerrard, depositing them into the UEFA Cup and across our path. We were now to face Rivaldo, certainly the single most famous player we had come across in this year's UEFA Cup. I do hope that his face is not still hurting from being hit on the leg in that painful incident down by a corner flag.

Looking at all the other results, we were now the second-highest-seeded team left in the competition, behind Parma, as Feyenoord, Ajax, and Valencia had been knocked out, spelling hard times for managers Gullit, Koeman, and Ranieri. The next day the latter two were both without jobs.

We were also by far the biggest club left, in terms of business turnover. And according to UEFA's own maybe too simple system of ranking points for this season's Euro games, we were top of all the teams in Europe not only in the UEFA Cup, but also in the Champignons League. This of course took no account of the fact that we'd been playing the likes of Panionios and Tbilisi, not Real Madrid or Barcelona, but so be it. Nevertheless, would there ever be a better chance of us progressing to the Final? The bookies, not weighed down by fifty years of bitter first-hand experience, installed us as competition favourites. The kiss of death!

Kalimera (with chips) – the odyssey returns

So we were in the last sixteen of the UEFA Cup as well as the Quarter-Final of the greatest Cup of all, and the next Euro round would bring another trip to Athens. I must admit that, on balance, I'd been hoping for Athens, as the city does have a wee bit more to offer than Sochaux. Unless of course you are into car plants in a big way.

Barry rang the day after the Heerenveen match with the dates sorted. Thursday March the tenth in Athens. Sarah and Chris would be in Cuba on their hols. Chris was looking forward to watching the match while smoking a geet big cigar, and had offered to apply for tickets for us. But Don had been in touch and reckoned his sources were an absolute banker. So rather than complicate the postal logistics and also run the risk of having too many, I told Chris and Sarah there was no need to apply on our behalf. And in a worst-case scenario, we would get in by hook or by crook.

For some obscure reason I had got it into my head that we were playing AEK Athens – but we weren't. It was Olympiakos. And strictly speaking, they don't play in Athens, but in the nearby port of Piraeus. So even if we won there, would it be a Pyrrhic victory? Their big rivals are Panathinaikos. And as we were to find out on the night, to chant 'Pan – a – thin - ai – kos' to the Olympiakos crowd is rather like insulting their grandmothers in a big way. It drives them absolutely bananas. And they were already half bananas to begin with – what noise! That side of their support put us to shame, but only that side. The partisanship makes us and the mackems look like blood brothers. Which, when you think about it, is not all that far from the truth. But even if I had turned up at the AEK ground, at least I wouldn't have been all that far away. It's certainly nowhere like the distance from Montpellier to Montbéliard, for example!

160

I didn't want to risk missing the flight from Brussels to Athens by sleeping in or being delayed on the Ring or something, so I decided to blast over to Brussels straight after work on the Wednesday evening. It was the usual two and a half hour or so sweep through the Ardennes, which is quite a pleasant run if the weather is okay. You go right through the middle of Battle of the Bulge country. Around Christmas 1944 the Germans launched a surprise counter-offensive with the aim of re-taking the port of Antwerp and thus stretching the Allies' supply lines and gaining more time to develop their so-called *Wunderwaffen* which Adolf reckoned, even at that late stage, were going to win the war for them!

Whereas the Toon beat Antwerp five-nil, the *Wehrmacht* didn't even turn up for their fixture there. Instead, they got bogged down fighting General Patton in the snow-covered rolling countryside of the Ardennes. But American defences were initially under-manned here, as they didn't anticipate any threat whatsoever. And as a result, Jerry enjoyed some considerable successes and in the end delayed the outcome of the war by, it is reckoned, around four months. But at the cost of a hundred thousand casualties. Mad, isn't it? Give me the UEFA Cup battles any day! Anyway, arguably *the* key battle was for the strategically important town of Bastogne, not far from the Luxembourg border. The Americans were encircled by the Germans there, but managed to hold out. The town has a fantastic museum that includes a lot of original equipment, uniforms and artefacts, and the 'tailor's dummies' wearing the uniforms have been very realistically given the actual faces of the combatants on both sides. It is well worth a visit. And afterwards you can have a reasonably priced meal in one of the café-restaurants on the main square. On display in that square is one of Patton's Sherman tanks! *Côté gastro*, as they say, the local speciality is very definitely *marcassin* – wild boar. Marvellous with a nice bottle of Mouton Cadet or a couple of Jupiler Pils to wash it down.

The Ardennes were a winter wonderland this darkening Wednesday evening. Even though we were well into March, spring still looked a distant prospect following a two-week cold spell that had seen much of Western Europe a few feet deep in snow. Mind, even the cold weather doesn't deter the Belgians from indulging in what must be their national sport, namely pulling onto the hard shoulder of the motorway to have a slash. It's amazing – surely by the first decade of the twenty-first century, mankind must have evolved the capability to last out until the next services. And since the whole of Belgium is only about the size of Yorkshire, the next services are never really that far away. But maybe old unpleasant habits simply die hard!

My plan was to stay at my usual hotel for trips to Brussels or for stopping over on the way to the airport. It's actually not in Brussels itself but just outside in a very pleasant little Flemish town called Tervuren. The hostelry in question is called *La Vignette* – it would probably qualify for just two stars, but it really is okay with clean, comfortable rooms and an adequate buffet breakfast. At the time of writing, bed and breakfast costs around seventy euros, and it is good value for money. Check out the website: www.lavignette.be. The location is perfect. If you are visiting Brussels, you can save a small fortune by staying there and not in a city-centre rip-off place. You only have to walk five minutes to a tram terminus, and the number forty-four will get you into town (including changing into the metro at Montgomery) in about forty minutes. And at the paper shop on the way to the tram stop, you can buy an all-day pass for the complete public transport network for only about seven euros, as well as same-day British papers (though inexplicably they don't have The Journal). The red-brick pre-War hotel also has a nice restaurant, and next door there is another restaurant called the *Chalet Vert*. It offers basic but steady Belgian fare at fair prices. My favourite there is *croquettes aux crevettes grises avec pommes frites*, which with a carafe of red wine and a couple of Primus Pils will only set you back about twenty euros.

Diagonally opposite the hotel is the Africa Museum, which focuses on Belgium's colonial past and some of its sins.

It is well worth a visit, and its grounds are just magnificent. Beautifully landscaped along the lines of stately-home gardens complete with a series of Paddy-Freeman-size lakes, they merge with the surrounding forest, the *Forêt des Soignes*, the green lungs of the European capital. Perfect for walking, jogging or cycling. And a must for all Napoleonic history buffs, as this is very much Battle of Waterloo country.

Because Tervuren is located just off the Ring, it is an ideal place to stop over the night before a flight from Zaventem and, again, *La Vignette* is a lot cheaper than anything around the airport. Hotel to airport car park only took about twenty minutes and I was soon checked in and on my way through Terminal A. As mentioned in *Toon Tales*, there is a smaller scale version of the Angel of the North on display in the concourse before the tunnel under the runway in Terminal A, so I naturally paid my respects by rubbing the Angel's toes and saying 'Bring us luck, marra!' Must take a black and white scarf to adorn it with next time! Barry was later to go one better and adorn it with a Toon top.

Read in The Times while waiting to board at gate forty-seven that Olympiakos had played their recent home games behind closed doors because of persistent crowd trouble. And on the Sunday before our Thursday night game there, their one-one draw away to PAOK Thessaloniki, who also have the good fortune to wear the black and white by the way, had also been marred by some nasty incidents that were to be investigated and possibly lead to further penalties. Plus, our match there coincided with the club's eightieth birthday. Okay, so it would be the first opportunity for their partisan fans to get inside their own ground for several weeks, and they had a birthday to celebrate. So the chances were that they would be well fired (as well, no doubt, as tanked) up. But would they be on their best behaviour? The memories of the first trip to Athens were totally positive. All the people we met, including Panionios supporters after their home defeat, had been really friendly. And the good people of

Heerenveen had made us very welcome indeed a couple of weeks earlier. Trouble was the last thing anybody needed...

On the actual subject of football, the article went on to say that Rivaldo would be their biggest threat, and Shearer (at thirty-four, two years Rivaldo's senior) was quoted as saying that older players tended to lose their legs, but not their brains. Were we going to be treated to the sight of both centre forwards shuffling around the pitch on a Zimmer frame while discussing the works of Aristotle, I wondered.

And so, faced with the prospect of encountering a bunch of heedbanging Greek loonies, I reflected on how fortunate we were that Barry had already arranged for us to meet our very own Greek minder, Thanos. Well, his local knowledge and lingo had already proven invaluable, with his tips to beware of the opposition's supporters, but to be sure to chant the team's 'Gavri' nickname at any opportunity.

Thanos, who is an ardent Panathinaikos 'Green Celts' fan, told us that they called the Olympiakos wallahs the 'Red Sailors' or preferably the 'Gavri', which apparently means some kind of stinky little fish, possibly anchovies, in an allusion to the Piraeus harbour area. It was clearly quite an insult. The joke was: what's the biggest frying pan in the world? The Georgios Karaiskakis Stadium, 'coz that's where Panathinaikos come to fry the stinking 'Gavri' tiddlers. The Gavri in turn call Panathinaikos the 'Vaseli'. Back in the sixties, before a derby match, the Gavri smeared the Panathinaikos dug-out seats with Vaseline, saying their arses were going to need it, in view of what was about to befall them. I'll let you work that one out for yourselves; suffice it to say that the Ancient Greeks reputedly invented it. Thanos' words of encouragement rang in our ears: 'I do hope you crush the Piraeus bastards'.

Our 'mackem' is harmless by comparison. I remember in the seventies that my Uncle Tommy would talk about the 'mackems and tackems', and I'm not at all sure when that got shortened to the 'mackems'. Any ideas? But I do know that it was never intended as a compliment. Yet the mackems themselves have taken it over and proudly call themselves 'mackems'. That surely is a compliment to us. And it makes a change, because in the past mackems have often claimed to be Geordies when abroad. But who could blame them for that?

It was time to get on the plane. Was a bit disappointed at not being Pan-piped aboard Olympic Airways flight 8144 (operated by Hellas Jet) by a delegation of the mini-skirted Greek Presidential Guard wearing those funny fez-like hats (just like that) or by nubile nymphs bearing complimentary *feta* cheese (actually cheddar would have done, as I was a bit peckish) to the accompaniment of some authentic cheese-shop *bouzouki* players. Still, can't have everything.

On a positive note, the brief exchange with the exceedingly bonny air hostess did increase my Greek vocabulary by a good fifty per cent. In addition to *kalimera* (with chips), I was reminded of the word '*yassas*', which from the context had to mean something along the lines of 'hello'. Unless of course she had mistaken me for Yosser Hughes (who looked uncannily like Souness, remember!) or Yasser Arafat. Made a mental note to learn Classical and Modern Greek sometime (in the afterlife). The captain came on and gave us the disappointing news that Athens was only a few degrees warmer than Brussels at about fifteen degrees, but at least it was dry, a phenomenon that Brussels hadn't experienced for more than a week.

We weren't long airborne and already the Alps were rising up majestically even above the blanket of cloud. Did Hannibal look down onto the tops of the clouds, I wonder? There they were, the cold, icy, rocky and eternal mountains. What a fantastic sight actually looking down onto their glacial splendour, their crevices, folds and lakes. Mind, the Rising Sun slagheap in Waalsend was more impressive in its heyday. Canny nature park, now though.

It was time for a bit bait, and te gan with it a couple of cans of Mythos beer. I knew from the Panionios trip that this was the beer of philosophers, 'coz when we all got pissed on it in Kolonaki Square we started philosophising like mad. Was this the favourite tipple of Aristotle (that bugger for the bottle) and Archimedes, perhaps? Alas and alack, the writing on the can told me they had only been brewing it since 1997. But hang on, maybe that meant 1997 BC.

Be that as it may, Mythos beer definitely makes you feel mythologically sky-high as you are whisked through the clouds on your winged chariot. There was Zeus over on the left having a bit practice at hoyin' thunderbolts, like. Definitely an omen for a Robert thunderbolt or two. And there was Mercury looking all mercurial. The gods were with us. And full marks to Hellas Jet for their in-flight catering. Certainly nothing Hellish about it. Their piping hot noodlos and tomatos saucios followed by a nice bit claggy sweet cakeopoulos get them three stars out of five from your correspondent (who is not in the habit of hoyin' stars aroond like Zeus lobs thunderbolts, I can tell you). You even get a Bailey's to round the meal off. And they give you a boiled sweet to suck during descent – I thought they went out in the sixties. A fine airline indeed.

On the foldy-down monitors, BBC World announced that oil prices had hit a new high that day, of fifty-three dollarouzos per barrelaika – so when would the Nana Maskara look-alike cabin attendant be coming round holding an urn asking for a fuel surcharge? They gave us real headphones, none of your air tube rubbish, and I flicked through the channels on the armrest controls. Easy listening, hard listening, Greek jabbering, and then 'Greek for Tourists'. What a great idea! They should copy it and have 'Larn yersel' Geordie' on Newcastle flights. A lot of it was too fast, but I found out for instance that *proto* meant 'first', so now we know what prototype really means. *Treno* was a 'train' which you could sort of guess, and *dexia* meant 'right', which is interesting as there's a Belgian bank which changed its name to that, and it also shows where dexterity comes from. It then went on to give useful phrases for everyday situations that you might find yourself in. Such as:

'Excuse me, Mr Riot Polis, but could you ask those crazed Olympiakos fans to stop hoyin' bottles and cigarette lighters at us, *parakalo*?'

'Not likely, you Eengleesh peegs.'

This caused a memory overflow, so the lesson endethed there. I switched back to BBC World and was informed that they're starting up cricket in America. In a 'lite' version, as scientific research had shown that the average American's attention span cannot accommodate anything which lasts longer than two hours fifty-four minutes. That should just about see them through stoppage time in a Man Utd match if they're losing in the ninetieth minute.

Nick the Greek plane driver (answers to the family name of Popoloposhlopodopoulos) got us to Athens bang on time, bless him. I was travelling light this time, and had borrowed Tina's best rucksack – which I was to return unscathed, under pain of not being able to borrow it again. This was great because it meant I didn't have to hang around waiting at the baggage carousel. This little ritual usually wastes precious minutes of drinking time. Mind, I usually take more baggage than a Roman legion with me – well a geet big Samsonite. But this time wor lass kindly helped, and so I was out of the airport and at the taxi rank in no time, and it was only three o'clock local time.

'Do you speak English?' I asked Nick the taxi-driver, who turned out to be Wassilis the taxi-driver who had worked in Berlin for ten years as a fitter and then moved back to Athens with his German wife. So we had great crack in our *lingua franca*, kraut-speak. Two of his three bilingual daughters were studying in Berlin. Another two years and he would jack in this lark. The stress, the traffic jams. Canny lad, was Wassilis. We agreed a price of twenty-five euros to the hotel. No need to switch the meter on – why add an extra burden to the already overworked taxi tax people? We flew along the new motorway, which for the first few clicks outside the airport ran parallel with the metro, likewise spanking new and EU or Olympics funded. Wassilis had left Greece before they had joined the then European Community. By the time he came back, the place had leapt out of the middle ages and into the twentieth century with a vengeance, most importantly of all leaping streets ahead of Turkey, apparently. It's amazing how much you can exchange and learn in a forty-five-minute taxi ride. Text message on the mobile.

'Omen. Saw two magpies at Hadrian's Gate.' It was from Barry.

Ah, but did you rip them open to examine the entrails for signs?

'This magpie has landed too, so three goals for the Toon!' I replied.

Prophetic, or pathetic, or what? Then it rang.

'We're in Piraeus, where are you?'

'*En route* for the hotel. I'll dump my gear and get back in the taxi and ring you back.'

That was fine by Wassilis:

'Another ten euros and I'll take you to Piraeus. And pick you up at the hotel at seven tomorrow morning. And I hope you piss on those Olympiakos tossers.'

Canny lad.

Great things mobiles, mind, aren't they? These precision last-minute Toon Army operations would be impossible without them! Except Barry's was on the blink and he was using Ashington Neale's. Did I have his number? Hang on, got it somewhere. Yes. In the meantime, Wassilis was well into his retirement plans, but hey it was good crack. How did their lass like Greece? Great. Hadn't spoken a word of Greek when they first moved down from Berlin, but now she was fluent. Not perfect, but fluent. That is pretty steady, thought I. She even spoke in Greek in her sleep. Wheyabuggama! As we wound our way through the congested Athens streets up the Lycabettus hill, Wassilis kindly explained the ancient mysteries of that word '*yassas*'. Apparently, the root of it means 'health' but it is used in a very versatile way indeed. It can mean 'hello', 'goodbye', 'cheers', 'bless you'...

Reached the hotel. Wassilis waited outside while I dived in to check in and dump my gear. Pretty much the same story as on the Panionios trip, when Chris and Sarah had been waiting at this same hotel ready to dive into my taxi. They couldn't make it this time as they had booked that holiday in Cuba well in advance. They no doubt wanted to trace the footsteps of the Cuba-based AWP series, which would be a bit difficult as most of that series was in fact filmed in the Dominican Republic. Never mind. Their plan for match day was to find a boozer with a wide-screen TV somewhere in Havana. Hmm, could be a bit difficult. But Chris would at least be puffing away on that geet big cigar.

Dived back out of the hotel and back into the taxi. And, after a journey of fifteen metres, back out of the taxi again and into the hotel and into the taxi again. I had left the e-mail print-out with everybody's mobile numbers in the room. All haste, no speed. Off we set again. Rang Neale's number and he passed the phone to Barry. The four of them were in the *Vosporos* restaurant overlooking Microlimano harbour, just a Shay Given clearance away from the football ground. That was a new one on Wassilis, but he said it wasn't such a big quarter down by the harbour and we'd find it no bother. After about twenty minutes, we passed the impressive-looking Olympiakos stadium. Milling around outside were a few supporters clad in their red-and-white striped shirts. Looked like a slightly different shade of red from the mackems, a bit lighter maybe, but an unfortunate choice of colours nonetheless. The stadium apparently had a capacity of thirty-three thousand and it was well and truly sold out for tonight. It had been built for the 2004 Olympics, and it was there that Olympic football of the female kind had taken place. A bit like mackem football, come to think of it. Another few minutes and we were in the harbour district. Wassilis stopped to ask a couple of Greek dolly birds if they knew where the *Vosporos* was, and they did. It was just around the corner.

'*Yassou*, Wassilis, see you at the hotel reception at seven tomorrow morning.'

So the rendezvous was successfully accomplished. Barry had arrived in Athens from Brussels the previous evening, and had had a bit time for some sightseeing, while Neale had arrived just before me. Don and Alec had come over on the day too, from Stansted by Easyjet for next to nothing! They had ordered two individual meals plus one for two persons, Donos and Alexandros, but it turned out that the mountain of meat was enough to feed a Blyth Spartan army, so I tucked in as well, and meanwhile the red wine was flowing freely. I could quickly see what had attracted the lads to this particular eatery. It was the delicious fare on view - the delicious waitresses, that is. Black skin-tight catsuits and tanned midriffs, who could ask for more?

You're right, Petros, we'd come to Microlimano specially to sample the freshly-caught fish dishes, and the *Vosporos* was the only harbour-side taverna which didn't serve fish, but when we spotted one of the skin-tight visions slinking across the road from the main restaurant to the harbour-side taverna, did that really matter? Maybe the two sirens who'd shown you the way actually worked there too?

We'd been hoping to invite our Greek minder, Thanos, to join us at the match and lead us in a few home-brewed Panathinaikos chants against the enemy, but unfortunately he wasn't able to make it, so we had a ticket spare. Attempts to persuade Calypso, one of the lasses, to take it and join the Toon Army catering corps proved fruitless, however. After the meal, which came to a very reasonable twelve euros apiece, it was *yassas* all round and off we set for the ground, which we had been told would be only a fifteen-minute walk up the coast road. En route, Barry told the full story of the two magpies landing at Hadrian's Gate:

Well, Pete, I was walking back through the grounds of Zeus' Temple from the Gate and past the Roman baths when

I spotted the pair of magpies I texted you about, flitting around by a little pool. To me, this had to be an omen. Like the two eagles sent down by Zeus in the Odyssey. You know how in Greek mythology the gods are always transforming themselves into animals to have their wicked way with the mortals? Clearly, what we had here were the spirits of the footballing gods coming down in the guise of Mags to worship at the temple before heading over to the match. I just had to take a photo, a really good one for the book, close up, of them standing side by side, with the Temple of the Olympian Zeus in the background. So I stalked them, trying to get the perfect picture, but every time I got all set, they pissed off again. So maybe those two goals were going to prove more elusive than we had hoped.

It had been a beautiful bright and crisp morning, so I'd decided to take a walk in the National Park that we'd skirted on the way back after our Paula marathon run. As you walk through, you find toppled and broken ancient marble columns, plinths and capitals strewn around more or less abandoned. They have such an embarrassment of riches that they don't seem to care. If the same vestiges were found in the Toon, they certainly wouldn't be left lying about for people to have picnics on, they would be turned into a heritage centre. Athens is like that – you find little open-air storage areas packed full of archaeological samples all over the place. As I strolled along, I gradually became aware of people looking at me. To me, it seemed quite natural to be walking around in a tee shirt, it was so sunny. But then I realised that everyone else was wearing fur coats, leather jackets, scarves and anoraks. I suppose they don't get many days when they can show off their winter clothes. It really got brought home to me when I passed by a bunch of well wrapped-up school kids. One pointed straight at me and shouted out to his pal, 'Hey, Tassos, *uno touristikos!*' Or words to that effect.

I took breakfast on the edge of the park in the Oasis taverna. Luckily they had an open-air part, because the inside was blindman thick with Greek cigarette smoke. I've never been in a smokier place. They don't do things by halves, the Greeks! I then passed by another military guard trooping up and down a big parade ground in the middle of the park and then headed down to the Temple of the Olympian Zeus and the neighbouring Hadrian's Gate.

Hadrian's Gate was a kind of Checkpoint Charlie in the ancient world. Yep, it was the same Roman Emperor who had our wall built who had this gate named after him. There's even a town named after him, Hadrianopolis, and a street in Sooth Shiels, not to mention the Emperor Hadrian boozer on Battle Hill Estate in Waalsend, and still less the Adrian Hotel in the old *Agora,* meaning 'market', square in *Plaka.* This gate had been integrated, apparently, in a kind of Athens Berlin wall if you see what I mean, which had separated the Roman sector of the city (probably the bit with the better sewers) from the Greek sector in Hadrian's time. Give those Romans their due, they certainly put themselves about.

By the time Hadrian came over to inaugurate the newly-finished Temple of the Olympian Zeus just outside the Gate in 131/2 AD, the Romans were well and truly the top dogs across the whole of western Europe and the Middle East. From Consett to Constantinople and beyond, what they said went. Hadrian reckoned the empire was big enough by then and decided to consolidate what they had and make its borders watertight to keep the riff-raff out. That was why he built his wall up our way. But hang on, if he was such a clever sod, how come he built the wall from Wallsend to Carlisle, yet had the gate built in Athens. That seems a bit stupid to me. Unless it was just an excuse to get away from their lass! 'A'm just gannin' oot te shut the gate, pet, a'll not be lang'. And then he hops on a boowert at Sooth Shiels (Arbeia) and has heesel a Mediterranean cruise followed by a binge in the Tavernae of Athena. Later on, the Emperor Trajan reckoned it was time to expand the empire again, and it wasn't long before present-day Romania came into the

Roman fold. Hence the name. You've got to admire these Emperors, though but.

The all-time great has to be Julius Caesar, mind. Writing during the reign of Hadrian, Suetonius (one of the chief imperial librarians, so with access to all the records) tells us what a gentle, mild-mannered and forgiving person Caesar basically was. When he finally got hold of the pirates who had previously captured and tortured him and then held him to ransom, 'He merely crucified them and did not make them suffer any other punishments'. Wow, my hero! How's that for forgiveness. Those pirates certainly got off lightly, didn't they? After all, he could have broken a few bones and lopped off a few limbs before the main event, if he had been in a bad mood. Such was his benevolent disposition on that particular occasion that apparently it was a toss-up between crucifixion and seventy-two hours of community service, cleaning out the sewers in the port of Ostia!

As you've heard, it was Hadrian and the Romans who completed the Temple of the Olympian Zeus, nearly six hundred and forty years after the first stone was laid. So there you go, the Ancient Greeks couldn't have been the clever shites they had made themselves out to be, after all. Their very own top god, and somebody else had to finish the job because they had presumably been getting stuck into the retsina a bit too often. A bit like they did in 2004 AD too. That would give us a brilliant chant with which to taunt the Olympiakos fans (to the tune of 'you couldn't sell all your tickets'): 'You couldn't finish all your temples, finish all your temples.' Or how about: 'You're Greek, and you know you are'?

As we got near the Georgios Karaiskakis ground, we could already hear the roar from within. The volume was so impressive that for one dreadful moment we looked in panic at our watches and wondered if we had missed the kick-off. But no, by now we were among a good few Olympiakos fans who clearly were not panicking. One of them suggested in a very friendly way that we should cover up our colours until

173

we were safely in our section of the ground, as there was no shortage of out-and-out lunatics in this neck of the woods. And we duly took his advice. Looking at our tickets, we saw we had to get to entrance twenty-four, or so we thought. To get to the ground we crossed a brand new concrete footbridge that also gave access to the equally new Neo Kafiro metro station adjacent to the ground. Bridge, station and ground were all less than a year old and everything was very impressive. There was another stadium just a few hundred yards away, which looked even more impressive in a curvy concrete Ullevi style. This was the Faliro Peace and Friendship Stadium used for volleyball, another remnant from the Olympics, which have certainly had a Greek dramatic effect on Athens.

Incredibly, the arriving away fans were not being segregated from the home support in the queues to get in. But when we were finally at the turnstile, we were told we had to go to a different one and so we backed up through the incoming home throng, mouthing *yassas* to all and sundry. We had to go back along the bridge, then down the steps before the metro and across a courtyard packed with hotdog stands, scarf sellers and the like. As he passed them, Donos couldn't resist buying another giant flag. We made our way to the ground-level turnstile where we could see plenty of Toon wallahs, including a few Toon lasses wearing laurel leaf crowns, Greek-goddess style. But there, too, we were mingling with Greeks headed for the adjacent turnstile, and where the two streams finally parted there was plenty of verbal abuse and ridiculously over-the-top gestures from the Greeks, none of whom were bearing gifts. But here at least there was a strong police presence that formed a kind of last-minute filter before we could pass through the turnstile. One yard away, when we'd long given up on selling the spare ticket, a Greek girl called out:

'Have you got a spare ticket?'

'We certainly do! That'll be twenty euros to you, pet, face value.'

'Thanks so much and *yassas*. You've saved my life!'

The turnstile was a very high-tech affair, and like many a high-tech device these days it was completely user-unfriendly. Like those digital car radios that must have caused a million car accidents because you can't simply twiddle a knob anymore but have instead to press buttons here and there to get the exact frequency. Give me the old variety any day. Well, this turnstile was a tight squeeze for big fat Geordie gits like me, for a start. But then you had to insert the barcode bit of the ticket to get the thing to open. Of course, we had all expected to show a ticket to some gadgy in the conventional manner, but here we were in an ecstasy of fumbling instead, with the result that it took twice as long as it should have done to get in. As we walked up the steps the noise got ever greater, and to our utter surprise we found that our section wasn't properly separated from their fans at all. The high-tech design merchants of Greece had certainly made some pretty stupid mistakes. Maybe that was why the Romans had found them such a pushover in ancient times. They were fine when it came to philosophy and technology. What was missing was plain common sense. Instead of a fence, there was a wall of polisses between us and their kop-type end, which was clearly full of lunatics. Gesticulating, hissing, and throwing things at us, they were, and the match hadn't even kicked off yet!

When their players came out, the noise was virtually deafening and stopped just short of taking the roof off. Flares and flags everywhere, including a massive version of the 'Gate Seven' flag which Don had bought. This was going to be a mighty test for the Toon's nerves. I wonder how many of our team of Given, Hughes, O'Brien, Bramble, Carr, Robert, Butt, Faye, Dyer, Kluivert and Shearer had ever experienced such a hostile atmosphere before?

As it happened, there were a good half dozen Greeks around us. Obviously some very nice people who just wanted to enjoy the game and soak up the atmosphere of being in with the Toon Army. And interestingly enough, they didn't even look over to the seething mass of lunatics, who by now were foaming at the mouth. Our Greek auxiliaries clearly knew that the home fans' bark was worse than their bite.

We would have been happy with a draw. Even going down one-nil or two-one would have been okay. But the reality of the night surpassed our imagination. In the early minutes, the Greeks were passing the ball about very neatly and the two baldy wingers were making some positive runs. Bramble got in a good tackle on Rivaldo, who collapsed as if stricken on the ankle by one of Zeus' own thunderbolts. Bramble got roundly booed every time he touched the ball after that. Apart from one mediocre free kick, Rivaldo was just a meaningless nothing hobbling around the pitch. He never really fully recovered from that terrible injury he suffered a few seasons ago down by someone's corner flag, did he? When he got hit on the leg and the pain went straight to his face. It's called short-circuited nerve syndrome. At least he didn't roll around holding his face this time.

One of the baldies looked like he was breaking free into the penalty area until Robert steamed back in to rob him of the ball and back-heel it out to Aaron Hughes. Then Amdy Faye slide-ruled a pass through to Dyer, whose shot ballooned back off the goalie, and just when he seemed poised to head it back into an empty net, a defender got back to put him off and the ball went wide. If their goal was at the Gallowgate End, then we were in the Popular-side corner of the Leazes, so we couldn't really tell from our vantage point whether it was a penalty or not. But the Spanish ref, Arturo Ibanez, was better placed to judge and he sent Georgatos off and we had a penalty. Georgatos couldn't believe it and stood behind the goal with his hands clasped onto his bald pate, looking like Uncle Fester having a nightmare. This was a triple whammy for the *Gavri*: a penalty, a man sent off, and he'd been their best player. Anyone who was there will never ever forget the sheer wall of noise that faced Alan Shearer. He must have nerves of steel. And bang – we were one-nil up. But only minutes later, bang, they were given a penalty too, when O'Brien challenged one of the Greeks and he went down very easily. And this was right in front of our eyes. We reckoned 'No way,' the ref must just be scared. One-one and the ground erupted in flares and an enormous roar.

And then Robert's free kick. Shearer chested the ball down to him and he was up-ended just outside the penalty area, again down their Gallowgate End. What a cracker, bent around the left of the wall with the silver-haired Greek national team goalkeeper left flat-footed. 'You're not singing any more!' Then another one of their players got sent off over on the far side of the pitch amidst scenes of confusion after the ref had played advantage when Butt had been fouled. The *Gavri* went mad and the noise went up to ear-bursting levels again. I think I might have heard them calling the referee 'Polyphemus', the Cyclops blinded by Odysseus. No one could deny that the ref was courageous, sending two of theirs off, and distributing yellow cards like they were going out of fashion. He and his assistants had to be very brave to run the gauntlet to get off the pitch at half time.

The talk in the away section was over whether we should go after them in the second half and settle the tie tonight, or play it carefully, make sure we gave the trigger-happy ref no reason to send any of our players off, and maybe sneak another goal. The nine men of Olympiakos came out with all guns firing like Butch Cassidy and the Sundance Kid, and forced us onto the back foot and into initiating Plan B whether we wanted to or not. The Greek crowd had decided that if they couldn't be their twelfth man, they sure as Hellenic were going to be their tenth and eleventh men and they made one almighty din. Amidst all the pandemonium, we kept giving the ball away and our lead didn't look at all safe.

A few of us started chanting '*Ga – vri, Ga – vri*', but it never really caught on in a big way – well, anchovies are small fry. But it did catch the attention of the Greek polisses who were two yards away and turned around at us with the look of someone who is thinking 'Are they singing what I think they are singing?' Imagine how a Newcastle polis would feel if he heard Greek fans behind him singing 'You Byker Bastards', and if that polis happened to come from Byker himself! We realised this possibility and so began preparing our excuses. 'Er, one of our subs is called Gavri, well actually that's just his nickname... er... honest.' But fortunately, the necessity didn't arise. We tried 'Panathinaikos - Panathinaikos' and that met with much greater success and furious looks from the *Gavri*.

On the hour, Dyer and Robert went off to a well-deserved standing ovation - okay, so what if we were standing already? Robert especially showed his appreciation to the Toon Army by applauding as he left the pitch. I suppose we could have stuck with our nine players, but Graeme Souness then ruthlessly decided to send Milner and Jenas on.

The other nine men had eventually begun to tire, especially Rivaldo, which was strange as he'd done nothing. He was substituted by another Brazilian, Giovanni, who had actually scored a goal against us when he played in the Champignons League for Barcelona. Olympiakos's other sub was the comically-named Pantos. Whenever he was in danger of being tackled from behind, the Greeks yelled, 'He's behind you.' And we replied, 'Oh no he isn't.' Then Milner made a great run down the left, raced inside, jinked past the defender and cut the ball back to Kluivert who drove a low, first-time left-footed shot into the left corner of the goal. He looked up to the Toon Army in the stand and rightly raised his arm in salute. Our worries were over. The Greeks went quiet for once as we went through the repertoire: 'Are you sunderland in disguise?' and 'Can we play you every week?' and 'You're not very good' and 'Can you ref us every week?' and 'There's only one referee, one referee' and the very ironic 'Happy Birthday', seeing it was the eightieth anniversary of their foundation. Shortly after, Shearer grazed the post with a tremendous low free kick from just outside the area, and after that the match wound down while we sang more and more songs. Mind, the noise from the Greeks actually got louder and louder too, with a long-running chant of 'Ole, Ole, Ole, somethinggreek, somethinggreek', and much brandishing of scarves, flags, and flares. At the final whistle, this welled up into massive boos and whistles aimed at the match officials. They aimed plenty of bottles and lighters at them too, and at us. The next morning, one of the Greek sports papers, 'Goal News', had a one-word headline, 'Clown', and a close-up of the referee.

Overall, we hadn't been too impressed by Olympiakos. They had their couple of baldy midfielders who were pretty good dribblers and crossers of the ball, but the rest were a bunch of shirt-tugging, heel-tapping, whingeing (and given half a chance, back-stabbing) play-actors, just like the eyetie teams of old. But it soon became apparent that they were playing out their roles in a Greek tragedy.

When the final whistle blew, the hatred was intense. Their crowd's behaviour was becoming more and more disgraceful. Objects had been hurled at the ref and at Souness when the half-time whistle went, and now plastic water bottles and cigarette lighters were being thrown our way. Alexandros got hit by some coins and one of the lighters. The Greek police were taking no action at all. Surely, they could at least have been taking photos or videoing the culprits with a view to picking them up later. But nothing. The polisses had shields and were interested only in shielding themselves. We wondered if they were up to this challenge. But gradually they pressed back the lunatics while we taunted them with 'You can't even throw straight' and 'What shall we do with Olympiakos? What shall we do with Olympiakos? What shall we do with Olympiakos, early in the morning? BAN, BAN, BAN the bastards' and, to the tune of 'Guantanamera', 'Banned by UEFA, you'll be banned by UEFA.'

And surely UEFA will have no option but to follow the Greek FA's example and ban them. Football does not need these people. They're not fans, they're scum. They do not deserve to be allowed into anybody's stadium. They are also as thick as pig shit. They seem unable to correlate their disgusting behaviour with the bans that have been imposed on them. Good riddance to the vermin. They will not be missed, the *Gavri*.

Because it was such an early kick-off, it didn't really matter that we were kept in so long. One hour of being targets for weak-armed bottle throwers. Eventually, the chief of the riot police called out 'Where is Kiss? I want to speak with Kiss. Come down here please.' After some confusion, the message was understood and Keith of Toon Travel came down to the front and the polith explained that the coaches were ready and their party should leave by the left exit while everyone else travelling independently had to leave down the right-hand stairs. We would be back in the city centre by about ten, so there was still plenty of time for a couple of pints and a bit crack with the locals. While waiting to be allowed on the bridge to the metro, people were meeting others they had bumped into at previous European games. Weren't you at that boozer in Heerenveen? Did you manage to get a ticket in the end? That sort of thing. Great crack. It turned out that one lad we bumped into, yet another Barry, lived in Deutschland, just down the road from Trier. It's a small world, the world of the Toon Army. Married to a Dutch girl who works in Luxembourg too. 'The one with great legs,' he said, to help pinpoint her. 'Oh, her.'

That crackpot who had been causing trouble at Panionios was also there, unfortunately. Pissed again and making a exhibition of himself with ridiculous gestures. Fortunately he was being completely ignored and ostracised. Perhaps he's highly strung – he should be.

Into the metro, a bit singsong for seven stops or so, and out we got at Monastiraki station in the lively Psiri quarter of downtown Athens. It was just about warm enough to sit outside for one, so that's what we did in one of the tavernas that line one side of the Monastiraki Square, site of the Sunday flea market. One or two Panathinaikos fans came over to offer their congratulations and express their satisfaction. We impressed them with our local knowledge of the anchovies.

We were itching for a bit bait and it was beginning to turn too cool to search too long. So we didn't hesitate to enter an inviting-looking and heaving eatery just on the corner. We trusted that we wouldn't be heaving after sampling its menu. There were plenty of people coming in after us to start their meal at eleven on a Thursday evening - did everybody have the Friday off? Surely not, but they'd already had another strike earlier in the day. This time it had been civil servants, not air traffic controllers. We went upstairs to the strains of bouzouki music and the smell of garlicky gyros. Pretty steady. As was the feta cheese and the moussaka and some more Mythos beer. On the next table were Gus from Minnesota, (echoes of the Fargo film again), and his daughter Megusta, who inexplicably was spending a year in Warsaw learning Polish. Presumably that was why they had come to Athens! Like the Minnesotan pensioners who'd taken our picture at the Olympic stadium at the end of our marathon run.

Megusta asked 'What's that name they call you sahccer fans?'

'Toon Army?'

'No...'

'The Magpies? The Mags? The Geordies?'

'No, you English fans have got a special name.'

'You don't mean 'hooligans', do you?'

'Yeah, that's the one!'

Barry explained to Megusta and Gus the difference between hooligans and the Toon Army. Megusta then tried to convince us that the Mexican Wave was invented in Minnesota. We begged to differ on that one, mainly because it isn't called the Minnesotan Wave. But is she right?

Must have been about half past one local time when we left the taverna. We parted company with Donos and

Alexandros in the now almost deserted Athens streets. By now, they knew the way to Amaryllis, their hotel. Barry, Neale and I quickly abandoned the original plan to walk back up the hill to the St. George and were fortunate enough to get a taxi. The ten-minute trip up the long and winding road cost all of two euros and fifty cents. It was about a quarter to two when I got to my room on the first floor. Had to gaze in wonder again at the Acropolis. This time my balcony afforded a square-on view. I reckon this room was next door to the one Chris and Sarah had had on the Panionios trip, 'coz this view was very like the one we had had from their balcony when we had soaked up the Athenian sunset and the Athenian beer. Then the phone rang.

It was Barry to say that highlights were being shown on Eurosport and that we were two-one up so I could still catch Kluivert's goal. Which I did, toasting it with two disgustingly expensive small bottles of the cool Heineken from the minibar. It seemed like it was just a few minutes later when the phone rang again with the six o'clock wake-up call! So it hadn't been more than four hours' sleep and a total of five hours' presence in the super-duper luxury hotel this time. Really, something further down-market, like a park bench maybe, would have done the job. (Sod that!) But the parting view across to the Acropolis in the dawning light of an early spring morning convinced me it had been worth the extra few drachma after all. Okay, so they have euros, I know, but drachma still sounds much more atmospheric, don't you think? But it has to be said that it is absolutely brilliant to be able to spend the same money just about everywhere in Europe these days. Such a pity that Britain hasn't cottoned on to that yet!

So it was a very short but action-packed stay in Greece the second time round, yet there was still a bit more adventure to come on the way back to the airport. While I was settling up at reception, (in the family we call it 'repception', 'coz that's what Tina used to say when she was little… funny that, Pete, because Brian used to say exactly the same too), I was approached by yet another Stavros the Big Fat Greek Taxi Driver, who was holding out his mobile in my general direction, saying 'Eats for you, probably'. I was very surprised, I suppose, as I don't know anyone in Athens, and nobody I do know could possibly, or even probably, know that I would be there at reception in the St. George Hotel at that particular moment and also conveniently know the mobile number of a taxi driver standing at the door! Except of course Wassilis – but it was a bit too early in the morning for me to work that one out in a hurry.

Wassilis' dad had been rushed into hospital and was very poorly, so would I take his marra's taxi instead and at the price of twenty-five euros that we had agreed yesterday? As Stavros came on my old friend Wassilis' recommendation, I reckoned he had to be as sound as a drachma. I had been speaking in English to the guy at reception (Alcinous, I think his name was), but after he had heard Wassilis and me talking on the phone in our teutonic *lingua franca* he too slipped effortlessly into very good German. I was suitably impressed and more than a little ashamed of my total lack of Greek. Must do something about that...

A few minutes later, I was certainly less than impressed by Stavros' driving. In fact I got off to a very bad start in Stav's cab, because the seatbelt in the front passenger seat was buggered. After I had struggled with it for a minute or two, Stav said ' 's alright', and muggins here says 'Okay'. You know how it is sometimes. You're so tired after just half a night's sleep following Toon victory celebrations, and you are not really switched on at all. You even somehow regard a Big Fat Greek Taxi Driver as being a figure of authority, and you are no more likely to contradict him than you would have contradicted your favourite primary school teacher (Miss Platt, at St. Aidans, Willington Quay, in my case - I didn't half have a crush on her) when she told you to stop deliberately belching in class. Of course I should have said 'Ya norron, Stav, bonny lad, a'm gettin in the back.' But I didn't, so more fool me.

To say he drove like a raving lunatic would be grossly unfair to raving lunatics, who are probably chivalrous white knights of the road by comparison. I told him there was no hurry, plenty of time for my plane, but Stav obviously wanted this fare out of the way as quickly as possible, either that or he had a one-way ticket to Mount Olympus. It was a bit like being in a Steve McQueen fillum as we tore and rattled and bounced down the narrow winding streets towards the city centre and out towards the airport. He had obviously bought this clapped-out diesel Merc from a retired Beirut terrorist, and its suspension had suffered from the impact of all those checkpoint car bombs back in the eighties. Stav looked as happy as Larry, however, with his beer gut pressed firmly against the steering wheel for good measure, thus leaving his hands free to light a tab and get on the mobile to their lass at the same time.

My subtle hints in the form of coughing and wheezing were to no avail, so I said in my slowest, clearest and most deliberate English:

'I have a smoke allergy, please don't smoke.'

'Smoke allergy? Never heard of that before.'

'Yes, er, it makes me cough.'

'Oh, right!'

And he threw his tab out of the window, muttering in Greek something probably along the lines of 'Smoke allergy, huh? So you live and you learn, already.'

The Merc may have been old and shrapnel-pock-marked from its Middle East campaign, but given an open road and the right kind of loving care its diesel horses could be coaxed and nursed up to one hundred and sixty km per hour in as many seconds – in a seventy zone. It was one of those moments when prayer is the only recourse. And then, surreally, he pulls back over into the slow lane, slams the anchors on, pulls onto the hard shoulder and screeches to a shuddering halt. We're just short of one of the mountain tunnels that adorn this gleaming stretch of what is a spanking new EU-financed motorway replete with high-tech warning panels reminding you alternately in Greek and English to 'respect the speed limit'. In the Stav vocab, this read 'show contempt for' rather than 'respect'.

'Is there a problem?' I sheepishly ventured, happy still to be alive.

'Back door's open, your side.'

Before I had time to say 'Don't close it till I climb in the back', we were once again hurtling down the road to damnation. Pretty soon, we were up there doing a ton again and I was remembering prayers I thought I had left behind for good in childhood.

A rosary, sermon and benediction later and we were pulling up outside the airport terminal and it was a very happy *moi* who got out. Curiously, the meter said fourteen euros, but Stav assured me that meant thirty, but what the hell? I was alive.

Only once do I remember having been even more relieved to get out of a road vehicle, and that was after a trip in a Bulgarian minibus to a monastery in the mountains about a hundred clicks from Sofia. It makes me think of Apocalypse Now – 'seventy-five clicks up river into Cambodia'. Coming back, the guy drove like the utter madman he was and at one point we actually took off from the road – I swear, we did! It was only a split-second or so, but we were airborne. A little further on, some gadgy started to overtake us but had to abort when a head-on collision with someone coming around the (blind) bend from the other direction looked inevitable. The abort manoeuvre was not of the put-the-brakes-on-and-slip-back-behind-the-car-you-were-overtaking variety. More of your swerve-onto-the-gravel-hard-shoulder-on-the-other-side-and-bounce-around-like-crazy-until-you-finally-skid-to-a-dust-swirling-halt type. Inch'Allah.

Having survived *Acropolis Now*, I checked in with loads of time to spare, so managed to doss for a bit lengthways on the chairs at the departure gate, and then doss some more on the plane, on and off. This dossing business, or alternatively getting mildly steamed, is actually a good strategy if you are afraid of flying. Either way, you are pretty much out of it. For more useful tips read on, you nervous flyers...

Try not to dwell on the fact that an aeroplane comprises hundreds of thousands of individual bits and thousands of assemblies, and that ninety per cent are safety-critical. In other words, if one of them fails, it probably means curtains. Though the curtains separating business class from us *hoi polloi* (funnily enough, that's Greek: *hoi* means 'the' and *polloi* means 'many' – it must be rubbing off) are actually among the least safety-critical of an aircraft's component parts, so don't worry unduly if the curtains jam as the stewardess is trying to pull them to before takeoff. By the same token, don't dwell on the fact that the proper maintenance of an aircraft depends on, well, human beings. People like you and me. People who occasionally have too much to drink and feel lousy the morning after the night before. People like irate Olympiakos fans who maybe got pissed after we beat them and then went home and had a blazing row with their lass, slept in the next morning and got to work ten minutes late, got a bollocking from the boss and spent the first hour fumbling around with their spanner and cursing a stinking rotten headache.

Nay, verily I say unto thee, dwell not upon suchlike things.

Arrived at Brussels bang on schedule and got back home in ample time to pick Tina up from her final dancing class in Luxembourg on the Friday evening. Her *premier bal* on the Saturday evening went brilliantly, despite my attempts at dancing. Mind, I went on a dancing course myself – a quarter of an hour's worth in our living room just before setting off for the ball. It was a great night and we didn't get back hyem till nigh-on four on the Sunday morning. So there was nothing for it but to sleep all day and get up just in time to watch our FA Cup Quarter-Final against Spurs. Watching it, I convinced myself it could be our season after all. (Will I ever learn?) Kluivert scored the only goal that counted in the match, with almost a repeat of his goal at Olympiakos, except this time he was fed by Shearer instead of Milner. The gods (and my personal household god Fortuna in particular) were surely with us. We had beaten seven and two half-man Chelsea, and then nine-man Olympiakos and now we beat Spurs one-nil when really they had an entirely justified penalty appeal turned down and a perfectly good goal disallowed.

Mind, Kluivert had an equally onside goal chalked off too. So that would have made the score two-one to us, because Shay would surely have saved their pen, he was in such fantastic form that Sunday! I was even beginning to warm (or thaw out, maybe) towards Souness, who, it has to be said in all fairness, was at least saying all the right things in his TV interviews. I particularly liked it when he was asked, before the Spurs game, if he was aware of the Geordie passion for the FA Cup. He replied 'I'm aware of the Geordie passion – full stop!' On this unparalleled run of luck, we would surely now be drawn against Blackburn in the semis (no disrespect, but they were definitely the preferred choice). In fact, they were the most popular team left in the Cup – everyone wanted to play them. We were duly drawn against Man Utd, of c(o)urse.

The following Thursday saw the Olympiakos return leg at St. James's. Olympiakos were naturally missing their two red-carded players, and one of the yellow-carded ones was out under the totting-up rule. It turned out to be a stroll, ending in a four-nil win with two goals from Shearer (he could have had four) and one apiece for Dyer and Bowyer. Dyer's back-heel into the left corner of the net was, in his own words, 'cheeky', and a bit similar to a goal Thierry Henry had scored early in the season, which led to the London media calling him a 'genius'. The same papers just said Dyer was 'cheeky'. Graeme Souness's experiment of playing Dyer up front with Shearer in a 'Bellamy' role worked out really well – it was one of Dyer's best ever games. Our seven-one aggregate victory could not fail to impress all of the other seven teams left in the competition. Sporting Lisbon went through at the expense of a battling and rather unlucky Middlesbrough, who just couldn't overcome the two-three reverse they had suffered in the home leg, missing a number of good chances to draw level and ultimately losing four-two on aggregate. Joining us in the draw were the very impressive AZ Alkmaar and Villarreal, as well as Parma, CSKA Moscow, Auxerre, and Austria Wien.

The draw took place on Friday, the eighteenth of March, and we ended up paired with Sporting for the Quarter-Final and the winners of the AZ Alkmaar v Villarreal tie in the Semi-Final. This looked to be the toughest half of the draw, with in my humble estimation any of these four teams likely to beat any of the other four in the eventual Final. Shows how much I know, you might be able to tell me later. We don't know yet. The stage was set for Sporting at SJP on the seventh of April, with the away game on the fourteenth.

Sporting Lisbon – four months on

What a week! On the Friday, we were happily digesting the excellent news that Alan Shearer had decided to stay on for an extra year, taking a player-coach role. Mind it was April Fools' Day, so we had to do some double-checking of the veracity of the statement. Things were really looking good. When Saturday comes, it all changes in the space of a couple of seconds. We lose to Aston Villa three-nil. Okay, we can accept that. But we also lose three players. Taylor sent off to loud cheers for deliberate handball and a John Wayne shoot-out acting performance as he saves a goal-bound shot. Okay, we can accept that too. Dyer and Bowyer sent off for fighting each other while we're actually attacking the Villa penalty area. We can't accept that. Nor can anyone in the world of football. You don't need us to remind you. On top of that, the Pope died the same day. 'Bowyer and Dyer, they'll be the death of m…,' he might well have said. At least that rather bigger event put us on the back pages instead of the front. Except in the Toon papers, of course, who always have their priorities tuned to the sensibilities of the Geordie nation. When I was little, I remember that there used to be fight bills posted around the Toon. White or yellow they were, filled up all over with black writing: St. James's Hall, I think it was called, main bout tonight Dyer v Bowyer, referee Gareth Barry. Thank goodness he acted fast to pull them apart.

I am writing this particular paragraph the day after the Bowyer-Dyer fight, so I don't know how things are going to pan out, but it's hardly going to be a week where everyone's going to be focused on the main task of beating Sporting. Because I think that is what we have to do. All the rest will be a distant memory in a few months from now, but winning a Cup will last us forever. So let's hope that whatever decisions are taken, all are done with the aim of giving us the best chance to go on and win something. Any drastic actions

189

against individuals can wait for later, in the summer break. That's the way I feel right now.

Even without the self-imposed troubles, we've got selection problems. Bramble is out for at least a month, and more likely six weeks, after a hernia operation performed the day after the victory over Spurs. Babayaro and Kluivert haven't been properly fit for ages. O'Brien's confidence is very low after a poor performance at the weekend. We go into the game in not particularly high spirits, but with the whole European football world looking on, wondering 'whatever will they manage to do next?'

Well it's late on Thursday night now and what we managed to do was win. A one-nil victory, and well-deserved it was. Despite all the Portuguese side's possession and superior passing, and play-acting and diving, we restricted them to a couple of half-chances and a very good Steve Harper save in the second half when he came on in place of Shay. On our side, we had an excellent goal by Shearer with a glancing header into the corner of the goal from a Robert free kick disallowed because the referee said it had been taken too early. The goal that counted involved the same two players, but this time it was a clever move with Shearer stepping away from the goal while Ameobi blocked Al's marker from following him. Robert's corner was pinpointed to just the right place for Shearer to stride in and propel a blockbuster header into the goal.

The defence was solid, with Taylor for the first time playing at centre half right from the start of a game and looking strong and decisive. He certainly is some tough customer for a nineteen-year-old. The way he shepherded one ball out with a Portuguese attacker punily bouncing off his back brought a big smile to everyone's faces. There were only a couple of shaky moments, one when Robert completely fluffed a clearance. But the defence can maybe breathe easier in the return game because Sporting's leading goal scorer Liedson got himself a yellow card which puts him out of the return leg.

Despite all his troubles, Kieron Dyer was as lively as he had ever been over the last few weeks and frightened the Sporting defence on a number of occasions. And when he came off after pulling up hesitantly half way through the second half, who else should replace him but Lee Bowyer? They lofted their arms and grasped hands as they passed each other. Now Dyer had been given a good reception at the start of the match by the crowd, but the cheer that they gave Bowyer must have brought a lump to his throat. We can't really say if he deserved it, but you have to salute our terrific fans for their loyalty to the greater cause. This was undoubtedly the moment of the night.

We had a number of other opportunities to score more goals, with both Ameobi and Milner guilty of not getting off the final shot when they'd both created excellent openings in breakaway moves towards the end of the match. On another occasion, Ameobi charged down the goalkeeper and would have scored into an open goal if play hadn't been stopped for his handball. But it was totally involuntary as the goalkeeper blasted the ball against him and he made no move at all towards the ball with his arm.

Winning was important, but not conceding an away goal was even more pleasing. Funnily enough, it was exactly the same score as in the home game thirty-seven years ago when Pop Robson got the goal. The tie's delicately poised and we've got it all to play for. If we can repeat the one-all draw from all those years ago, then we're through again. And if Ameobi and Milner had both 'converted their chances', as they say, then we could have afforded to lose four-one in Lisbon and still go through on the away goals rule. Let's hope it doesn't end with a penalty shoot-out!

Sporting in Lisbon

Wasn't it good to be contemplating a trip to the springtime warmth of southern Europe with a good home result in the bag? Give us that any day if the alternative could have been facing postponements because of a few snowflakes settling on the reclaimed wastelands of Teesside. Maybe we'd felt a little bit sorry for the Boro when they lost out to Sporting, but there's no room for sentimentality here. We could, however, take heart from Middlesbrough's performance in Lisbon as they really missed a host of chances to bring their tie level.

Before we boarded in Brussels, we took the sensible precaution of rubbing the feet of the Angel of the North in Terminal A for good luck. I actually went one step further this time and draped my Toon top over the shoulders of the Angel and took a good photo. All this before a world-wide audience of streams of businessmen and tourists descending the escalator and no doubt wondering who this gadgy was performing some kind of ritual ceremony in front of some straight-winged, straight-spined statue in the departures hall. We couldn't do much more to ensure our good luck, could we?

The Virgin plane was nicely on time, leaving at a quarter past seven in the morning, with me happily settled into a front row seat with loads of legroom, and Neale further back down the plane having a good lie-in. The plane was maybe two-thirds full. We were lucky that we didn't choose the SN-TAP airlines alternative, as their plane was cancelled! We were also lucky that we were travelling on the fourteenth of a month rather than the twelfth or thirteenth, because on those days of each month the planes are full of pilgrims heading from all over the place to the shrine of Fatima, north of Lisbon. We were latter-day pilgrims, precisely one day later, headed for the shrine hidden somewhere in the José Alvalade XXI Stadium. The first time I visited Lisbon was on one of those Fatima days and it was only later that I'd found out why I had been accompanied by a host of nuns and monks, priests, the elderly and the infirm. I'd been wondering what I'd stumbled into.

It reminds me of the morning of the Arsenal FA Cup Final day. A bright warm spring day saw many of us congregating in Trafalgar Square. Another coincidence that, because Trafalgar is of course a Cape to the south of Portugal owned by those other inhabitants of the Iberian peninsula, not the Portuguese. A further coincidence there, because this year is the two-hundredth anniversary of the great sea battle, with celebrations planned in the Toon because of the aforementioned Lord Collingwood connections. He went to my school, you know. Mind, he wasn't in my year. He was Nelson's right-hand man, wasn't he? And we all know that Horatio needed a right-hand man more than most, in view of his major deficit in that department. The square was almost exclusively black and white, save for a few tourists taking photos. How would they have explained those photos when they got home to Minnesota, or Tokyo?

'Who all those stlipy guys alound you?'

'Oh, they cockneys. In Rondon, they arrl dless in brack and white and go singing in square on Sarraday morning. It a tladition.'

'Ah so…'

They too must have been wondering what they'd stumbled into.

Portugal has the great good fortune and taste to be on our wavelength in more ways than one: not only are they our oldest allies, sharing several common enemies over the years (they can't stand mackems), but also they have chosen to stay in the same time zone. It's not so much the same wavelength as the same longitude, come to think of it. Mostly because their country is in just the right place on the map, just about due south of Greenwich. When you live *sur le continent*, the enjoyment of heading to England, or Portugal, is further enhanced by the knowledge that, every morning you're there, you'll get an extra hour to snooze and/or take a leisurely breakfast, with your body clock being one hour ahead on euro-time. We arrived not long after nine, after almost three hours of flying. The airport even had a UEFA Cup carpet, which you had to walk along to get to passport control. They were taking things seriously, hoping that it was going to be Sporting walking victoriously down this carpet after the away leg of the Semi-Final on their way to playing the Final in their own ground.

We met up with a couple of fellow Toon travellers who were also musing on how to get into Lisbon toon, and since there were four of us we thought we might as well all go together in a taxi. They had come in via Frankfurt from Manchester, which seemed quite an imaginative route, and must have got up even earlier than us. The crack was of course about the prospects for the match, and we learned that Robert had made some kind of outburst and was unlikely to play. This didn't bode well. Still, everyone was hopeful that with a bit of luck we could scrape through, possibly on away goals. The ride into town only takes perhaps twenty minutes, and it cost us the princely sum of six euros, less than four airport bus tickets. We got out with our fellow travellers at their Sheraton Lisboa Hotel and, after our *aux revoirs*, walked on to the giant Marques de Pombal roundabout and down the main Avenida de Liberdade to our Hotel Jorge V. The Marques de Pombal was responsible for planning and re-building Lisbon with its impressively grand boulevards and squares after the giant earthquake of All Saints' Day, 1755. That was the earthquake that tipped the scales for Voltaire and convinced him once and for all that this wasn't the best of all possible worlds, and so he wrote *Candide* to get his point across in a comical vein.

I'd chosen the Jorge V hotel partly on the basis that it was called Portuguese George, a bit like the Greek George hotel we'd stayed at in Athens, and partly because the girl at reception was called something that sounded like Cunégonde. There was a bit of a mix-up at reception, however, as they'd lost our reservation and the hotel was full. Some ridiculously optimistic guy by the name of Pangloss had got one of our rooms, apparently. Luckily, we had a copy of the e-mail booking correspondence, and after a spot of foot and room shuffling (it beats foot and mouth) they were able to offer us a two-room suite for the price of a single room for Neale and me, and a double room for Sarah and Chris, who were due to arrive around lunchtime. I am not sure what the other guests thought of their more densely-packed accommodation, but we were happy. So maybe this was, after all, *le meilleur des mondes possibles.*

Pete sadly had had to call off his trip to Lisbon at short notice as his Mam had become very ill and died on the thirteenth. So he was of course back in Geordieland this time.

To pass the time on the plane, I'd looked through the in-flight magazine and read the sightseeing recommendations. Virgin's is one of the better ones for advice, though it maybe tries to be a bit too trendy for its own good. What you really need is a picture and a description of the authors to be able to know whether you should take any notice of what they advise. They told us to take a walk around the old Alfama district, located on one of the seven hills on which Lisbon is built. I thought that was Rome! The *Castelo de Sao Jorge* sits atop the hill. That also reminded me of Saint George on Mount Lycabettus in Athens. This opportunity to kind of re-trace our footsteps rather appealed, so Neale and I followed the beckoning of the blessed Virgin and hiked our way up to visit Saint George in his castle. What a great view you get of Lisbon and its harbour and the *Rio Tejo* estuary from up there - well worth the entrance fee we'd had to pay.

There was a bunch of about fifteen people huddled over by the ramparts, and it was apparent from the bright lights and umbrella-shaped reflectors that they were filming. On closer investigation, we learned that they were making an advert for the local brew, 'Super Bock'. Why do they need fifteen people to take a video of a girl holding up a glass of beer to the horizon? They were having trouble with the look of the beer and kept pouring out new glassfuls. Then, sacrilege of sacrileges, they started pouring away the televisually unsatisfactory ones down the castle drain.

'What a waste! It can't taste that bad, can it?' we asked, appalled.

'Pass 'em over here and we'll save you the effort of having to pour it away.'

They weren't too friendly. In fact, they told us to go away, to mind our own business and not to take any pictures. So we took a few pictures holding up one of the discarded bottles. It's a free world, isn't it? And we'd even paid to get into this particular part of the free world!

You don't get much to eat on Virgin unless you pay through the nose. Mind, their coffee's the best you can get while airborne. So after a leisurely and late breakfast in the Castle grounds, we strolled on down the hill to meet up with Don and Alec in the square beside the city-centre *Rossio* station. They had found the attraction of Super Bock at sea level greater than a mountain climb. In their company were 'Ginger' Kev (Kevin Keegan signed his arm), last seen in Breda and Sochaux, and Rick, with whom we'd shared extortionately-priced drinks in the team hotel in Basel.

There was quite a crowd of Toon wallahs in the square and the atmosphere was most welcoming. The Super Bock was flowing freely and quite right too, as it really is rather super. Though maybe they should ask their PR people to be a little bit better at PR.

It took Sarah and Chris a while to find us, because unbeknownst to us there are two squares beside the *Rossio* and they'd been looking for us in *Praça Dom Pedro V*, while we were in *Praça da Figueira*. Luckily, Sarah and Chris hadn't noticed any problem at all at the hotel, so the re-arranged booking had gone very smoothly. There were hordes of street sellers trying to off-load their hoards of eighties mirror shades, but they weren't finding many takers at all. They were getting to be a bit of a pest. When the next seller came along, he suddenly found himself with one of the Toon Army up alongside him, marching on the spot with his arm around his shoulder and bursting into a raucous chorus of 'Is this the way to Amarillo', Peter Kay style. The same thing happened to the next, and the next. It caused great merriment, and it had the desired effect, as no more hawkers dared approach us. They couldn't work out what was going on, and still less what was likely to happen next.

We still had our ten tickets between Neale and myself, what with every man-jack of our belt-and-braces applications all coming up trumps. (How about that for a mixed metaphor?) We had three from our season ticket applications, three from our better-connected friends, and four in the Sporting seats from Amadeu, Pete's Portuguese colleague who'd been down in Lisbon for a holiday at Easter. Asking around in the square, we found that we weren't the only ones with spare tickets. Don and Alec told us that they'd passed by the ground on the way down to the city centre and had seen people queueing up. That was it, probably the only way we were ever going to off-load ours was to go up to the ground and see if anyone in the queue would take them off our hands. Down in the town, they were just about as saleable as eighties mirror shades.

By contrast, there was a national shortage of tickets for Sunday's Semi-Final in Cardiff and we had quite a bit of ticket-swapping to do. We'd all brought our tickets to Lisbon to share them out in the sunshine. Brother Ian had managed to get me one ticket just behind the goal, but I was hoping to find two together so that I could be beside son Brian. Don had a spare ticket up near the half-way line. Sarah had a seat beside Chris up in the back row of the gods, but through unfortunate timing Sarah had pre-arranged to go to Holland on a business trip. The solution was that I swapped with Chris so that he could have Don's spare seat, Brian and I would use Chris and Sarah's seats, and Neale would take Ian's spare seat. Got all that?

I borrowed Don's Lisbon Metro-Mover ticket and headed up on the green line to the *Campo Grande* stop, right outside the José Alvalade XXI Stadium. I got chatting to a pretty blonde girl sitting next to me who turned out to be English and who worked in a language school right beside the ground. She was working in evening classes, otherwise she might have come along, but she promised she'd ask some of her fellow teachers whether they would like to buy some of our tickets. In any event, there weren't all that many punters queueing up and I wasn't too hopeful of success. By chance, the first group of lads I asked were seven Danish tourists, and so it was out with my best *Dansk*. I thought I was going to sell them nearly all of the eight tickets straight off, but then they stalled when I explained that four were in the Newcastle end and four in with the Sporting fans. Understandably enough, they wanted to sit together, so we asked the box office if they had three tickets in the same block as our Sporting tickets, but they didn't. So it was back to the drawing board. Then someone with a Lancashire accent pitched up in the company of three Portuguese. He preferred to be in with the Newcastle fans, but his friends wanted to be in with the Portuguese. Same problem again! But this time I was in luck as the Lancashire lad was really keen on being in with us and he eventually overcame quite a bit of reluctance on the part of his pals, and he bought all four Toon tickets. After that, I just walked up to Portuguese fans as they approached the box office and sold the other tickets as two pairs. All in all, it only took about a quarter of an hour, and instead of looking at a loss of about two hundred euros, we were all square, give or take a few euros. Then it was back down on the Metro to meet the others and take in a few of the Lisbon sights.

Sarah and Chris had been looking up things to do and suggested a ride up to the *Bairro Alto* in the old *Santa Justa* cast-iron lift designed in 1901 by a disciple of Gustave Eiffel, of Tower fame. It creaked and groaned as it raised us up from ground level to the top where there was a footbridge across onto the *Bairro Alto* hill. All well and good, but the footbridge was closed, and of course they had 'forgotten' to tell us that when we'd bought the tickets. This explained why they had told us that we could only buy return tickets, when we'd actually wanted singles to take the lift up and then stroll back down the hill. Still, it was a good view from the top, which we had plenty of time to admire in the half an hour or so that we had to queue up behind all the other dupes to get the lift straight back down!

We couldn't face walking up the hill after that, so instead we had a bit wander around the town. For reasons best known to himself, Don decided to help some ladies to clean their shop windows with a big mop. It was clear that initially they weren't quite sure what to make of this kind offer, but when they saw the great job Don was making of it they were very grateful and posed for photos.

After all that hard work, it was time for pre-match eats in the *Rua Portas de Sao Antao* pedestrian zone. The two most typical choices on the menu were pork and clam stew and *bacalhao* salted, dehydrated cod. By Poseidon, was that fish salty! While we waited for it to be re-hydrated and prepared, we tucked into mounds of delicious *iberico*-style ham, *manchego*-style cheese, and olives. I must look up the Portuguese equivalents of the more familiar Spanish names.

They're probably pretty similar words anyway, because that's how it is between Portuguese and Spanish. Oftentimes there's just one letter difference between the two. For instance, if it's an 'n' in *San*, the Spanish saint, it's an 'o' in Portuguese *Sao*. A Spanish garden is a *jardin*, but it's a *jardim* in Portuguese. While in Spain we *vamos a la playa*, it's off to the *praia* in the Algarve. The languages really are very close. There again, sometimes Portuguese is just like English and nothing like Spanish: *cha* is exactly equivalent to our cup of char, both coming from the Chinese word for tea, while the Spanish call it *té*.

On the way up to the ground on the Metro, we got talking to a young Sporting supporter. He was probably about fifteen years old, very polite and spoke beautiful English. He said he and his *amigos* already had four tickets for the Final, which they'd got through the uefa.com Internet sale. It had been organised in February exclusively for Portuguese locals and had sold out in about fifteen minutes. We'd tried to get tickets through our Portuguese friends, but they couldn't even log on to the site, it was so log-jammed. We joked with him that we'd meet up after the match and buy his tickets from him, as by then, he'd not be needing them any more. We hoped.

We were in the section down by the corner flag in the equivalent of the end of the Milburn Stand nearest the Leazes. It's a clean, modern stadium, decorated in a strange mosaic of pastel colours, predominantly green and yellow, but with seats in plenty of other colours including white, mauve, orange and pink. It looks a bit like a flower-strewn meadow. Like the Olympiakos stadium, or in fact like St. James's come to think of it, transport is ideally organised with the Metro station just a minute's walk away.

Our side had a few changes compared to the home leg. Most notable was the absence of Robert, which we'd heard about earlier. Apparently, he'd opined that we were not playing as well as last year. Not many would have disagreed with him, but maybe he could have left it unsaid for a little while longer. We also had Titus Bramble back, only four weeks after his groin operation, which must have been a medical record. Dyer was also playing despite having ongoing hamstring problems. Rested from Premiership duties, he and Bowyer would, we hoped, both be able to expend their energies to good effect. The team was Given, Bramble and Taylor in the centre, Carr and Babayaro as fullbacks, Jenas, Faye, Bowyer and N'Zogbia in midfield, and Dyer playing with Shearer in attack.

The game began in much the same way as the SJP leg had been played, with Sporting's players again giving our lads a lesson in close control and how to pass the ball to one another. We were defending the end nearest to the Toon supporters in the first half. The atmosphere in the home section was very much as it is at St. James's nowadays: subdued. With our Olympiakos experience still fresh in our minds and still ringing in our ears, this was a bit of a letdown. But the Toon Army was in good voice, if a little apprehensive. It certainly is true that, if you want to be surrounded by singing and excitement, you need to go to a Toon away match.

Luckily, just like in the first leg, the Portuguese were very shot-shy. They played neatly and brought the ball up to our area, but were very reluctant to take the responsibility to get it into the box. Our defence, with Titus and Taylor at its heart, was looking rather comfortable. And then, half way through the first period, Dyer burst down the right, into the penalty area and put the ball through Ricardo's legs and into the goal. Pandemonium! An away goal! Now Sporting would have to score three goals to beat us! The way we were playing at that moment, it looked a tall order. Bramble and Taylor were defending solidly, and Dyer was terrorising them and could have scored twice more if he hadn't been flagged just offside. Bowyer too had a great chance when Shearer presented him with an opportunity right in front of the goal, but he skied it over. Back in Geordieland, meanwhile, Pete was avidly watching events unfold from the temporary sardine tin that was the Cumberland Arms on Tynemouth Front Street.

Too right I was, Barry. I had inexplicably got the timing all wrong (my internal clock must still have been on Central European Time) and had crow-barred my way into the stowed-out bar just after Dyer had scored. In fact, they were just showing the slow-motion replay. This was in the big lower-level bar area of the Cumberland, as opposed to the narrower upper-deck bit. Like I say, it was jam-packed and you were having to ask people to pass money to the barmaid for you and hand your pint back over tops of heads. Most of us were focused on the giant screen in front of the window facing onto Front Street, but at the back of the bar area there was also a small telly which some people were watching. I had managed to get to a standing-sardine position somewhere in the middle and was watching the giant screen. But a few lads and lasses in front of me were watching the smaller telly behind me. So as I gazed forward mostly over backs of heads, quite a few faces were looking back over my head. It was a strange sensation. The place was absolutely buzzing. What a fantastic position the Toon were in, though but: two-nil up on aggregate with about a third of the second leg gone. That looked briefly like an unassailable lead! The beer was gannin' doon nicely and I started to work out arrangements for getting to Alkmaar. We later learned that Steve over in the Netherlands had gone one better and already become the proud owner of an AZ Alkmaar membership card in the hope of a chance for a Semi-Final ticket. Still, one consolation for him this year was that his adopted *ersatz* team Sparta won promotion to the top flight of Dutch football after a three-year absence. Sausage-side, however, both Rot-Weiss Essen and Eintracht Trier were relegated from the German second division. Such is life. Bet you were all in a very optimistic frame of mind over in Lisbon.

You bet we were. And if we could sneak another, or at least hold out to half time, we would surely stand a great chance to make it to another Semi-Final. But we couldn't. Just a few minutes before the break, Titus unluckily only managed to deflect the ball on to Niculae who scored with a header to bring his side level on the night. And Sporting would have scored another had it not been for a magnificent bit goalkeeping from Shay just before the whistle blew for the break.

Talk at half time was over whether we could hold on. We were still ahead, and they still needed to score another two goals to overcome our away goal advantage. In the queue for the drinks stand, I met Clarky from my old school, last seen in Sochaux, and I distinctly remember holding up three fingers and saying 'They need to score three goals, man, we're going to be alright.' Clarky was hopeful, but he wasn't so sure.

The half-time crack in the Cumberland was very much centred on a forthcoming weekend shopping trip to South Shields being organised by the Tynemouth Ladies' Sewing Circle. Only kidding: the bar staff were rushed off their feet as just about everybody was ordering their refills, and the loud and general consensus was that we were going to squeeze through in the end. Alkmaar, here we were coming...

The first disappointment when the teams came back out was that Jenas wasn't with them. He'd been harrying their midfield pretty well, but he'd damaged a calf and couldn't continue. Luckily, the RSPCA didn't find out about the calf business. His replacement Milner is a different kind of player. While he couldn't do the harrying job that Jenas had done so well, he did have a real chance to score from a Dyer cross with his first touch. Surely that would have been the killer blow, but it wasn't to be. Sporting came at us early in the second half, but we were withstanding the challenge pretty well until two more injuries followed in quick succession. First Bramble was in trouble, obviously not fully healed from his operation, and he was replaced by Andy O'Brien. Then Dyer pulled up in the middle of a run and it was clear his hamstring had tightened again. There was still half an hour to go and we were now deprived of three of our best performers in the match so far. Kluivert came on for Dyer, but the challenge that he presented was not the same as Dyer's and the Portuguese defence seemed to breathe a collective sigh of relief.

I happened to look up at the stadium clock as it showed twenty minutes to go. The score was still one-one and we were hanging on. I thought to myself that these next twenty minutes were going to decide a lot of people's happiness, and for some even their future careers. I still held out some hope, but at the same time I felt there was an inevitability about what was unfolding before our eyes. One minute later it was two-one when a fluffed clearance by Andy O'Brien landed unluckily at the feet of Sporting captain Pedro Barbosa. Given pushed his weak shot away, but again it fell nicely for the Portuguese and Sa Pinto had the easy task of rolling it into the net. Now we were only leading because of our away goal. The Portuguese section of the stadium, which had been very quiet up to now, came back to life and they started waving their flags.

When the other side's got no goals with nearly half the game gone, scoring three looks like a pretty tall order for them. But when they only have to score one more with twenty minutes left and you're short of three of your best players, you're just waiting for it to happen. We didn't have to wait long. With just over ten minutes to go, they got a corner and Beto headed it in. The whole energy of the Toon following slumped in direct proportion to the outburst of joy from the massed ranks of the Sporting crowd.

Back in the Cumberland you could have heard a pin drop. Even in the Kronenbourg you could taste the bitterness of disappointment and our old friend despair. 'A divvent believe it, A just divvent believe it', people were heard to say as they virtually sobbed into their pints. Was there any way back?

No, there didn't seem to be, even though just one goal would have restored our overall lead. We did our best to raise the spirit of the team and they did rally back, and Faye and Kluivert both had chances which they might have taken on another occasion, but it was all to no avail. And as we pushed more and more men forward in increasingly desperate attempts, Rochemback broke through with time just about up to make it four-one. What was the difference between three-one and four-one? At least it showed that we'd been trying to fight back.

In many ways it was like the Marseille Semi-Final of last year all over again. Too many injuries, both physical and psychological, tearing at the fabric and gnawing at the spirit of the team. Last year, the one key injury had been to Jonathan Woodgate. He'd played in the first leg and turned in a sterling performance, but had been injured before the away leg. This year the injuries happened in the middle of the game itself. We weren't the same without Jenas, Dyer and Bramble. And now we had to go to Cardiff without them too.

We congregated back in the same bar in the same square as in the afternoon, and we were soon joined by Sarah and Chris's friends Eric and Pat from Worcester and their friends Peter and Clive from Carlisle and the mythical Alan from Gateshead, whom Pete first met in Zurich and who by strange coincidence also is a friend of Sarah and Chris's friends. We'd all met pre-match in Heerenveen, at the pizzeria, and they would all be in Cardiff too. We also met up with the two lads who'd shared the taxi with us that morning. It's a small world. And we got talking to a lad called Steve, who told us he worked in Luxembourg, like wor Pete. On further investigation, we learnt that his wife worked in the same complex as Pete. It's a small, small world after all. Disney wrote a song about it, and a very catchy one too.

Talking of songs, Clive is a great singer. A booming Geordie voice, full of confidence and indomitable spirit, and a cheery face crowned by a Sporting/Toon scarf worn as a bandana. Just what we needed to raise our spirits, forget the disappointment, and gird our loins for the challenge of the weekend to come. Like the bard and minstrel Homer telling stories of heroes from a bygone age, Clive went through his full repertoire and we joined in as many of the verses as we knew of 'The Blaydon Races' and 'Cushy Butterfield', before he finished them off solo for us. And then he moved on to a long medley of songs from the Fairs Cup and Supermac eras. 'Wisht lads, haad yer gobs, an' aa'll tell yiz 'boot the Cup', 'No says Joe, I don't think so', 'Supermac, Superstar', 'Frank Clark knows my fatha', and countless others. He knew verses that no one else had ever heard before and he was absolutely magnificent. It made us all proud to be Geordies; Geordies browbeaten but unbowed. There couldn't have been a better way to end the evening. Well, maybe if we'd won...

The cold light of morning told us that, once again, our pilgrimage had faltered. The road to Fatima had proven too hard for this band of disciples and our journey had been cut cruelly short. So too had the paths of Auxerre, beaten by CSKA Moscow by the same four-two aggregate score as ourselves, Austria Wien, who drew one-one but lost out to Parma on away goals, and Villarreal, narrowly beaten three-two by AZ Alkmaar. As we took our seats on the blessed Virgin's winged chariot we saw around us several fellow travellers who truly had been to the shrine of Fatima and were returning home with spirits restored and faith renewed. Not having benefited from the same holy experience, we would have to rely on our own inner belief in the suspension of reality to get us through the trials of the coming weekend.

After we landed, I had the chance to find out a little of what it's like to be an airline pilot. I got off the plane just about first, but I realised straight away that I'd forgotten my jumper, so I had to go back to fetch it. I had to stand at the front beside the stewardess and wait for everyone to file off, and as they left, everyone started to say goodbye and thanks for a good flight, not only to the lassie but also to me. With my white shirt and black trousers, they thought I was the pilot, so I got into the spirit of things and started to shake their hands for a laugh. 'Thank you for flying Toon Airways.' A nice way to round off the trip. For me, and for my passengers, too, I hope.

Now where exactly is Cardiff? I'd only been to Wales for a total of about four hours before, and all of that time was spent driving to and from the Irish ferry port. I had hardly had time to stand still in Wales. It's not an easy place to get to from the Toon. The only ways to do it in a day and be *compos mentis* by the end were to go on an organised coach (but it's a long, long trip) or one of the supporters' special chartered flights to the little Cardiff airport. Coming from Belgium and not being able to avail myself of those alternatives, an overnight stay was going to be necessary and it didn't take me long to work out that staying in Cardiff was not an option. For a start, the hotels apparently double their prices for match weekends, and in any case they were all full.

We weren't the only ones coming from afar for the match. Don told us about his friend Ashley, also from our old school. He had had quite a week. Ashley had come over from Canada to a business meeting in Nice, had diverted through London to meet Don to go to the Spurs game before heading back home to Canada, done a couple of days' work and then got right back on a transatlantic plane to come to Cardiff. How's that for dedication? And how did things look on Tyneside, Pete?

Well, Barry, I had some time on my hands on the Saturday and was in need of a long walk and some space. So what better place to go for both than Tynemouth Long Sands? And that little café on the beach just down from the Grand Hotel does a grand sausage and bacon sarnie (with a bit red sauce, please). And to go with it a nice mug of coffee and the Times, interspersed with a terrific view of the North Sea. There were plenty of white horses out there in the breeze. From the café, I walked along the beach and on to Cullercoats, from where I took the Metro into the Toon.

Although the place was half empty, even around the Monument, there was still an air of tangible expectation and excitement, as there just has to be on the day before Newcastle play in the Semi-Final of the Cup. Half way down Dean Street on my way to the Quayside, I bought the Chronic, and the drift of the back page was that we weren't going to win but everybody was going to have a good time regardless. Carried on down under the Tyne Bridge then along the Quayside to the egg-slicer and crossed into Piggy's-Waistc't, as I wanted to have a look inside the Sage slug-whale. Canny place, mind. In the cafeteria, I had a proper read inside the Chronic, which was full of interviews with the Toon Army. Between the various accounts I gazed up and over towards the Toon skyline, inevitably reflecting on the fact that there hadn't been an FA Cup victory parade since 1955. The Chronic told me that the Toon Army were travelling by coach, train and plane. One lot were travelling up to Edinburgh to catch their plane there! A few die-hard optimists said we would win, but most people were being realistic. One lad was quoted as saying it would be a very close-run affair, 'right up to kick-off'. I liked that.

Walked back into the Toon over the Tyne Bridge and met up with our Ireland-based marra Mike for a pizza at that great little place at the bottom of Westgate Road (Roma, I think it's called) opposite the Old Assembly Rooms. This was an appropriate venue, as Mike, Chris, Barry and I had originally planned to attend the Cuths annual gala dinner and piss-up in the Assembly Rooms on the fifteenth of April. As an RGS Old Boy, Barry wouldn't normally have attended a Cuths Old Boys' gathering, but this year's guest speaker was none other than Sir Bobby himself, so Barry was keen to go - despite threats of being chinned as an RGS intruder. A few weeks before the scheduled event, however, we all got word from the organisers that the dinner was being postponed until the 27th of May on account of the fact that so many Old Boys were planning to travel to Lisbon and/or Cardiff. Now where else would such a dinner be postponed because of football commitments? Glasgow and Liverpool, maybe, but that's about it! Mike had made arrangements to visit his Mam over that weekend and didn't want to disappoint her so had come to the Toon anyway. After the pizza we thought it might be a good idea to go to the pictures and we watched '*Der Untergang*' (Downfall) at that arty little Tyneside Cinema on Pilgrim Street opposite what used to be the Odeon. What an appropriate choice of title for this week of NUFC woe: Downfall! But as we were watching the film and reading the subtitles where necessary, thirty-three thousand of the faithful were slowly but surely making their pilgrims' progress towards Cardiff and possibly the Holy Grail. So what were your travel options, Barry?

One possibility was to fly to Bristol, which has a decent airport with international flights, but I worked out that the only way to get back was to fly out on Monday morning at about six o'clock, as there were no flights on Sunday evening. As it turned out, Bristol would have been a very bad idea anyway, because the train line to Cardiff was closed for repairs. Then I had the idea of making a family weekend of it and going across in the car through the Channel Tunnel. I checked the trains to see where they stopped, and found that you could go from Reading to Cardiff on a direct train in an hour and a half. Reading sounded like a good strategic point as it was very close to Legoland and that surely was an attractive prospect for the whole family, including me. I think it's a great place. The service and the quality are far better than the likes of Euro Disney.

As we drove round looking for the Holiday Inn Express, we passed by an old prison. This must have been the site of Oscar Wilde's 'Ballad of Reading Gaol.' As Oscar might have said, 'To lose one match four-one may be regarded as a misfortune; to lose both would look like carelessness.'

It was only a week after the Royal Wedding, so we had a trip around Windsor too. I wonder if Windsor is the only castle with a string of souvenir tat shops and burger bars on the other side of the street? What must the Queen think when she looks out of her windows and sees the view? Her windows face the other way, I suppose. But at least one of the white-painted buildings houses a hotel, with a good old-fashioned carvery restaurant on the ground floor. You can't beat a good English carvery. Just what we needed to set us up for the rigours of the next day's trip. The shops were full of Charles and Camilla souvenirs and we got ourselves a very presentable giant Union Flag tea towel with their portraits on. It looks canny good on my office wall, like, and everyone can see it when they walk in. No one quite knows what to make of it. What's that, Pete?

Well I for one certainly don't know what to make of it, Barry! You could always use it to wipe your shoes if you have the misfortune to tread in something at half-time on a future European adventure, like that lad in Heerenveen! It's a pity they didn't sell black-and-white-striped People's Republic of Geordieland tea-towels instead!

Very true. Anyway, this was our fourth FA Cup game this season playing London teams: Yeading, then Chelsea, then Spurs, and now Manchester. And after Blackburn had been knocked out the day before, we were going to face a fifth, Arsenal, in the Final if somehow we could survive against Manchester.

With the Millennium Stadium being a big ground and with most tickets going to the teams' fans instead of to sponsors and hangers-on for a change, there were around thirty-three thousand seats for each team and just about everyone who applied got tickets. I was just thinking, if we'd been allowed by the 'save the dogshit' brigade to build our big new stadium on Leazes Park, we might well have been playing the Semi-Final at the New St. James's instead of in Wales. After all, the result down in Lisbon meant that there was a good chance that Sporting were going to play the Final at their own ground, so why couldn't we have played this Semi-Final at St. James's? By the end of Sunday, an awful lot of people were going to be wishing that the game could have been played anywhere but Cardiff.

The reason was the disastrous transport provision. You would think 'First Great Western', who run the iron horses down south and west, would have worked out that the number of travellers was going to be somewhat higher than on your average sleepy Sunday morning. Do 'iron horses' make you think of cowboys? Does 'Western'? Well, so should 'First Great Western', because wild-west cowboy style is the way they run their operation. It had all started the day before when I called into Reading Station to pick up the tickets which I'd bought over the Internet from Belgium. They have a website which gives you a code number. You key it into a ticket dispenser and it prints out your tickets. Unfortunately, the website doesn't allow you to reserve seats from abroad, so I went into the Travel Office.

The lady told me that it was impossible to book seats, so I asked if I would still be able to catch the train. She said that there was no guarantee as a lot of people would be getting on in Paddington and I'd just have to turn up and hope. I told her that, if this was likely to happen, then I'd rather have my tickets refunded and I'd go by car instead. But she said I couldn't have the money back as I'd paid over the Internet so it was not her problem. It was between the Internet firm and me. I asked if I could speak to someone else and she said there was no one else! I gave up and went outside to look for the Station Master. He was a lot more helpful. He asked who had served me and, when I told him, he said that I must have been the fiftieth person to complain about her and that she was for the high jump, but the company rules meant that, at the moment, she was protected somehow. He reassured me that we should be alright to catch the train. To be sure, I decided we'd turn up early and catch the first possible one.

Brian and I were in the station before half past eight. On the way, we'd spotted a dog's turd in the shape of a cross. It must have been a religious dog, maybe a Saint Bernard? Perhaps this was a good omen, though maybe we should have stepped in it to make sure of our good luck. (And you could have put that Royal tea-towel to some good use – this an aside from Pete). The first thing we saw in the station was a monitor with a blue stripe across our line showing that the

8.38 Reading to Cardiff injun was not running. No one knew why. This was not the best of starts. The next train wasn't due for an hour or so, so we got ourselves a cup of coffee and went out onto the platform where we bumped into Stuart, the Manchester supporter who'd bought our spare ticket off us on the tram in Basel last season. Small world, yet again. Stuart had enjoyed his night out with the Toon in Basel, and was quietly confident that he was going to enjoy his afternoon in Cardiff. Then we bumped into Neale, which was less of a surprise, as he'd been toying with the idea of catching the train with us from Reading if he could persuade their lass to get up early on Sunday morning and drive him down from Suffolk.

Eventually the train pulled in and, of course, it was stowed out with everyone who'd been planning to catch the first train in Paddington too. We piled on to the first carriage and found ourselves riding shotgun in the caboose. The platform attendant got very officious and told us all that the train wouldn't be leaving until we moved out of the guard's van. But of course that was impossible as the adjoining carriage was jammed solid. That's why we were in the guard's van in the first place. After some negotiations, the town's lawmen came and guaranteed that if we got out with them they'd find us a space further down the train. Everyone dismounted and moseyed on half-way down the platform, where we were branded and shoehorned in again.

We got talking to an Australian couple, possibly called Bruce and Sheila, too, who were squashed in the end of the carriage with us. They said that it was their first ever football match and they'd be supporting Manchester, because they'd won Manchester-section tickets in their church raffle in London. Typical Manchester supporters. Then another coincidence, because who should squeeze past us but Clive. Not Clive the singer, but Clive, Chris's BBC colleague and son of Eric and Pat. And through the mass of standing fans, Clive pointed out Chris sitting half-way down the carriage.

Small world again! They'd been lucky and jumped on first at Paddington.

We trundled through various stations until we were ambushed at Swindon. Somehow, the First Great Western livery stable owners out in this Wild West frontier town decided that the train was now overcrowded and they demanded that a hundred and fifty hostages would have to get off and take their chances on the next stagecoach. Funny that, because no one got on in Swindon, so how could it be overcrowded now, when it had been allowed to leave all the previous stations? Of course, no one got off, as no one believed they would be allowed on the next train, which was surely going to be just as crowded. They said there was another wagon train just twenty minutes behind which we could catch, so we all decided to wait until that train arrived so we could check it out for space. Twenty minutes came and went and no train turned up, which convinced everyone even more that they were just feeding us lies.

The lady platform attendant was getting hysterical because only a few people had got off, and she said she was going to get the sheriff to take us all off the train. But when the posse from the local law came along, they were on our side and said they didn't blame us for stopping on the train and they would do the same themselves. They clearly thought, like us, that First Great Western was speaking with forked tongue. The fat controller lady still wanted another hundred people off the train. She said there was going to be an express directly to Cardiff. Would you have believed her? Well she didn't lie about it being an express train. In fact, it was so fast that it didn't even stop at our station!

An hour went by and it was getting uncomfortably close to the point where the train wouldn't have time to get us to Cardiff. High Noon! The polis told us that the promised train actually was just outside the station at last, and the cowboys had told them that it would leave before the one we were on. We had a look to assure ourselves and decided we might as well get off the first train and catch the new one, otherwise we were never going to make it. The tumbleweed rolled down the platform as we watched our new train pull in. As soon as it arrived, the first train left before they opened the doors for our new train.

We found some seats so we could sit down for the first time since we'd had our breakfast five hours earlier. The new train went even slower than the first and kept stopping out in the boondocks. Rail works at Dead Man's Gulch meant we had to be diverted via Cheltenham, or Gloucester (that's Trier's twin town, by the way) or some place like that. We were past caring. We limped over the mighty Severn, way upstream of the two Severn Bridges, rumbled past the monolithic block of Oldbury Nuclear Power Station and eventually staggered into Cardiff. We ran through the pouring rain and got to our seats at ten to two. Thanks very much, I don't think, to FGW. More than five hours for a ninety-minute journey. They used to say that the Great Western Railway's initials, GWR, really stood for God's Wonderful Railway. Well in that case, FGW must actually stand for Forget Going West. How were things stottie-side, Pete?

Well, Barry, by now I was firmly established in the Last Chance Saloon (the Cumberland Arms again), getting in my second pint of Kronenbourg sarsaparilla as kick-off time was rapidly approaching. (By the way, 'sarsa' means Bramble, so I chose knowingly.) This time it had been just impossible to get into the main bar area through the door on Tynemouth Front Street, so I had tied up the horse and moseyed up that little alleyway and pushed open the swinging doors into the saloon through the back entrance. As a result, I was on the upper deck but managed to get right through to the top of the steps looking down into the bar area and across to that giant screen again. And just like for the Sporting game, half the heads were turned to the giant screen, the other half towards the little telly at the other end. It was a strange sight, as it looked almost as if one half of the punters were not speaking to the other half and had simply turned their backs.

Nothing could have been further from the truth, however, as we were definitely United in the cause. The atmosphere was brilliant and the place was just buzzing with the pre-match crack. Again, people were being realistic but determined to enjoy the occasion anyway.

To get served, I was passing my money down a human chain to the bar and getting the beer via the same route in reverse. Some kind soul also sent a couple of serviette-wrapped sausages up the chain with the pint, as the management had done us proud with a terrific sausage and fried bread spread in the best tradition of Geordie pubs. You just cannot beat the Tyneside pubs and clubs, can you? And what I particularly like about the boozers in North Shields and Tynemouth is the fact that they so rarely have their names changed. The Cumberland has been the Cumberland for as long as I can remember, and that goes back to some under-age drinking of a Friday lunchtime back in the early seventies. Had a summer job as a petrol-pump attendant just around the corner opposite Knotts Flats, and Friday dinner was fish and chips at Marshalls followed by a pint in the Cumberland. Come to think of it, the interior of the bar area hasn't changed all that much since then either – which is great. And the Turk's Head is still the Turk's Head, the Gib is the Gib, and the Sally the Sally. It's the same throughout Shields... the Gunner, Ye Olde Hundred, etc. There have been some exceptions, however, and if you get into a Shields taxi and ask to be taken to the Wooden Dolly, the chances are the driver will ask 'which one?'. To which wor Mick once famously replied: 'the one that hasn't been called that for the past twenty-five years, of course.' Yes, time grinds along slowly in North Shields, thank goodness. It's such a pity that so many boozers in the Toon have had their names changed. But to me, the Printer's Pie is still the Printer's Pie and always will be...

An interesting feature of the Cumberland is that it doesn't say Ladies and Gents on the doors of the corresponding facilities. It doesn't actually say anything. Instead, there are illustrations. One is of a seagull, the other of a buoy. Now you can work out the buoy pretty quickly, but a seagull? It must have puzzled many a Geordie lass. Maybe it's a gurl? But today this was no place for Blackadders or Slackbladders, as it was well and truly stowed out, with the start of the FA Cup Semi-Final now just seconds away and no time left to battle your way to the bog, whether you were a seagull or a buoy! How was the build-up going in Cardiff, Barry?

Well, the magnificent atmosphere and the wall of noise in the Toon section ensured that all the trials and tribulations of the wagon train were instantly forgotten. We asked our neighbours and they told us that the team was Given, Boumsong replacing the newly injured Bramble alongside Taylor in the centre, Carr and Babayaro as fullbacks, Butt, Faye, Robert and Milner in midfield, and Ameobi partnering Shearer in attack. We had a seagull's eye view from right up in the last row of section U2, to the left of Shay's goal. We were ideally placed to watch Ronaldo take his tumble in the opening minutes and referee Mike Riley point immediately to the penalty spot. What was that pointing for after all? If he was pointing for a free kick, he's a very bad aim. So we survived that scare, but we couldn't survive for long. The wide-open prairies of our left side were being patrolled with little assurance or application by Babayaro and Robert and were happy hunting grounds for Neville, Ronaldo and Rooney.

We were protected from the elements by the roof, but the stadium authorities left the central section open, so the pitch and the players were left fully exposed to the torrential rain. For some reason, our players were less able than the opposition's to keep their feet in the slippery conditions. This led directly to the opening goal as first Babayaro's and then Boumsong's boots lost their grip, allowing Ronaldo the time to measure his cross to van Nistelrooy, who turned and guided the ball beyond Shay's outstretched fingertips. One-nil, and it had been coming. And it pains me to say it, but you've got to admit that the second goal was beautifully executed. Scholes rose to deflect an inch-perfect cross from Ronaldo over and out of reach of Shay Given and into the far corner of the goal without taking any of the pace off it.

In between times, we'd had our moments. We'd been the first to gain a corner, and a little later Robert had been put through but had been felled by a typically cynical Keane foul about twenty-five yards out. On both occasions, Robert had wasted the chance with a poor kick. Shearer got kicked in the head by Ferdinand for his troubles and was down for a few minutes while he received treatment. But if our players were losing on the pitch, we were winning hands-down on the terraces. It was the full Phil Spector wrap-around Byker Wall of Sound versus the Sunday School raffle prize-winners. No contest. The Sunday Schoolers must have felt as overwhelmed as we did when faced with the Marseille masses last year. Wave upon wave of songs and chants crashed upon the helpless banks of seated Manchester supporters cowering over on the other side of the field. You pitied them. The Manchester players and manager must be ashamed of them. We all know their captain is. And so too must be the small core of good and true supporters who follow them around to away grounds outside of London. It made you feel proud and very lucky to be there in the midst of a special occasion. Proud, no matter what was happening out on the pitch.

Dead right, Barry. The Soond o' the Toon came across beautifully on the big-screen telly (and the little ones) at the Cumberland, and plenty of us in this Last Chance Saloon were enthusiastically joining in the singing. The Toon Army were just outstanding, and the entire Geordie Nation was a proud witness. Managed to grab another couple of Cumberland sausages to go with my half-time pint. Did youz get some scran where you were?

I'm sorry to say the half-time catering was almost non-existent, Pete. Who ate all the pies? Arsenal and Blackburn on Saturday, that's who! The only 'food' they had in our section was crisps. How many of us did they think were coming?

We're not Blackburn, you know. They had left huge swathes of seats empty the day before, even though they had less than half the distance to travel that we did. The caterers didn't explain that you couldn't get pies or anything until you got to the front of the queue, then they told you to go somewhere else half-way around the other side of the ground. And then when you got there, all they had were manky half-cooked hot dogs.

The support got even better (if that is possible) in the second half, especially after Shola scored. Even though in our heart of thirty-three thousand hearts we knew it was hopeless, there rose a belief that we could score another, and we roared louder and louder. 'Toon, Toon, Black and White Army', as loud and as insistent as against Spurs in the Semi-Final of yesteryear; 'We are the Geordies'; 'Newcasserl, Newcasserl, Newcasserl'; plus the loudest 'Blaydon Races' we'd sung in a long while. There really was only one United that day: players and supporters United. There was another team with a similar name, but they were players and disparate onlookers. 'Four-one and you still can't sing' summed it up all too well.

Shola's goal came straight from the kick-off. It was only a pity that it wasn't from the second half kick-off, but from the re-start after their third goal. Otherwise, maybe we could have had some kind of a chance. Straight after the Ruud boy had got his second after good work from Butt combining with Rooney, Jean-Alain Boumsong bypassed their midfield with a through ball to Alan Shearer, who played it into space in the penalty area directly in front of where we stood. Shola ran on and threaded the ball underneath Howard's end. We celebrated as if it were one-nil, not one-three, and kept on going until the end of the match. Seven goals went into our net between Dyer scoring the opener in Lisbon and Shola's goal. Is that some kind of record? Our players had a good go, and a second goal was on the cards on several occasions in the following quarter of an hour, which was by far our best period of the game. But like so many times this season, and this week even, we made the chances and half-chances but no one was able to convert them into an end product. And then as we pressed forward, often with five up in attack like Manchester had been in the first half, the ball came out on the break to van Nistelrooy. He generously laid it off to Ronaldo to stroke it calmly beyond Shay's reach and it was four-one. Lady Bracknell would not have approved.

On the final whistle and after most of the team had come over to salute, we ran back to the station in the now monsoon-like rain. We mistakenly took the long way round, and when we got there the Wild Westerners were still up to their tricks, this time carefully corralling everybody up like cattle outside in the wet. How thoughtful! We needed to get back for our Channel Tunnel booking, so I showed our Belgian ID cards and explained our problem and they let us through to the front and eventually onto the platform. But the guards thought we were trying to escape from Wales and shouted 'Shut the doors, don't let them on.' We had to wait for an hour to catch the next train, but at least we got seats. The mad rush meant that all we'd seen of Wales was their football pitch and the inside of their Central Station. Pity really, because people say it's a good place. As we have been saying for fifty years now: 'Maybe next year!'.

Yeah, maybe next year (again). Maybe then pigs will fly at long last! Man U's man of the match was definitely Nicky Butt, and he fully deserved Ferguson's congratulatory embrace on the final whistle. Butt-features sportingly declined to go and salute the Toon Army. Well done, Butt, you have shown us your true colours, and we have seen red. It's here for you to read in black and white.

Lisbon again - Sporting v. Say Ess Kah

Pete wasn't interested in yet another Final without the Toon, but like last year UEFA had been very considerate and they'd booked the Final for the school half-term week, so I decided we'd still go and make the last leg of our pilgrim's odyssey into another family holiday.

This was the fourth time we were going to see Sporting play this season! The pre-season Newcastle-Gateshead tournament, then the home game in the group stage, then the away leg of the Quarter-Final, and now the Final itself. We couldn't make it to the home leg of the Quarter-Final. And to think that with fewer injuries, and with fewer squandered chances, especially in the home Quarter-Final, it could have been us.

In the meantime, I'd been up in Newcastle for a long weekend on the occasion of my fiftieth birthday, and had witnessed one of the finest displays of aerial prowess ever seen at St. James's. This far surpassed anything that famous headers of the ball like Wyn the Leap, or Gary Speed, or Alan Shearer had ever managed: the paper dart display put on at the Crystal Palace match when everybody made planes out of the green 'Pepperami' hot dog adverts that were stuck in plastic bags on the backs of our seats. It was the most memorable thing that happened all afternoon during the nil-nil draw. The best one flew down from the back of the Leazes and stuck like a javelin into the ground just a few yards to Shay's right.

We'd never had a holiday in Portugal before, and everybody was looking forward to it. I had booked us all onto the early Virgin flight on the Sunday before the match and we decided that we'd just hire a car and drive off and look around for a good place to stay rather than book up in advance. With Sporting being in the Final, we thought that that there wouldn't be a big demand for hotels as the supporters would all be locals, and we didn't expect all that many Muscovites would be making the trip either.

CSKA Moscow had strolled past a very young Parma team three-nil in the second leg in Moscow. The Parma club's priority was to escape relegation, so believe it or not they sent out a second team for a European Semi-Final. If only the draw had given us them instead of Sporting! The second leg of the other Semi between Sporting and AZ Alkmaar had been a great game, with the advantage switching back and forth throughout. It was all level on aggregate after ninety minutes, so it went into extra time. AZ Alkmaar scored in the first quarter hour of overtime, and up until the last minute, they were hanging on to a three-one lead, which would have seen them go through four-three on aggregate. Then, instead of running down the time, they allowed Sporting to get a goal kick, which goalkeeper Ricardo hoofed up field and the Portuguese got a corner. Ricardo then raced up into the penalty box and caused mayhem, and in the confusion the ball was headed in. It was just like the scenes when Bellamy scored the late winner at Feyenoord. What an incredible game. I felt sorry for AZ because they had the better of the play and had a really fast and skilful Moroccan winger called Tarik Sektioui, who would look geet good in a black and white shirt. They also had a tough and dirty veteran called Barry van Galen who elbowed at least two different Sporting players but never got caught. I don't know if they'll do anything with the video evidence. If I were Graeme Souness, I'd take one look at the video of Sektioui and sign him up forthwith.

On the ticket front, we had both applied for a pair of Final tickets even before the Quarter-Final games were played. And about two weeks before the Final, we were informed that we had succeeded in getting two, on the strength of Pete's application. Last year, remember, we had both been successful and got a total of four tickets. So, for the second year in succession we had secured tickets for the UEFA Cup Final. Had our luck now run its course, we wondered? If the

Toon ever reach the Final, will we get tickets? Who knows? It could be a purely academic question for some time to come...

UEFA said the tickets would be sent from HQ on the ninth, which was cutting it fine, as Barry and his family were flying from Brussels on Sunday the fifteenth of May. UEFA had also said that the tickets were being dispatched by a courier service, so that would speed things up, wouldn't it? Not necessarily! Because the whole courier service thing is based on the premise that someone will be at home to open the door. In other words, they are geared exclusively to business customers! If no one is there, the courier will not just pop the tickets through the letter box the way the postman would. Of course, no one was at home when TNT brought the merchandise on the Wednesday. But they left a little card to say they had called (one white duck on the wall!). This farce was enough to make me want to explode, alright. I rang the number on the card they had left. I was talking to a lassie in Saarbrücken:

'Could you maybe deliver them to me at my office here in Luxembourg? Or maybe to my marra in Brussels?'

'No.'

'Would you agree that this is rather a crap sort of service? Could the guy not simply have popped them through the letter box like a postman?'

'No. We're not allowed to do that. We're a courier service, you see?'

'It's a bit pointless really, isn't it, being a courier service but not actually delivering?'

'The customer's always right, Sir'.

'Can't this be sorted some way?'

'Well you could always send us an e-mail authorising us to pop the tickets through the letter box like a postman.'

'Well I'll do that, then'.

It really is farcical, isn't it? It would have made far more sense for UEFA to send the tickets by post. If you are not in when a recorded delivery arrives, at least you get a card which you can take to a local post office and collect the tickets that way. But TNT's office in Saarbrücken is a good hour and half's drive away. In other words, a morning off work. But the e-mail did the trick and the tickets were at home waiting for me when I got back from work on the Thursday evening. But there was still a problem. If I posted them on the Friday, there was no guarantee that the pony express would get them to Brussels in time. There was only one thing for it. Rendezvous in the Ardennes, Battle of the Bulge style...

We agreed to meet up roughly half-way between Brussels and Luxembourg at the Wanlin services that I told you about earlier: known to insiders as 'the Pyramid', because it looks rather like, well, a pyramid – it kind of straddles the *autoroute*.

It was stottin' doon on the Saturday morning. But, never mind, we both got to the Pyramid from our respective sides of Battle of the Bulge country and made the rendezvous in good time, a bit like spies parachuting in behind enemy lines. It probably looked a wee bit suspicious, like, when the envelope containing the tickets was exchanged for cash! John le Carré himself couldn't have set it up better! So we had a leisurely, if conspiratorial, breakfast and discussed the chances of Newcastle actually going anywhere next season. We accordingly parted company and headed back to Brussels and Trier in a state of abject depression.

Mind, Pete, it certainly was lucky I'd booked the plane for Sunday, not Saturday! It's strange how all three trips I've ever had to Lisbon have coincided with the mid-month Fatima pilgrimage days. Is it fate? This time we were a couple of days behind the pilgrims heading to Fatima, which meant that when we arrived in Lisbon airport just after nine in the morning we met hordes of them making their way back home. We collected one of the hire cars the pilgrims had abandoned and took the 'second circular' Lisbon ring road, passing by the Sporting Lisbon and Benfica grounds, both gleaming after their renovations for the Euro 2004 Championships. My colleague Mario had given us a few tips on places to stay, so we spent most of the day making a sightseeing tour.

We first passed through Estoril and Cascais, where the Laureus (never heard of them) world sports awards were being staged at a very plush-looking open-air venue on the cliffside. Apparently, David Beckham, Kelly Holmes, Michael Schumacher, eventual winner Roger Federer, and other luminaries were around, but we didn't see anybody to add to our celebrity encounters list, just lots of black-windowed limousines. Just round the corner was the *Boca do Infierno*, the Mouth of Hell, where the sea roared loud enough to make Hell's own teeth rattle. It was then on to the wild Atlantic rollers crashing onto the *Praia do Guincho* surfing beach, which leads up to the most westerly point of the whole European mainland at *Cabo da Roca*. Some young English heavy-metallers were having their publicity photos taken, striking poses on the cliff's edge. None of us could recognise them.

From the cape, we headed inland and up the steep mountain road to Sintra, the old centre of which shares with Hadrian's Wall and a hundred or so other sites the distinction of being a World Heritage Site. The little old village with its steep, narrow paths grew up to serve the National Palace at its centre. In the surrounding wooded hills, there are scores of imposing villas, the country residences of the nineteenth and early twentieth century rich. By far the most impressive and outlandish is the *Palacio de Pena*, a fairytale palace and luxuriant park built in 1840 for Ferdinand Saxe-Coburg, naturally a relative of our own royals, who was later installed as King of Portugal. Those Saxe-Coburgs certainly had a way of getting themselves good slots, didn't they?

As we wandered around the village, picnicking on the local speciality pastries of *queijadas de Sintra* and *pasteis de nata*, and very good they are too, a local guide told us that it was only five minutes up to the *Palacio*, so we set off up the steep hill. Half an hour later and exhausted, we concluded that she'd probably meant by car, not on foot! She obviously had, because in fact it took more like ten minutes by car. We then pointed the nose downhill towards Lisbon, crossed the River Tejo via the 'Twenty-fifth of April' Bridge, and drove a half hour south to the beach resort and still-active fishing harbour of Sesimbra, where we decided to stay, following Mario's recommendation.

We spent the days up to the Final on the beach in the warm sunshine, and on occasion braving the springtime cold of the Atlantic to have a swim in the sea. One day, we drove along the fantastic cliff road into the Arrabida National Park and passed the early afternoon in the tiny harbour of Portinho de Arrabida, which is well worth a visit out of season. Apparently it gets too crowded in the summer, but in mid-May we were nearly the only tourists there. It was a very similar experience to being in the Smögen harbour before last year's Gothenburg Final. You can stay in rooms in a couple of the little white harbour-side houses. We continued on to Setubal (pronounced 'Shtoobal' – there are lots of Sh's in Portuguese), of Vitoria Setubal fame. We took the quarter-hour ferry ride to the sandbar peninsula of Troia, spotting a school of dolphins on the way. It seems that the tower blocks at the end were begun in the seventies as an exclusive development for the ruling military *élite* of the time, but construction was halted by the revolution. They have only recently re-commenced building them, and I stayed in one of them a few years ago at a conference. The wide, white-sand beach is about twenty kilometres long, natural and unspoilt. We spent some time watching a couple of professional windsurfers from Australia and Poland with AUS 0 and POL 25 on their sails, testing out new board and sail designs in the wide bay between Troia and Arrabida. On the way back, we returned to Portinho de Arrabida for an evening meal of grilled fresh *sardinhas* and *caldeirada* fish stew in the harbour-side Restaurante Farol. It was a perfect day out, and a good end to our stay in Sesimbra, as the next day was Cup Final day in Lisbon.

We returned to Lisbon over the incredible eighteen kilometre long *Vasco da Gama* Bridge, further upstream over the *Rio Tejo*. It makes landfall just beside the new *Parque das Naçoes* exhibition park where the Expo 98 was staged, and which is the site of Europe's largest aquarium, the *Oceanàrio de Lisboa*. We spent a couple of hours there in the company of shoals of screaming school-outings kids aged from about three upwards with their bellowing teachers. It was quite a loud experience, much louder than the stadium later on. At the end, I asked our kids what they'd liked best. For Brian, it was the flashlight fish, which live in the darkest depths and flash their blue lights on and off. For Sarah and Emilie, it was the sea otters:

'We like them because they float on their backs and eat their food off their tummies. And we know what you like best, because you told us.'

'What was that, then?'

'The herrings. You said they're delicious.'

The weather couldn't have been better – a cloudless sky and twenty-nine degrees – and the Sporting and CSKA fans were making the most of it, gathered together in good-humoured rivalry in the area around the *Praça de Figueira* (the scene of our late-night singsong session the previous month), where the local TV had set up a giant screen to view the match and were busy running an all-day show of fun and games. To the obvious bemusement of the locals, the Russians had been taking full advantage of the Portuguese brewing and vineyard products on offer in the many bars and cafés lining the streets and squares of the *Baixa* downtown area. Their 'Say Ess Kah' chants echoed around the narrow streets. It was a staggering spectacle, in all ways.

We met five Celtic fans who were camouflaged in nearly the same colours as the Sporting fans, but their slightly lighter green hoops gave them away. Like us, they had bought their tickets in the UEFA Internet lottery, and were having a great time. *Déjà vu*, or wat? The five of them go to all the big European Finals. We then took a trip on one of the old yellow trams, just to see what they were like climbing the steep, narrow, winding streets up to the castle. We stood on the back platform and were surprised when we caught sight of a couple clinging India-style onto the outside of the tram, with their fingers poking through the crack between the door and the jamb. Each time the door opened at a stop, they jumped down just in time to stop their fingers getting chopped off. We were sure they were going to be scraped off when the tram took a bend and ran up too close to the side of some scaffolding or the corner of a house, but somehow they survived.

Then it was up to the Jose Alvalade XXI Stadium for the Final. The XXI stands for twenty-first century, by the way. We met some Toon fans just outside the ground. Most had come from Consett, but one had come from South Africa! There were more Celtic fans too, and when we got inside and were standing in the long queues for the drinks and hot dog stand, we met a lone Boro fan. He'd been very optimistic and ordered his ticket back in the spring too. Hey, maybe the Toon, the Celts and the Boro should meet up every year for European Finals, whether any of our teams are there or not. Who gives a shite? It's great fun either way!

Our seats were close to the half-way line, and in the top tier, from where we had a good view of the match. Before the game we'd been neutral about whom to support, but one sight of the tiny contingent of three thousand CSKA fans up against the massed ranks of forty-five thousand Sporting supporters convinced us that we had to do our bit to help the Russians. *Davai, Ivan!* They call themselves the 'Army Men', so two of the Toon Army joined the Army Men for the evening. They also had a giant banner saying the 'Gallant Steeds', which somehow sounded rather poetic. Even in our supposedly neutral UEFA section, we were surrounded by thousands of Sporting fans. To us, it didn't seem fair that a team can play a major Final at their own ground. The home advantage is too much of a head start, and I really think something should be done about it, by having a back-up location. Just like last year, it was disappointing to see a fair sprinkling of empty seats all around the ground, including beside our seats. Brian and I were able to spread ourselves over four seats, so we were very comfortable.

The match began in a similar pattern to our Quarter-Final, with Sporting passing the ball neatly, but to no great effect. The much taller Moscow defence and midfield coped very well, and Sporting had very few opportunities to break through until just before the half-hour mark, when all of a sudden the ball broke free just outside the penalty area and Sporting's Rogerio scored with a powerful rising shot. Sporting tried to press home their advantage, but the CSKA defence continued to look fairly comfortable and in the few minutes before half time the Russians had a couple of chances to equalise. In fact, the Brazilian with the fifties pop star name, Vagner Love, really ought to have scored when he was put through, but he scuffed the ball feebly with only the goalkeeper to beat.

After half time, CSKA looked increasingly comfortable and it wasn't really too much of a surprise when they equalised through defender Berezutsky. The little corner of CSKA Army Men went crazy with delight and the ones down the front got their tops off and waved them round their heads. Could have been the Toon Army Men!

Coming up on the Metro, one of the Sporting fans sitting opposite us had said the huge crowd advantage could actually work against Sporting if they got into difficulties. This is exactly what happened when Zhirkov nipped in between the Sporting central defenders to push the ball past Ricardo for the second CSKA goal. There were scenes of pandemonium in the little Russian corner, while the silence on all other sides was absolute. When passes went astray, there were cries of frustration and exasperation, and no one started up a chant or a song to show support for their team. The CSKA players must have been lapping it up.

The sequence of play leading up to the third goal was stunning in its irony and shift of emotions. The ball was in the CSKA penalty area and Tello's thunderous shot ricocheted off Rogerio, rattled the left-hand post and shot across the face of the goal. Goalkeeper Akinfeev managed to grab the ball and thwart the host of Sporting players scrambling to get across to stab it in. The goalie passed it out to CSKA's other Brazilian, Carvalho, on the left wing and in a flash it was in the Sporting penalty area where Vagner Love made amends for his earlier miss by side-footing it into the goal. Three-one! We'd seen all the goals down in our half of the pitch. The Sporting fans slumped in their seats. One second they thought they'd surely equalised, ten seconds later they were down and out. Does it sound familar at all?

Brian and I were laughing out loud – we couldn't believe it. Then we realised someone else was laughing too, and when we turned around there was a Leeds supporter, accompanied by his wife. He goes to all the big Finals, though in view of past events he was giving Istanbul a miss this year. The four of us were the only ones with a smile on our faces on this side of the pitch. The place was like a morgue. Then the zombies got up and left in increasing numbers (and this is the Cup Final, remember?). Hugo Viana came on as an eighty-seventh minute substitute, courtesy of NUFC letting him extend his loan spell, but he did nothing to raise his market value. Pity he couldn't have scored a couple of goals so we could get back a bit more of the huge transfer fee.

The game petered out almost in silence, except of course for the exultant Army Men in the far corner. We couldn't see what happened, but for some reason the riot police laid into them just as the game ended and pushed them further back into their corner. But it did nothing to dampen the celebrations when the CSKA team ran over to salute their fans. The team changed into gold shirts for the medal ceremony and the ticker tape in the Russian flag colours of red, white and blue sprayed over the assembly. They had said before the game that they hoped to emulate the Greeks of last year and come through as the unfancied outsiders to win, and they thoroughly deserved it. The biggest boos at the medals handout were directed at referee Graham Poll and his English assistants. The Sporting fans certainly had gripes with a few of his decisions.

Last year, Sarah had been determined that she would find a giant UEFA Cup Final banner as a souvenir, but they were all high up the lampposts and impossible to reach. In the end we'd found a consolation of an advertising hoarding which was being dismantled. This year she desperately wanted the real thing. So the next morning we went back to the ground to see what we could find. One of the UEFA staff told us that the best plan would be to keep a lookout during the day and try to spot the dismantlers. Just as we were leaving, that's exactly what happened. They had just begun taking the banners down and putting them on the back of a little truck. They kindly said we could have one as a souvenir, and it now looks great hanging in the garage (*déjà vu* again?).

CSKA Moscow's achievement was admirable. Being on the outer edge of Europe, their odyssey had been longer than any other team's in the competition, but they'd shown the fortitude and determination to meet all the challenges put in their way. To overcome the unfair home advantage that Sporting benefited from was a great exploit and they are fully worthy of the highest praise. Some time, I hope someone might be able to say the same about the Toon.

If it's going to be next year, which seems as distant and unlikely a prospect as ever, then the place to be is our old friends PSV Eindhoven's Philips Stadium on the 10th of May 2006. See you there, with or without the Toon!

How fitting that the last word, albeit vicariously, should go to Sir Bobby. The Saint Cuthbert's Old Boys' Dinner should have taken place, as explained, back in April. But that had collided with too many Old Boys' appointments with destiny in Lisbon and Cardiff, so it had to be put off. One-nil to common sense, for a change! Because unlike UEFA, the organisers of this particular event are truly in touch with reality. So the gala dinner finally took place on the twenty-seventh of May.

Chris and I met up in the Printer's Pie at six o'clock. Nothing unusual about that, you might think, except that Chris had just blasted up the M1 from the smoke to be there, and I had woken up in Germany in the morning, taken Tina to school in Luxembourg, then driven back to Deutschland and then back to Luxembourg with Stephie to get the plane to Paris and our onward flight to the Toon. Phew! Pause for breath... Not bad going, eh? Chris duly appeared with our fellow Cuth, Keith from Gosforth, who was doing the driving and so modestly ordered just a bottle of broon. Keith often appears on TV and radio quiz shows and sometimes uses Chris and Sarah's season tickets when they can't get up from the smoke. So who invented the Mexican Wave, Keith?

We made our way over to the Old Assembly Rooms, just next to Dr Gibbs's of Blaydon Races fame, in good time for more pre-dinner drinks at about a quarter to seven, hoping very much for a photo opportunity with Sir Bobby in the reception area where we had posed with Big Jack a year earlier. No sign of the Great Man at that stage and we were thinking he'd be coming just before kick-off, which proved to be the case. Chris's cousin Jimmy, who has a season ticket for the same section as Chris and Sarah, rang to say he was outside so Chris, who had his ticket, nipped doon to get him in. Then it was a couple of rounds at the bar, where predictably I thought I recognised loads of people from thirty-odd years ago. Though mostly wrong, I was right on a couple of occasions, including in the case of the legendary Stan Eardly (raise, step and play) and equally legendary Harry Potts, who haven't changed a bit, since last year! Very sad I was to learn that Mr Baron had died. He tried to teach our class geography back in 1967 and was still teaching at the Cuths when I went back there to give my little talk on the Monday after the Man U. game back in the autumn. What a bummer of a result that was! Once again, Sting didn't turn up; so if you're reading this, Gordon, get your arse along there next year and give us a song or two.

The Spug-managed glorious class of '74 was well represented and the crack was grand. Next year's collective 50th birthday celebrations in the Potato Republic (land of many of our forebears) promise to be something special, though but! Learned from one lad the interesting fact that the Newcastle Polish Club, of which his Dad is a member and which apparently was on its last legs, has been completely rejuvenated by the influx of loads of Poles, including bus drivers specially recruited from Cracow! Imagine the courage it must take to up sticks like that, probably without a brilliant command of English, never mind Geordie! And having to learn to drive on the wrong side of the road, to boot! Now their bairns and grandbairns will definitely all have Geordie accents. Mind, I hope they also learn their parents' language for good measure. A few generations back, immigrants just about everywhere thought it best for their kids to speak only the language of the new country, as they reckoned that was the way to get on. But what a fantastic advantage to grow up with an extra language in this day and age! Great, isn't it? Another generation of the Toon Army arriving on Tyneside and very welcome they are, too! That's the way it has always been with Tyneside's hard-working immigrants. And our happy gathering in the Old Assembly Rooms bore witness to that very fact. The building dates back to 1776, and you can be sure that hardly any of the Old Boys' forebears were on Tyneside back then. The first big wave of Irish immigration, for example, didn't get into full swing until almost a century later. And at a rough guess based on the names of the people I knew at school, I'd say that ninety per cent of those present were of Irish extraction, followed by maybe seven per cent Italian, two per cent Polish and a few unknowns. Those percentages now look set to shift a bit in Poland's favour. And yet we're all second, third or fourth generation Geordies. Black and white to the core. Howay the Toon!

Mind, there were a few mackems in the room, it has to be admitted, and at the charity auction a signed safc ball fetched a good few quid. But it was a member of the Toon Army who started the bidding off with a cry of 'A'll gi' ye fifty quid te borst it!' A signed Shearer shirt went for 750 quid, I think it was, and an England shirt signed by Sir Bobby fetched over a grand. All for charity, mind, to which the Great Man even contributed his speaking fee!

The evening was once again compèred by the brilliant Spike Rawlings, who had us roaring in the aisles with laughter at times. Although it was an Old Boys' occasion, there were a handful of ladies in the room. Speculation that a few lads had had a sex change with spectacularly good results was quickly quashed, however, when we found out the school at last has some lady teachers. Sighs of relief all round.

After the meal and a few more Spiky gags, we were told there would be a little break in proceedings to answer nature's call, i.e. get another round in. As we wandered along the corridor, who should be coming the other way but Sir Bobby himself. And he very kindly agreed to let us take a great picture of him and Chris, which we proudly feature in this here book. Back at the top table, he also kindly took the time to sign his autograph for what looked like just about everybody in the room! And Chris also got a dedicated Sir Bobby autograph for Sarah.

Then at last it was time for the Great Man to speak. But it was a while before he could actually do so, because the entire gathering stood up to chant: 'There's only one Bobby Robson, one Bobby Robson...' Sir Bobby told us his whole life story, with a good few anecdotes that went down very well, particularly his account of the time he told Gazza he was as daft as a brush. What was crystal-clear throughout his speech was that Sir Bobby is one of us, black and white through and through and truly in love with the Toon. And the Toon, as we all know, loves him! Indeed, he told us that - like yours truly - he was born pretty much nine months to the day after a Newcastle FA Cup Final victory. And we remembered that we had heard on the radio around the time of his 70th, the day of the away game at Bayer Leverkusen, that Yoko Ono had been born on exactly the same day as he had. Make a good pub quiz question, that would. So John Lennon not only lived on Newcastle Road near where Liverpool's Strawberry should stand, but their lass was born on the very same day as wor very own Sir Bobby. 'Imagine!', he must at one stage have said to himself, filled with Toon inspiration. Is that spooky, or wat?? Another fact to remember, Keith!

Sir Bobby went on to jokingly refer to the fact that some of today's players earn in a couple of minutes what most professional footballers earned in a week during his own playing days! He also told us he once actually scored a goal against Newcastle for Fulham at Gallowgate. And you know, you could honestly tell from the tone of his voice that he hated doing so! Well wouldn't you? Sir Bobby is of course a true gentleman, and didn't comment at all on the way he was treated by NUFC back in the autumn of 2004. Nor did he comment on how the team had performed under new management this season. He didn't have to, because we had all reached our own verdicts on those matters and gave free expression to our feelings at the end of his speech when we again all stood up and, after prolonged thunderous applause, started singing and kept on singing till hoyin-oot time. And the words we sang are the best words with which to end this book:

THERE'S ONLY ONE BOBBY ROBSON!